No King But Caesar
&
The Return of
The Melchisedec

A Layman's Study...

No King But Caesar
&
The Return of
The Melchisedec

A Layman's Study on Faith, Religion &
the Antichrist From the Covenant Perspective

*A*dvantage
BOOKS

Dewayne A. Pattie

No King But Caesar & The Return of The Melchisedec by Dewayne A. Pattie
Copyright © 2022 by Dewayne A. Pattie
ISBN: 978-1-59755-685-9

Published by: ADVANTAGE BOOKS™ www.advbookstore.com

All Scriptures within quotation marks are quoted from the Holy Bible King James Version, Public Domain.

Library of Congress Catalog Number: 2022932216

Names:	Pattie, Dewayne A., Author
Title:	*No King But Caesar & The Return of The Melchisedec*
	Dewayne A. Pattie
	Advantage Books, 2021
Identifiers:	ISBN (print): 9781597556859, (mobi, epub): 9781597557009, (hardcover): 9781597556903
Subjects:	Christian Life: Inspirational

First Printing February 2022
22 23 24 25 26 27   10 9 8 7 6 5 4 3 2 1

Use of Scripture and Definitions

All Scriptures quoted are from the King James Version of the Bible unless otherwise noted and will appear in *italics*. I believe the italics will aid in identifying the quote from the common text.

I have made every effort to preserve the quoted Scriptures as they appear in the Bible, including quoted punctuation. Inasmuch as the Elizabethan English used by the KJV translators follows different rules than our Modern English, sentence punctuation in this book will appear outside the quotation marks when quoting from the Scriptures. While this may appear to be a departure from accepted norms, I believe the reader will find this acceptable to preserve the integrity of the Scriptures. Only ellipsis have been added within quotation marks when necessary to show the quote as a fraction of the Scripture referenced.

All emphasis by **bold** or <u>underlined</u> type found in Scriptural quotes has been added by me, DP.

<u>Underlined</u> words will usually appear in pairs or multiples to emphasize their juxtaposition, even if they are separated by several paragraphs.

Book/Chapter/Verse references in **bold** indicate a "Scriptural quote" either before or after the reference. If the reference appears after the quote, it will be in parentheses.

(See or see also references in parentheses) indicate Biblical citation of the subject matter in discussion.

The proper names of "Holy Ghost", "Holy Spirit", and "Glory of God" are used interchangeably in this book.

All definitions offered for words in English are derived from the "American Dictionary Of The English Language" / Noah Webster 1828 / Facsimile First Edition / Published by Foundation For American Christian Education / ISBN 0-912498-03-X.

All definitions offered for words in Hebrew or Greek are derived from the "Dictionaries Of The Hebrew and Greek Words Of The Original, With References To The English Words: By James Strong, S.T.D., LL.D." found in "Strong's Exhaustive Concordance Of The Bible" by James Strong / Published by Hendrickson Publishers PO Box 3473 Peabody, MA 01961-3473 / ISBN 0-917006-01-1.

1 Corinthians 2:13 *"Which things also we speak, not in the words which man's wisdom teacheth, but which the Holy Ghost teacheth;.."*

Table of Contents

A Layman's Study...

Preface

Early in my Christian walk with the Lord Jesus Christ I felt compelled to study God's Word. It was through reading the Bible in private that I came to know the Lord Jesus Christ as my personal Lord and Savior. From that time, I have been inwardly compelled not just to study God's Word, but to apply it to every aspect of my life and also to share that life-transforming knowledge with others. I realize today that the urgency that still compels me to seek God's Word for understanding and knowledge is the "calling" the Lord Jesus has upon my life and that calling is to serve the Body of Christ unto its edification as the Holy Spirit prompts me.

About twenty years ago the Holy Ghost flashed a vision before me. The vision was simply a hand with a pen held so as it was writing. I knew immediately what the Lord was saying to me and I responded with a very casual, "OK Lord. Just tell me what you want me to write and I will write it." As the urgency to study persisted I became frustrated that the Lord didn't tell me what to write. Even as years of study permeated my thoughts, I could not figure out what it was He wanted me to write about. Then a television ministry mentioned that "Fasting restored the vision." After about three days of fasting I heard the proverbial bell, "*Ding, ding, ding*...the things you have been led to study are the things the Lord wants you to write about."

After twenty years of my best and not so best efforts I can honestly say that God's grace and my merits are not even comparable. His gifts and manifestations forever exceed my abilities. His longsuffering endures beyond my folly. His correction is sweeter than the fulfillment of all my aspirations. By His loving-kindness I am reconciled to the Truth and I am planted therein "like a tree by the waters", without which I would surely stray. In this I give thanks first and foremost to the Lord Jesus Christ, who saved me and called me. Without His guidance this work would not be possible.

The book you now hold is the third revision in this effort. Initially I thought a collection of teachings on the covenant and various precepts would suffice the Lord's intentions in the reader towards producing a right relationship with Him. And the Lord was none too blunt when He let me know that I had hurriedly published an unfinished work. This third revision now encompasses a much broader scope than I could have possibly envisioned for the book twenty years ago. It is therefore my hope that God has also shaped and matured my person into a companion suitable for the subject matter of this book.

As all ministers should be subject to their flock, I am happy to present you with this work, "No King But Caesar & The Return of The Melchisedec" for your reading enjoyment, your learning, your examination, and if necessary your rejection. No part of this book should be considered as exhaustive or all inclusive for matters of doctrine. There is only one source that is an Inspired and completed work; that is your Holy Bible. Please read it. If you feel that something contained within these pages is written in error, please defer to the Holy Scriptures and pray for this author. I claim only the Grace of God, which He gives abundantly to all who call on the name of the Lord Jesus Christ.

I would enjoy hearing from you and your experience with this book.

Very Truly Yours,

Dewayne Pattie
PO Box 404
Estill Springs, Tn. 37330

Introduction

As we read the Holy Scriptures, we are drawn to the conclusion that God has appointed an end to this present condition of humanity. One of the questions the disciples asked Jesus was, "*...what shall be the sign of thy coming, and of the end of the world?*" (**Matthew 24:3**). In the Epistles of the Apostle Peter, he writes of the "last time, last times, and last days." As well, the last "time" and "days" are mentioned in the Apostle John's Gospel, Acts, the books of First and Second Timothy, Hebrews, James, Jude, and most notably The Revelation. The Apostle Paul speaks definitely about this time in **1 Corinthians 15:52** when he says: "*In a moment, in the twinkling of an eye, at the last trump: for the trumpet shall sound, and the dead shall be raised incorruptible, and we shall be changed.*"

Today, in this late hour, we have already seen many of the prophecies concerning last day events come to pass. For example, the re-gathering of National Israel as prophesied by Isaiah, Joel, and Jeremiah is a clear indicator of our time. The apostasy of the church from the Apostle Paul's warning to Timothy of "perilous times" (2 Timothy 3:1), of "grievous wolves" (Acts 20:29), and John the Apostle's vision of a Laodicean age from Revelation 3 are none too subtle warnings that last days are upon us. Apostasy of the church? Oh Yes: **1 Timothy 4:1** "*Now the Spirit speaketh expressly, **that in the latter times some shall depart from the faith**, giving heed to seducing spirits, and doctrines of devils; ² Speaking lies in hypocrisy; having their conscience seared with a hot iron; ³ Forbidding to marry, and commanding to abstain from meats, which God hath created to be received with thanksgiving of them which believe and know the truth.*"

Even now, in the geo-political realm, we see the dynamic nature of nations and kingdoms and powers as God raises up one and throws down another. These events also were prophesied millennia ago as God brought forth prophecy from the relationship between Daniel and Nebuchadnezzar, and from men like Ezekiel, and from the Apostle John in the New Testament.

But the greatest evidence of the hour that we live in is on the inside. In the collective psyche of humanity, the Witness of God is playing out as a fascination with all sorts of mysticism and spiritualism, and even in the occult as a lost world grasps for answers in the midst of uncertain times. The popularity of television shows on humanity's false prophets or apocalyptic events to come attests to the subconscious knowledge that something big is about to happen. And whether that evidence on the inside is turmoil, anxiety, or despair for the unbeliever or whether that evidence is peace, hope, and glad expectation for the believer, the Holy Spirit is speaking to hearts and minds everywhere saying, "Soon."

Even as the fascination with mysticism and the like is portrayed as harmless by profiteers, the deluge of information that has been ushered in by the age of technology has brought with it a great diversification of ideas and a great deal of confusion and uncertainty concerning near-future events. It is not just a proliferation of new ideas, but old ideas are being cut and spliced, altered, and malformed so that new, mutant and tortured fruit is fast becoming a staple for a society, "*...that cannot discern between their right hand and their left hand;*" (**Jonah 4:11**).

However, God has not left us without comfort to wander in bewilderment as the unstable and unlearned wander from doctrine and belief system to doctrine and belief system. God has established us on the Rock, and the Path, and He has given us Light that He might reveal all things necessary for us to complete our journey through this present time.

The aim of this study is not to make predictions or to bring charges against any person or people group. The aim of this study is to discover (uncover) the subtle nature of the enemy of our souls as it has been revealed in the Holy Scriptures, to set in a proper context ideas and principles previously thought of as being disconnected or perhaps irrelevant one to another, and to laud the Lord Jesus Christ as King of kings and Lord of lords!

In this study we will examine such subject matter as: Covenant Principals and Fundamentals, Adam's Nature, The Angelic Worship of God in Heaven, The Fall of Lucifer, The Knowledge of Good and Evil, The Inter-Relationship of Covenants and Dispensations, The Restoration of the Trinity of Man, The Relationship of Law and Grace, The Man of Sin, and The Ministry of Melchisedec.

As we transition into the body of this text, and since God is the Beginning and the End, let us also begin with a brief look at God.

1 John 4:12 "*No man hath seen God at any time...*"

It would be impossible to teach every aspect or feature or manifestation of God, or any part of the God-head, as indicated by John the Apostle in 1 John 4:12. A similar Scripture appears when the Apostle Paul writes in **1 Timothy 6:16**: "*Who only hath immortality, dwelling in the light which no man can approach unto; whom no man hath seen, nor can see: to whom be honour and power everlasting. Amen.*" So we will attempt to focus on those aspects of God that relate more closely to this study.

Revelation 10:6 declares that time itself is in subjection to the Word of God. When we read in **Genesis 1:1** *"In the beginning..."* we understand that it is a reference to the beginning of time and not the beginning of God, for God is infinite and without measure. The fact that God is sovereign over time was not lost to the Prophet Isaiah, wherefore he said in **Isaiah 46:10**: *"Declaring the end from the beginning, and from ancient times the things that are not yet done, saying, My counsel shall stand, and I will do all my pleasure:"* Only the Creator of time can declare the course of time. And the beauty of prototypes and foreshadows and prophetic events and spoken prophecy within the Word of God, is that they also point to God's sovereignty over His physical creation as the creation interplays with time.

If we continue to read in Genesis chapter 1, we find that God created the heaven and the earth by the power of His Spoken Word. In **Genesis 1:27** we read: *"So God created man in his own image, in the image of God created he him; male and female created he them."* Here is where we begin to notice pattern. Pattern is evident in every Word that God has spoken, but we begin to notice the pattern in that God made man to reflect Himself.

Likewise in **Genesis 1:14**: *"And God said, Let there be lights in the firmament of the heaven to divide the day from the night; and let them be for signs, and for seasons, and for days, and years:"* In **Psalm 50:6** the psalmist Asaph says, *"And the heavens shall declare his righteousness:..."* Again the signs point us to God, the Creator and Initiator, who patterned His creation to reflect some part of Himself. This is much the same way that modern artists affirm self expression. What is happening within the inside comes to the outside. With the physical and the outward creation pointing to God, surely all of Scripture would lead us to look at our Heavenly Father.

John 1:1 *"In the beginning was the Word, and the Word was with God, and the Word was God. ² The same was in the beginning with God. ³ All things were made by him; and without him was not any thing made that was made. ⁴ In him was life; and the life was the light of men."*

John 1:14 *"And the Word was made flesh, and dwelt among us, (and we beheld his glory, the glory as of the only begotten of the Father,) full of grace and truth."*

The Word of God is His chosen means of expression. It is His expressed will. And yes, God has put His signature on all of His creation. Just as it was in the beginning, we see signs that point us to God; so even now from His Word, we see that wise men were looking for the signs and, *"have seen his star..."* (**Matthew 2:2**). In **Luke 21:25** the Word of God Himself declares: *"And there* shall be <u>signs in the sun, and in the moon, and in the stars</u>; and upon the earth distress of nations, with perplexity; the sea and the waves roaring; [26] Men's hearts failing them for fear, and for looking after those things which are coming on the earth: for the powers of heaven shall be shaken. [27] And then shall they see the Son of man coming in a cloud with power and great glory. [28] And when these things begin to come to pass, then look up, and lift up your heads; for your redemption draweth nigh."

If one could read the stars, they would not tell us our fortune. But they would literally read," In the beginning God...", for "the heavens declare His righteousness." But God gave us His Word knowing that man would need a more intimate and personal and direct way to hear from God. In addition to personal application, the Word of God is much more objective for understanding future events than reading the stars. **Revelation 19:13** tells us, speaking of Jesus: "...and **his name is called The Word of God**." In **Matthew 4:4** Jesus testifies: "Man shall not **live** by bread alone, but by every **word** that proceedeth out of the mouth of God." So God is **life** as we read in **John 1:4**: "In him was **life**; and the **life** was the light of men."

It would be easy to become lost in Scripture as we show the relationship of one verse and book to another and to the whole. So it is necessary to begin now to "rightly divide" the Word of Truth. (See 2 Timothy 2:15.) You will need your Bible for this study.

1

Covenant Principals & Fundamentals

Jeremiah 31:31-34 *"Behold, the days come, saith the LORD, that I will make a new covenant with the house of Israel, and with the house of Judah: ³² Not according to the covenant that I made with their fathers in the day that I took them by the hand to bring them out of the land of Egypt; which my covenant they brake, although I was an husband unto them, saith the LORD: ³³ But this shall be the covenant that I will make with the house of Israel; After those days, saith the LORD, I will put my law in their inward parts, and write it in their hearts; and will be their God, and they shall be my people. ³⁴ And they shall teach no more every man his neighbour, and every man his brother, saying, Know the LORD: for they shall all know me, from the least of them unto the greatest of them, saith the LORD: for I will forgive their iniquity, and I will remember their sin no more."*

What is "Covenant?" I asked myself. I have looked at the examples of covenant in Scripture. I have looked at how covenants were instituted, their symbolism, their ceremony, and their effect and power or rather their authority. I have searched out the definition of the word in different languages.

When we look at the definition of "covenant" in the English language the word basically means "to join, agree, or bind together." We are all probably somewhat familiar with this idea. The word is often used in legal documents and has this very quality or essence. But the word origin in the Hebrew language of the Old Testament means "to cut." The sense of the word is to separate, purge, or purify and is akin to "winnowing."

At first glance, these two definitions appear to be contradictory. But a deeper look shows that God's use of covenant in Scripture validates both definitions. For example, God used one covenant, initiated through Moses, when He brought the children of Israel out of Egypt. (See Exodus 19:5.) Egypt represents a type of spiritual bondage. But then He used a different covenant, initiated through Jesus, to bring us into Spiritual liberty. This is represented in the Old Testament by Joshua bringing the children of Israel into the Promised Land. (See Joshua 24:14-27.) So Moses brought out but Joshua brought in. Moses separated from but Jesus joined to. (See Ephesians 2.)

John 12:24 *"Verily, verily, I say unto you, Except a corn of wheat fall into the ground and die, it abideth alone: but if it die, it bringeth forth much fruit."*

When we look at hundreds of direct references to covenant, and perhaps many thousands more indirect references to covenant in the Scriptures, we understand, in a general sense, that covenant is God's way of initiating change. In a more specific sense, it is God's way of bringing in the new through the old, or even of birthing life through death.

Elements/What Covenants Are Made Of

As we begin to look at a few covenants from the Scriptures, we will notice the five fundamental elements that constitute a covenant, and their use as the parties entered into a covenant relationship.

1) VOWS or DECLARATIONS would be made indicating the participants TERMS and/or INTENTIONS. The terms establish and retain the basis for the agreement. The terms define the nature of the relationship between the participants. The terms set standards and expectations of conduct for the participants. And the terms bind the participants with default options and parameters. In our relationship with our Heavenly Father, the terms of the Covenant are found in the entirety of the New Testament. **Hebrews 8:13** *"In that he saith, A new covenant, he hath made the first old. Now that which decayeth and waxeth old is ready to vanish away."*

2) An EXCHANGE of garments, rings, jewels, or other items that bore a person's identity was made. Often the item would be a clan or tribal identifier and the exchange would signify that family status or identity, and authority was now bestowed upon the participant. **Revelation 19:8** *"And to her was granted that she should be arrayed in fine linen, clean and white: for the fine linen is the righteousness of saints."*

3) There would be a SACRIFICE/SHEDDING OF BLOOD to seal the covenant. From the expectation, "Till death do us part" testifies that covenants ratified by blood can only be nullified by blood. The action of sacrifice in covenant not only ratified the covenant but also in unison with the TERMS established default options and parameters. For example, if an animal was sacrificed in making the covenant, then an animal could be required when the covenant was broken. In regards to the shedding of blood, if the participants mingled their

own blood this was also the mechanism that imparted their nature one to the other. **Hebrews 13:12** *"Wherefore Jesus also, that he might sanctify the people with his own blood, suffered without the gate."*

4) A CHANGE of a person's name would often take place. This indicates that a CHANGE in their NATURE or CHARACTER was imminent. Almost always the change of name would be in the "weaker" participant. **2 Peter 1:4** *"Whereby are given unto us exceeding great and precious **promises**: that by these ye might be partakers of the **divine nature**, having escaped the corruption that is in the world through lust."* **Promises** are Covenant "Vows".

5) A WITNESS would be established as proof of the covenant. It was the evidence and was also called a TOKEN, MEMORIAL, TESTIMONY, or TESTAMENT. Often it was the SCAR or MARK in the flesh from which the participants mingled their own blood. The act of mingling the blood has been portrayed in more than one television movie by two men that cut the palm of their hands and then join their hands together. **Romans 2:29** *"But he is a Jew, which is one inwardly; and circumcision is that of the heart, in the spirit, and not in the letter; whose praise is not of men, but of God."* (See also Deuteronomy 10:16.)

With one exception, there is no set order or procedure to follow when establishing a covenant. The exception being of necessity that VOWS, TERMS, or DECLARATIONS would be made before the SHEDDING OF BLOOD or SACRIFICE. Take the marriage covenant process (ceremony) for example: the marriage is not consummated until after the vows are spoken. Of necessity, why would we sacrifice when we are uncertain as to what we agree upon? How do we come into agreement unless terms are declared? The standards that modern society practice in dating and in marital relationship often stand in stark contrast to the pattern for covenant that was designed by our Loving Creator. To state the concept bluntly, "No sex until marriage." We will discuss this further. But know that God doesn't expect a lost world to bear witness to His plan of redemption.

With the exception being stated, we will move on to note that all five elements are not necessarily found in every covenant. It is also evident in Scripture that one element or event could serve to establish and satisfy another element. For example, the sacrifice could become a memorial meal;

that is "a witness". Or creating a scar or mark in the flesh (a TOKEN) would satisfy the SHEDDING OF BLOOD.

In fact, a covenant can be evident anywhere in Scripture where two or more parties come together in agreement, with only one or more of the five elements being in place. For example, **Acts 23:12-15** tells us that more than forty Jews, *"...bound themselves under a curse, saying that they would neither eat nor drink till they had killed Paul."* Talk about flirting with death. Let's not! While this particular covenant does very little to reflect God, it is a covenant nonetheless. (The KJV translators assigned the word "conspiracy" to the verse while translating from the Greek. The same "conspiracy" comes from a word in the Hebrew defined as "a compact" or an "agreement".)

This brings us to the point that some covenants more accurately reflect God than others; particularly, the covenants that God Himself has participated in! There are several notable covenants found in Scripture and I list a few of them here for your convenience and study.

Notable Covenants

1. Adam & Satan* Implied and reviewed retrospectively through the persons of Esau and Jacob.

2.	God & Adam	Gen 3:21
3.	God & Cain	Gen 4:15
4.	God & Noah	Gen 6:18; 8:20; 9:17
5.	God & Abraham	Gen 13:14-17; 15:1-18
	Conveyed to Isaac	Gen 17:19-21
	Conveyed to Jacob	Gen 27:37; 35:10-12
6.	Abraham & Abimelech	Gen 21:27
7.	Isaac & Abimelech	Gen 26:28
8.	Esau & Jacob*	Gen 25:25-34; 27:11; 27:36-37
9.	Jacob & Laban	Gen 31:43-54
10.	Judah & Tamar	Gen 38:12-27 (Matt 1:3)
11.	God & The Nation Israel	Ex 19:5; 24:3-8
	2nd Covenant	De 29; De 32:1-43
	Retrospective Review (Marital)	Ezek 16**
12.	Joshua & the Nation Israel	Josh 24:14-27
13.	Rahab & the Spies	Josh 2:12-14,17-21 (Matt 1:5)
14.	Ruth & Boaz	Ruth 3:9; 4:9-10 (Matt 1:5)
15.	Jonathan & David	1 Sam 18:1-4
	2nd Covenant	1 Sam 20:11-23
16.	God & David	2 Sam 7:4-16; Ps 89:3-4
17.	God & Mankind	The New Testament

* In the covenant between Adam & Satan and also the covenant between Esau & Jacob, please notice the obvious omission of bloodshed.

** In Ezekiel 16 God is laying out His charges against Israel as an unfaithful wife, just as He required a man to do before the High Priest when a man sought divorce for infidelity.

Examples and Precedents

The essence of covenant that lends itself well for God's use is it's pliability. In our human nature we like to classify and define things, as well as concepts. It helps us to categorize and to separate, as we contextualize the thing defined against some standard or another. But, that same essence of pliability often makes covenant hard to recognize. The untrained thought process doesn't equate the covering by God of Adam's nakedness to a part of a broader covenant experience. In this life, we may at some time see a tragic event leave a person naked or even under-clothed for the scenario they are in. It's only just an act of compassion for us to try to cover them. The natural thought is, "This is all God was trying to do with Adam and Eve, right?"

God didn't design a rigid format for making covenant, and we don't find a pattern for rigidity in the Scriptures. What we do find are patterns where certain elements of covenant produce similar results. As we build "line upon line and precept upon precept," these patterns begin to stand out like registration marks for the work of art that is ultimately completed one layer at a time.

The Example of Marriage

Ephesians 5:22-33 *"Wives, submit yourselves unto your own husbands, as unto the Lord. [23] For the husband is the head of the wife, even as Christ is the head of the church: and he is the saviour of the body. [24] Therefore as the church is subject unto Christ, so let the wives be to their own husbands in every thing. [25] Husbands, love your wives, even as Christ also loved the church, and gave himself for it; [26] That he might sanctify and cleanse it with the washing of water by the word, [27] That he might present it to himself a glorious church, not having spot, or wrinkle, or any such thing; but that it should be holy and without blemish. [28] So ought men to love their wives as their own bodies. He that loveth his wife loveth himself. [29] For no man ever yet hated his own flesh; but nourisheth and cherisheth it, even as the Lord the church: [30] For we are members of his body, of his flesh, and of his bones. [31] For this cause shall a man leave his father and mother, and shall be joined unto his wife, and they two shall be one flesh. [32] **This is a great mystery: but I speak concerning Christ and the church.** [33] Nevertheless let every one of you in particular so love his wife even as himself; and the wife see that she reverence her husband."*

Of all the covenant relationships found in Scripture, it is the marriage covenant that best reveals the intimacy that God desires to have with His Church. (I capitalize Church here and after to emphasize the Mrs. Jesus Christ status that God has bestowed upon us.) In **Jeremiah 31:31-32** God said that by His covenant He was a husband to Israel: *"Behold, the days come, saith the LORD, that I will make a new covenant with the house of Israel, and with the house of Judah: ³² Not according to the covenant that I made with their fathers in the day that I took them by the hand to bring them out of the land of Egypt;* **which my covenant they brake, although I was an husband unto them, saith the LORD***:"* God also said to Israel by Isaiah the Prophet in **Isaiah 54:5**: *"**For thy Maker is thine husband***; the LORD of hosts is his name; and thy Redeemer the Holy One of Israel; The God of the whole earth shall he be called."* Furthermore, inasmuch as the Scriptures testify of Jesus Christ, it is more than plausible that most of the examples of husbands found in Scripture represent some aspect or other of His relationship with us.

Though we have already mentioned the marriage covenant ceremony, there is still want of explanation. I say this with all gravity, because there is a disconnect between God's intentions for marriage and the world's actual application of marriage. If, in the here and now, we set our eyes on the wrong examples, our thoughts on what marriage is supposed to be will be skewed. Not that every marital relationship is wrong, but how the world views marriage often creates misconceptions and wrong expectations within marriages. For example, let's expose a Satanic half-truth about marriage through a question: "Does marriage allow two people to act as one? Or does marriage allow two people to become one?" Let's move on.

In the Christian marriage ceremony, vows or terms are easily recognized as the focal point of the process. The vows declare our intentions to unite ourselves to our beloved and only to our beloved. We speak our vows in full view of God's officiating minister, family, friends, enemies, and a larger community to which we are accountable, and these bear witness of our covenant. I say this is the focal point because vows and witnesses are required to legalize the agreement.

There is usually the giving of the ring in the marriage process. While it is not required by law, the giving of the ring also bears witness to the covenant. It says, "Where you go, I go; there is another in this with you." The giving of the ring is symbolic of the two participants becoming one; it is an outward show.

Then there is often the change of name by the bride. It doesn't just reflect the bride taking on the nature of the groom; it authorizes her to act in his stead. There are many New Testament verses where Jesus authorizes His Church to use His Name and then there are the examples of the Apostles making use of it. In orthodox Hebrew circles, it is held that the man's job as husband is to reach up into the heavenly realm and pull down God's intentions for the family. The woman's job as wife, is to then reach down into the earth and pull up or materialize those same intentions. In other words, she operates in her realm on his behalf. If we view the man as the head of the wife, as the Apostle Paul states in Ephesians 5, then we can also spiritualize Proverbs 31, which correlates to the orthodox Hebrew view of marriage as a relationship between God and His Church. When I read Proverbs 31, I struggled with why she did all the work while he sat in the gate with the elders until I learned this principal. This proverb shows the relationship between Jesus Christ and His Bride. The Scriptures testify of Him. This will also become an important step in understanding prophecy.

Proverbs 31:1 *"The words of king Lemuel, the prophecy that his mother taught him."* King Lemuel is King Solomon. His mother is Bathsheba.

For the sacrifice in marriage, or in this case the shedding of blood, we look to the Hebrew marriage ceremony given by Moses in **Deuteronomy 22:13-21**: *"If any man take a wife, and go in unto her, and hate her, [14] And give occasions of speech against her, and bring up an evil name upon her, and say, I took this woman, and when I came to her, I found her not a maid: [15] Then shall the father of the damsel, and her mother, take and bring forth the tokens of the damsel's virginity unto the elders of the city in the gate: [16] And the damsel's father shall say unto the elders, I gave my daughter unto this man to wife, and he hateth her; [17] And, lo, he hath given occasions of speech against her, saying, I found not thy daughter a maid;* **and yet these are the tokens of my daughter's virginity. And they shall spread the cloth before the elders of the city.** *[18] And the elders of that city shall take that man and chastise him; [19] And they shall amerce him in an hundred shekels of silver, and give them unto the father of the damsel, because he hath brought up an evil name upon a virgin of Israel: and she shall be his wife; he may not put her away all his days. [20] But if this thing be true, and the tokens of virginity be not found for the damsel: [21] Then they shall bring out the damsel to the door of her father's house, and the men of her city shall stone her with stones that she die: because she hath wrought folly in Israel, to play the whore in her father's house: so shalt thou put evil away from among you."*

From God's design of the female body and by the instruction of Moses, we understand that God intended for blood to be shed when consummating the marriage. The cloth of verse 17 was the blood-stained bed sheet where the consummation took place. This token or evidence of the bride's virginity would have been presented by the groom to the parents of the bride on the first night of her wedding. Before we go further, let's maintain the perspective. The marriage ceremony is only an example of the Covenant that Jesus made as a man, on behalf of humanity, when He shed His Blood on the cross and then presented it to the Father in Heaven. The Scriptures bear witness of Him. And, when the Bride of Christ is carried to the consummation in Heaven, there will only be one standard: can we present the Blood of Jesus as evidence of our faith in Jesus Christ? Just as all aspects of the human body are subject to frailty, some women may not bleed the first time they have sexual intercourse. Nevertheless, from God's design of the female body, and by the instruction of Moses, we understand that God intended for blood to be shed when consummating the marriage.

Moreover, in the man's body, God instructed the male child to be circumcised on the eighth day. God had told Abraham and his descendants to keep circumcision in their flesh as a token of the covenant between him (Abraham) and God. This instruction by Moses is also found in Leviticus 12:3 and is important to the marriage covenant process, because during the consummation the seed of copulation passes through the token of the covenant. That token is circumcision and is the sign of the covenant that God made with Abraham (a scar in the flesh); thus conveying covenant virtue upon the seed. So in the male anatomy, blood was shed by man to God. In the female anatomy, blood was shed by woman to her husband. (See also 1 Corinthians 11:7-9.)

God created and gifted sex to humanity as an integral part of marriage to reference His relationship with His Church. In the marital context of love and mutual desires and mutual consent, sex is regarded by our Creator as innocent as a baby that doesn't know it's own nakedness. Even in marriage, sex is not supposed to be the fulfillment of carnal needs, but it is the fulfillment of a relationship based in love. Carnal needs/desires cannot be fulfilled, only appeased for a time. Neither were carnal needs made by our Loving Creator, but they are the product of a fallen humanity.

It would be hard to imagine two becoming one without the physical union of sex. Because the marriage so closely represents the God/Church relationship, it can be said that the purpose of marriage is sex. Let me explain: I don't need a covenant to love somebody. In fact the Lord commands me to love others. I don't need a covenant to be friends with somebody, or to enjoy their company. I don't need a covenant to serve or help somebody, even if they are the opposite sex. I could hire a servant to wash my socks and clean the house, without a covenant. In addition, my marriage is just as valid if I don't have children. I was married long before my wife and I had children.

Suppose we never had children; would the marriage have been or become less valid? Children are not the purpose for marriage.

But it is the coming together physically that requires a covenant. From the list of Notable Covenants, there are several examples of hostility between participants just prior to them making covenant. The examples are numerous enough that this author can say without trepidation that covenant is the mechanism that brings two people that were contrary to each other into harmony with each other. No matter how we say it, it is probably a gross understatement to say that fallen man is antagonistic toward our Holy God. Conversely, God's Holiness doesn't commune with wickedness. From the beginnings of time, we see Lucifer cast out of God's presence in Heaven and man cast out of God's presence in the Garden of Eden. The cherubim with the flaming sword in Genesis 3:24 were not just to deny us the benefits of the garden, but were also there to prevent our haphazard encounter with God's Holiness. Think of the awe-full power of God used to speak billions of suns into existence. Literally, it is the power to speak an entire realm into existence. That realm is what we call the universe; and this is small in comparison to the fullness of the Holiness of our Creator. **Job 37:22** says: *"...with God is terrible majesty."* Of the most well known covenant in Scripture, the Apostle Paul says the law *"was added because of transgressions,.."* (Galatians 3:19). The transgressions were acts by Abraham's descendants that were contrary to God's nature.

But now, from the complete revelation of the Scriptures, through covenant, Jesus has made for us the way back to God. **2 Corinthians 5:17** *"Therefore if any man be in Christ, he is a new creature: old things are passed away; behold, all things are become new. [18] And all things are of God, who hath reconciled us to himself by Jesus Christ, and hath given to us the ministry of reconciliation; [19] To wit, that God was in Christ, reconciling the world unto himself, not imputing their trespasses unto them; and hath committed unto us the word of reconciliation. [20] Now then we are ambassadors for Christ, as though God did beseech you by us: we pray you in Christ's stead, be ye reconciled to God. [21]* **For he hath made him to be sin for us, who knew no sin; that we might be made the righteousness of God in him.***"* Verse 21 is the exchange of natures within covenant which allowed God to join Himself to man **for that purpose!**

So we can say, children are the natural result of a right relationship between spouses. Think about it: if our children are the purpose of our covenant, or if our children hold a position of preeminence in our heart over our spouse, then we allow division from our spouse. Our children end up with two separate parents within the marriage. It's tantamount to the Church esteeming its members in higher regard than it does Almighty God. In this context, we can easily label the misguided affection, most often by the mother, as a form of idolatry. Perhaps you think, "Oh, that's a hard thought." OK then, let's contextualize a little further: Did God save you and call you to minister to others simply to grow His Church? Did He save you for what you could do for Him? Will He still love me if I never win anyone to Jesus? Or did He save you because He loves you and wants a relationship with you?

In **Genesis 29:31-34**, the narrative recounts how Leah, Jacob's wife, thought that her children would serve the purpose of perfecting the union that she had with Jacob. In verse 32 she says: *"...now therefore my husband will love me."* Similarly, in verse 34 she says: *"Now this time will my husband be joined unto me, because I have born him three sons:.."* As I read the words of Leah, I can't help but feel the loss that she suffered as her hopes of a right relationship with her husband were unfulfilled. No doubt that realization of "I'm rejected" would displace the overwhelming joy and intimacy she should have felt each time she pulled her son(s) to her breast. In nursing her children, Leah's thoughts of, "You didn't work." and "You failed." would infuse themselves within the bond between Leah and her children as they gazed into each other's eyes. In all probability, Leah would grow to understand her mistake, but the years of hurt and rejection that were directed into her sons would not be inconsequential. We have but to read the Scriptures to see the effect.

But Jacob had two wives. For lack of a better word I will say that Leah was "imposed" upon Jacob as his first wife. The Scriptures tell us that Jacob was less than enthusiastic to have Leah as his wife. The wife that Jacob loved was Rachael. Jacob pursued Rachael to the point he was willing to work twice as long as agreed to obtain her. While we should never dismiss the individual application of the Word of God to our lives, we would be negligent to overlook the broader truth in this story. Allegorically, Leah represents the World's relationship with God and Rachael represents the Church's relationship with God. Applying the Word individually to our lives allows us to understand that the World (Leah) hopes to be received by God through its merits or by what it can produce. But the Church (Rachael) is already received by God's Love.

Galatians 4:27 *"For it is written, Rejoice, thou barren that bearest not; break forth and cry, thou that travailest not: for the desolate hath many more children than she which hath an husband."* (See also Isaiah 54:1.)

Therefore, that same freedom that your obedience-oriented ministry offers over a results-oriented ministry will allow husbands and wives to thrive together in a right relationship when applied to the marital relationship. The right relationship is defined by the Apostle Paul in Ephesians 5 and is summed up as, "Husbands love your wives. Wives submit to your husbands." This relationship is repeated in Colossians 3:18 and referred to in 1 Peter 3:1-7. If your marriage is less than amiable today, then I encourage you to apply yourself to the pattern designed by our Loving Creator, and see as His blessings follow. God gifted the relationship of husband and wife to humanity to show Himself as a loving husband to His Church.

The writer of Hebrews declares in **Hebrews 13:4**: *"Marriage is honourable in all, and the bed undefiled: but whoremongers and adulterers God will judge."* Biblically, all sex outside of marriage is referred to as "fornication." From Ezekiel 16:29-38 the word "fornication" is even applied to idolatry. There is an unlearned type of false doctrine circulating among Churches today that says the definition of fornication is limited to pre-marital sex. This false doctrine is not validated by Scripture, but is refuted. Examine closely **1 Corinthians 5:1**:*"It is reported commonly that there is fornication among you, and **such fornication as is not so much as named** among the Gentiles, that one should have his father's wife."* Is it just me or is it any less an act of adultery for a man to have his father's wife than if he had his neighbor's wife? She certainly is not engaged in pre-marital sex, but rather extra-marital sex. The word extra-marital denotes sex outside the marriage and is rightly called an act of fornication by the Apostle Paul. The quote, *"such fornication as is not so much as named"* infers that there are different types of fornication, and that type of fornication by a married person is elevated to the act of adultery while retaining the nomenclature of "fornication." The sin of adultery in this instance was initiated through the act of fornication. There is a type of adultery that does not involve fornication; it is still adultery. I will discuss it in "Thoughts on Divorce" in the "Appendices" section of this book. In this verse from 1 Corinthians 5:1, "father's wife" is present tense. In all likelihood, she was only one wife of several, as the practice of polygamy was common in that time and place.

The Old Testament Scriptures tell us that Reuben, the firstborn son of Jacob, lost his birthright when he committed this very act against his father, Jacob, when he "defiled" his father's bed. (See 1 Chronicles 5:1-2.) The word defile means to corrupt something that has been set apart (sanctified). Losing the birthright was no small punishment. As the firstborn son, Reuben was entitled to at least a double portion of the inheritance, and some theologians say as much as half. More importantly, he (Reuben) was removed from the right to become the head of the family when Jacob would die. Consequently, the ensuing kingdom would be given to Judah and the priesthood would be given to Levi. This is not a small penalty for what many people today simply dismiss as a small "indiscretion."

The consequences of sexual deviation from God's intent cannot be overstated. When Judah casually committed an act of incest with his (deceased) son's wife, while thinking she was a harlot, it cost his family ten generations of separation from God's congregation. The act of illegitimate sexual intercourse brought illegitimacy upon Judah's house, so that a gentile named Caleb would have to represent the tribe of Judah when they received their inheritance of the Promised Land. The name "Caleb" means "dog", and us gentiles were commonly referred to as dogs by Abraham's descendants; and yes, that included Jesus. (See Psalm 22:16; Matthew 15:26.)

Deuteronomy 23:2 *"A bastard shall not enter into the congregation of the LORD; **even to his tenth generation** shall he not enter into the congregation of the LORD."*

This verse is actually a reference to a person "misbegotten" through incest or adultery according to Mosaic Law. It would not be until King David that the required ten generations would be fulfilled from Judah's transgression.

Sadly, King David also would fall into sexual transgression when he committed adultery with Uriah's wife. If we have been in Church for any amount of time then we have most likely heard the "thou art the man" sermon where the Prophet Nathan confronts King David concerning his misdeeds inflicted upon Uriah. We have learned that as a result of those misdeeds, God told King David, *"...the sword shall never depart from thine house;"* (**2 Samuel 12:10**). Moreover, we have heard of the judgment of God that, *"...the child also that is born unto thee shall surely die."* (**2 Samuel 12:14**). From the way these judgments were stated by God, we could assert that David's actions simply opened a can of worms upon himself: one of those "Uh-oh" moments. If these were the only consequences for David's transgression, we could probably rest in that assumption. But these were not the only consequences for David's transgression.

The Scriptures are detailed as this chapter in King David's life unfolds and culminates with Absalom attempting to usurp his father's throne. In honoring God, and Jerusalem as God's dwelling place, King David would abdicate the throne of Israel rather than fight in the city to retain his throne from Absalom's coup. In his retreat, King David left several of his wives in Jerusalem. Subsequently, the counselor Ahithophel advised Absalom to, *"Go in unto thy father's concubines,"* in an effort to solidify Absalom's popular support by his political base. **2 Samuel 16:22** *"So they spread Absalom a tent upon the top of* *the house; and Absalom went in unto his father's concubines in the sight of all Israel."*

So, here we go back to the words of the Prophet Nathan that we don't usually hear about as a result of King David's transgression. **2 Samuel 12:11** *"Thus saith the LORD, Behold, I will raise up evil against thee out of thine own house, and I will take thy wives before thine eyes, and give them unto thy neighbour, and he shall lie with thy wives in the sight of this sun.* [12] *For thou didst it secretly: but I will do this thing before all Israel, and before the sun."* No wonder we don't hear much about this particular consequence. It's a hard thing to think that God would take a wife from a man and then give her to another man...while said first man was still living! We would obviously be wrong in assuming that God, as Sovereign Creator, is bound by laws and commandments that He intended for a fallen humanity.

The signature of God in the whole matter is the place where "they spread Absalom a tent." The top of the house was the top of the king's house where King David was when he first saw Bathsheba, Uriah's wife. The place where lust and adultery entered into King David's heart was the very place where God exacted judgment. In God's economy the punishment is a reflection of the crime. As I read this account from the Old Testament, the New Testament verse comes to mind: **Galatians 6:7** *"Be not deceived; God is not mocked: for whatsoever a man soweth, that shall he also reap."* It was no simple can of worms that King David opened up. It was God defending His institution of covenant. In this episode alone, the judgment that God pronounced upon King David's house cost David the lives of three of his children, and the incestuous rape of his virgin daughter, Tamar. Again, no small penalty for what many people today casually dismiss as "indiscretion."

So let's end the discussion on fornication where we began it. From 1 Corinthians 5:1-13 the Apostle Paul tells us that fornication is still sin. He goes on to say that while we may not be able to get away from fornicators of this world, as Christians we are to separate ourselves from fornicators within the Church. As Judah was separated from the congregation of the Lord for ten generations, the simple act of personal excommunication within the Church is a way that lets the offender know that they stand in transgression. The ultimate hope is that they will be convicted in their own heart of their wrongdoing, and return to a right relationship with the Lord Jesus Christ; as God still defends His institution of covenant. It is this author's opinion that excommunication should be a last resort, and that a person excommunicated should have the preeminent place in our prayers. If I faced the impending amputation of an infected body part, I probably wouldn't be praying for much else; likewise the Body of Christ cares for its members as well. (See also 1 Corinthians 6:18; 7:1-2)

Well, now I've gone and done it. I've called people misbegotten, adulterers, fornicators, dogs, and bastards, and I have even used the word "sin." God was adamant in the period of the law because the Scriptures testify of Jesus Christ. God wanted us to know of certainty that Jesus Christ, our Great High Priest, was not conjured into this existence by the mingling of the desires of man and God. But rather, Our Great High Priest was the Holy Offspring of God the Father. The commandments to the Nation of Israel pertaining to sexual purity were largely to protect the "Promise" to Abraham that his physical seed would produce the Messiah. This is the primary reason God didn't allow Israel to intermingle themselves with their surrounding nations. As the Son of God, Jesus Christ is without fault or blemish or failure or anything less than perfect, as humanity has come to recognize and accept its own faults as the norm. Nevertheless, I guess I can expect to be crucified for breaking the world's great commandment; that being "Tolerate everything and everybody." How dare I hold the Word of God above the world's expectations? My response to the world and to the Christian that has succumbed to the world's demand for conformity... God didn't call me to apologize for Him. But rather, He commands me to love those that are contrary to their own selves so much that I would hazard myself to save them from their folly. If your young child wandered onto a busy street would you find agreement with him? Or would you offer a direct correction? God's love requires more from us than the world's tolerance. **Proverbs 27:6** *"Faithful are the wounds of a friend;.."* Besides,... this is a Bible study.

For more verses on excommunication see: Rom 12:4-8/Matt 5:29-30/Mk 9:43-47; Rom 16:17-18; 1 Cor 16:22; Gal 1:8-9; Tit 3:10-11; 2 John 9-11; 2 Thes 3:6; 2 Thes 3:14; 1 Tim 6:3-5.

For verses on unbelievers in the Church see: Acts 20:29-31; 2 Pet 2:1-22; 1 John 2:18-19; Jude 4-19; 2 Cor 11:1-15; 2 Tim 3:1-9.

2 Corinthians 6:14 *"Be ye not unequally yoked together with unbelievers: for what fellowship hath righteousness with unrighteousness? and what communion hath light with darkness?* [15] *And what concord hath Christ with Belial? or what part hath he that believeth with an infidel?* [16] ***And what agreement hath the temple of God with idols? for ye are the temple of the living God;*** *as God hath said, I will dwell in them, and walk in them; and I will be their God, and they shall be my people.* [17] *Wherefore come out from among* *them, and be ye separate, saith the Lord, and touch not the unclean thing; and I will receive you, [18] And will be a Father unto you, and ye shall be my sons and daughters, saith the Lord Almighty."*

Amos 3:3 *"Can two walk together, except they be agreed?"*

God & Noah

Gen 6:18 God initiates the covenant with Noah.

Gen 7:1 God declares Noah's righteousness. **Hebrews 11:7** *"By faith Noah, being warned of God of things not seen as yet, moved with fear, prepared an ark to the saving of his house; by the which he condemned the world, and became heir of the righteousness which is by faith."* Righteousness which is by faith is the garment that covers our soul and is represented physically by fine linen clean and white. (See Revelation 19:8.)

Gen 8:20 Noah sacrifices and offers by fire.

Gen 9:8-11 God declares His intentions.

Gen 9:12-17 God establishes the rainbow as the witness; here called a "Token."

God & Abraham

Gen 12:1-7, 13:14-17 God initiates the covenant with Abram and declares His terms and intentions.

Gen 15:1-6 God declares His intentions to provide Abram with seed.

Gen 15:6 God declares Abram's righteousness (again by Faith).

Gen 15:9-10 God instructs Abram on the sacrifice. The heifer, the she goat, and the ram were each divided into two equal pieces. The pieces would have been sawn right down the middle and laid a few paces apart from each other; thus prefiguring the division God would suffer within Himself as Jesus became sin for us. (See 2 Corinthians 5:21.)

Gen 15:17 God passes between the pieces of flesh.

Gen 17:1-22 God reiterates His intentions and terms.

Gen 17:5 God changes Abram's name to Abraham. From this point of time in the Bible Abraham is always referred to as Abraham. Only twice after this is he referred to as Abram and both times are references to a pre-covenant time.

Gen 17:10-11 God instructs Abraham to keep circumcision in his flesh as a "Token" of the covenant. These instructions were binding upon the descendants of Abraham.

Gen 17:15-16 God conveys this same covenant to Sarai (Abraham's wife) and changes her name to Sarah. He also declares His intentions to "bless" her with children.

Gen 17:19-21 God names Isaac. Then He declares to Abraham His intentions to establish this same covenant with Isaac. Verse 21 is important because it differentiates the descendants of Abraham. Although many tribes descending from Abraham keep circumcision as the sign of the covenant, God said *"But my covenant will I establish with Isaac, which Sarah shall bear unto thee at this set time in the next year."* (**Genesis 17:21**). Isaac is the seed of promise. This is a foundational stone for building the New Testament doctrine of "Salvation by Grace." (See Galatians 3:16.)

Ex 2:24 This same covenant is conveyed upon and through Jacob. We will discuss Esau later. (See Galatians 3:16.)

Gen 32:28 God changes Jacob's name to Israel.

Gen 32:32 A witness "unto this day".

In both the covenant with Noah and the covenant with Abraham, God places a great emphasis upon the "seed." The account starts with the phrase in **Genesis 6:1**: *"And it came to pass, when **men began to multiply**..."* From Genesis 6:18, God's instructions to Noah were to bring his wife and sons and their wives with him into the ark. The animals were also to come into the ark, *"the male and his female."* According to **Genesis 7:2-3**, the purpose was *"...to keep seed alive upon the face of all the earth."*

As we move into the covenant that God made with Abraham, the first thing that stands out is God's promise to give seed to a couple that were beyond childbearing age. **Genesis 17:17** *"Then Abraham fell upon his face, and laughed, and said in his heart, Shall a child be born unto him that is an hundred years old? and shall Sarah, that is ninety years old, bear?"* It's a simple concept; God does what man cannot do. Isaac and the events in his life will become a prototype or a prefigure of Jesus Christ. The plan of salvation that Isaac foreshadows and literally carries in his DNA is God's plan and not man's.

Gen 15:2-5 The discussion is of Abraham's seed.

Gen 15:13-16 The discussion is of Abraham's seed.

Abraham himself will prove to be a personification of faith just as Moses was a personification of the Law. In that regard, the seed is still of God. In Genesis 15:18 a promise or declaration is made to the seed.

In Genesis 17 the entire chapter pertains to the seed. **Genesis 17:11** *"And ye shall circumcise the flesh of your foreskin; and it shall be a **token of the covenant** betwixt me and you."* **Genesis 17:13** *"...and my covenant shall be in your flesh for an everlasting covenant."*

Again, the seed would pass through the sign (token) of the covenant. The virtue of God's covenant Promise to bless all the families of the earth was conveyed to and through Abraham's seed as it passed through the sign of the covenant. This happened from one generation to the next generation, until that Promise was fulfilled in the birth of our Lord Jesus Christ.

In Genesis 20, there is an interesting story of Abraham as he journeyed into the land belonging to Abimelech, the King of Gerar. After seeing Sarah, the King took her for himself. But God, intending to preserve the promise *"...came to Abimelech in a dream by night, and said to him, Behold, thou art but a dead man, for the woman which thou hast taken; for she is a man's wife."* (**Genesis 20:3**). After Abimelech made restoration to Abraham, the Scripture tells us, *"So Abraham prayed unto God: and God healed Abimelech, and his wife, and his maidservants; and they bare children. For the LORD had fast closed up all the wombs of the house of Abimelech, because of Sarah Abraham's wife."* (**Genesis 20:17-18**). Without knowing, Abimelech invoked God's law of reciprocity. By tampering with God's seed, Abimelech brought a curse upon his own! God actually told Abimelech that His whole house stood in jeopardy of death. The Pharaoh of Egypt also faced this consequence when he dealt with Abraham in a similar situation.

In Genesis 21, the seed of promise sprouts and begins to grow in the birth of Isaac. The posterity of God's Promise is the story of the Bible. The Promise is eternal life given to us; that is, to any person and all people that call upon His name. Eternal life is the product of God's covenant with Abraham and is fulfilled in Jesus Christ. I encourage you to immerse yourself in the source of Life, the very Word of God. The same Word that produced Jesus Christ through the nation of Israel will also produce Christ in you. The Apostle Paul says in **Colossians 1:25**: *"Whereof I am made a minister, according to the **dispensation** of God which is given to me for you, to fulfil the word of God;* [26] *Even the mystery which hath been hid from **ages and from generations**, but now is made manifest to his saints:* [27] *To whom God would make known what is the riches of the glory of this mystery among the Gentiles; which is **Christ in you, the hope of glory**:"*

At the risk of getting ahead of myself within this study, I want to point out that God has divided the pre-designated time span of the physical creation into seven eras, also called ages. In each of those ages, humanity found itself enveloped in the characteristics of the age and in its own collective nature. As each age gave way to the next, and as humanity moved into new stages, God also changed the way that He interacted with humanity. We call these changes "**dispensations**." God's covenant with Abraham began the fourth dispensation of time; we call this fourth dispensation the dispensation of "Promise." From the verses that attest to the covenant, Genesis 12:1-2 are the first to record the terms or declarations of the covenant. Genesis 15:17-18 records the "cutting" of the covenant, and this would become the actual day the fourth dispensation began. So, three dispensations of time are contained in the first fifteen chapters of Genesis. This is why I say the Bible is the story of the posterity of God's Promise. We will discuss dispensations further as we move through this study.

Now, please allow me to backtrack a little here and speak about Ishmael from the perspective of **Galatians 3:16:** *"Now to Abraham and his seed were the promises made. **He saith not, And to seeds,** as of many; but as of one, And to thy seed, which is Christ."* Ishmael was the son of Abraham and Hagar. Hagar was Sarah's handmaid and she was of Egyptian ancestry. The particulars of the account are found in Genesis 16, 17. What is observed but not stated is that Abraham's relationship with Sarah was based on love. Abraham's relationship with Hagar was not based on love, and **Ishmael was not conceived by a promise of God** but rather by the desire of the flesh.

In this current age of international terrorism, it has become quite trendy for ministers to commonly label people of middle eastern descent as "Ishmael." While quoting from Genesis 16:12, these ministers point out the similarities of the Scripture with the nature of the terrorists originating from that area of the world. I must disagree with the practice. At the time Ishmael was born, we can easily note that numerous people groups were already established in the land. Genesis 10:15-20 gives a thorough list of those people groups. Abraham himself was a tenth generation descendant of Shem, the son of Noah, thus giving ample time for nomadic and situational migrations, both into and out of the land. Further, we should not overlook that Ishmael's mother was Egyptian.

With this in mind, we understand that God's use of Ishmael in the Scriptures is not to represent a specific people group, but rather represents an attribute found in all human flesh. Even though certain people groups were often found to embody certain characteristics or traits, God's use of the people group is to teach us to identify the traits and how we may be affected by them.

This is the case whether the traits are good or bad. Ishmael is the product of fleshly desire: namely, self-sufficiency, self-reliance, or self-fulfillment. This is the attribute or nature that was imparted to Ishmael by Abraham and Hagar, as Abraham tried to fulfill God's Promise to him by his own efforts. Since the Scriptures bear witness that Ishmael is antagonistic toward Isaac, it would not be farfetched to correlate these desires of the flesh as being antagonistic toward the Promise of God.

Galatians 4:22 *"For it is written, that Abraham had two sons, the one by a bondmaid, the other by a freewoman.* ^{23} *But he who was of the bondwoman was born after the flesh; but he of the freewoman was by promise.* ^{24} *Which things are an allegory: for these are the two covenants; the one from the mount Sinai, which gendereth to bondage, which is Agar...."*

These two covenants are God-cut. The covenant cut at Mt. Sinai is the covenant between God and the nation Israel, and is represented allegorically in Hagar. The other covenant was cut at Mt. Calvary between God and all of humanity through Jesus Christ and is represented allegorically in Sarah. (**Biblical allegory is a real life person, thing, or event that represents a larger event or idea.**) Pertaining to these two covenants, please compare Deuteronomy 6:25 against Galatians 3:21. We will look at these two covenants further as we progress.

In summary: The covenants between God & Noah and God & Abraham emphasize the seed.

Jacob & Esau

Isaac was the son of Abraham. Esau and Jacob were the twin brothers born to Isaac and Rebecca.

Gen 25:25 (Covering) *"And the first came out red, all over like an hairy garment; and they called his name Esau."*

Gen 27:11 (Covering) *"And Jacob said to Rebekah his mother, Behold, Esau my brother is a hairy man, and I am a smooth man:"*

Gen 25:30 (Name) *"...therefore was his name called Edom."*

Gen 27:36 (Name) *"And he said, Is not he rightly named Jacob? for he hath supplanted me these two times:"*

Gen 25:30 (Terms) *"And Esau said to Jacob, Feed me, I pray thee, with that same red pottage; for I am faint:"*

Gen 25:31 (Terms / Exchange) *"And Jacob said, Sell me this day thy birthright."*

Gen 25:34 (Meal) *"Then Jacob gave Esau bread and pottage of lentiles; and he did eat and drink, and rose up, and went his way:"*

Both the exchange of garments and/or a change of name indicate a change of nature, person, or position. While this covenant has the feel of a simple business transaction, the effect was much more profound as Esau and Jacob literally traded places. Esau, being the elder, would have been heir to the birthright and to the covenant promises made by God to Isaac and Abraham. But in this case, one covenant made void the other. Esau would forever lose his birthright and the posterity of God's Seed and the relationship with God that came with it. The covenant between the two brothers would alter the destiny of each man in his own life and the destiny of his own descendants in the annals of eternal history. This fact is evidenced in Genesis 27:37, 28:10-22, 32:28, and 35:10.

Gen 27:37 (Witness, Evidence, Exchange) *"And Isaac answered and said unto Esau, Behold, I have made him thy lord,..."*

Gen 28:14 (God's promise to Abraham conveyed to Jacob) *"And thy seed shall be as the dust of the earth, and thou shalt spread abroad to the west, and to the east, and to the north, and to the south: and in thee and in thy seed shall all the families of the earth be blessed."*

Gen 32:28 (Name change) *"And he said, Thy name shall be called no more Jacob, but Israel: for as a prince hast thou power with God and with men, and hast prevailed."*

We will see this covenant again as it parallels the Fall of Adam in the Garden of Eden. This covenant between Esau and Jacob emphasizes the exchange of natures or the trading of places.

God & The Nation Israel

Ex 19:5 (Terms) *"Now therefore, if ye will obey my voice indeed, and keep my covenant, then ye shall be a peculiar treasure unto me above all people: for all the earth is mine:"*

Ex 24:3 (Terms) *"And Moses came and told the people all the words of the LORD, and all the judgments: and all the people answered with one voice, and said, All the words which the LORD hath said will we do."*

Ex 24:4 (Witness) *"And Moses wrote all the words of the LORD, and rose up early in the morning, and builded an altar under the hill, and twelve pillars, according to the twelve tribes of Israel."* (See also Genesis 31:44-46; Joshua 4:2-9.)

Ex 24:5 (Sacrifice) *"And he sent young men of the children of Israel, which offered burnt offerings, and sacrificed peace offerings of oxen unto the LORD."*

Ex 24:6 (Sacrifice) *"And Moses took half of the blood, and put it in basons; and half of the blood he sprinkled on the altar."*

Ex 24:7 (Vows/Terms) *"And he took the book of the covenant, and read in the audience of the people: and they said, All that the LORD hath said will we do, and be obedient."*

Ex 24:8 (Sacrifice) *"And Moses took the blood, and sprinkled it on the people, and said, Behold the blood of the covenant, which the LORD hath made with you concerning all these words."*

Ex 40:34 (Covering) *"Then a cloud covered the tent of the congregation, and the glory of the LORD filled the tabernacle."*

De 6:25 (Covering) *"And it shall be our righteousness, if we observe to do all these commandments before the LORD our God, as he hath commanded us."*

Predicated upon the seemingly minor "if" in Deuteronomy 6:25, this covering is not the covering for our soul that was imputed to Noah and Abraham. The covering offered by Deuteronomy 6:25 is most closely described in the dialog between God and Job in **Job 40:10,14:** *"Deck thyself now with majesty and excellency; and array thyself with glory and beauty."* *" Then will I also confess unto thee that thine own right hand can save thee."* (See Acts 15:10-11.) Contrast Deuteronomy 6:25 against Galatians 3:21.

In this covenant between God and the Nation Israel, the emphasis is, without question, on the terms. The terms of this covenant became known as, and are still referred to, as "The Law of Moses". This is the covenant that God cut at Mt. Sinai. While there have been many attempts to separate or distinguish the individual ordinances of this covenant into the categories of "civil, moral, and/or ceremonial laws," the Scriptures themselves consistently contradict this idea.

Consider:

James 2:10-11 *"For whosoever shall keep the **whole** law, and yet offend in **one** point, he is guilty of **all**. [11] For he that said, Do not commit adultery, said* *also, Do not kill. Now if thou commit no adultery, yet if thou kill, thou art become a transgressor of the law."*

Galatians 3:10 *"For as many as are of the works of the law are under the curse: for it is written, Cursed is every one that continueth not in **all** things which are written in the book of the law to do them."*

Galatians 5:3 *"For I testify again to every man that is circumcised, that he is a debtor to do the **whole** law."*

Moreover, there are examples in all three classes of law where the penalty for infraction is death: Deuteronomy 17:8-12 (Civil), Leviticus 10:1-2 (Ceremonial), and Exodus 21:15-17 (Moral).

If these Scriptures aren't enough to bind the individual ordinances of the law into a singular, cohesive, authoritative instrument, then I would simply refer back to **Exodus 24:3:** *"And Moses came and told the people **all** the words of the LORD, and **all** the judgments: and **all** the people answered with **one voice**, and said, **All** the words which the LORD hath said will we do."* (The **Emphasis is mine.** DP) If there are Scriptures that allow man to divide God's terms for this covenant, I have not found them!

In similar fashion, this covenant promotes the idea of maintaining fundamental distinctives. That is, the covenant has ordinances to promote self-preservation. It operates independent from any other covenant or outside source of contamination or compromise. **Leviticus 19:19** *"Ye shall keep my statutes. Thou shalt not let thy cattle gender with a diverse kind: thou shalt not sow thy field with mingled seed: neither shall a garment mingled of linen and woollen come upon thee."* "Don't mix your seed" and "don't mix your garments" are easily recognizable as principals applicable to any covenant. We cannot take promises or vows from one covenant and apply them to another. While the terms of this covenant convey an importance upon the "seed", as also spoken in the previous covenants, this particular verse in Leviticus 19:19 teaches us to segregate one covenant from another. (See Matthew 9:16-17; Galatians 5:4; 1Corinthians 7:39.) We will maintain this principle as we move through this study.

As we look at covenant as an institution, in light of the New Testament, we are brought to the understanding that the seed is not our fleshly offspring as it also pertained to Abraham, Isaac, and Jacob. For God, *"...hath made of one blood all nations of men for to dwell on all the face of the earth."* In fact, "seed" is "faith" itself, as received through the Word of God.

Mark 4:13-14 *"And he said unto them, Know ye not this parable? and how then will ye know all parables? [14] The sower soweth the word."*

Romans 10:8 *"...that is, the word of faith, which we preach;"*

Romans 10:17 *"So then faith cometh by hearing, and hearing by the word of God."*

1 Peter 1:23 *"Being born again, not of corruptible seed, but of incorruptible, by the word of God, which liveth and abideth for ever."*

As we continue this study, we will rely more heavily on this principle. The seed is faith.

Ruth & Boaz

Ruth 3:9 (Covering) *"And he said, Who art thou? And she answered, I am Ruth thine handmaid: spread therefore thy skirt over thine handmaid; for thou art a near kinsman."*

Ruth 4:10 (Witness) *"Moreover Ruth the Moabitess, the wife of Mahlon, have I purchased to be my wife, to raise up the name of the dead upon his inheritance, that the name of the dead be not cut off from among his brethren, and from the gate of his place: ye are witnesses this day. [11] And all the people that were in the gate, and the elders, said, We are witnesses."*

The entire story of Ruth is a beautiful representation of how the Gentile Church would be grafted into the family of Abraham through her covenant with the "Kinsman Redeemer". The narrative is rich in symbolism and allegory, as the lives of Ruth and Naomi foretell of the relationships of the Church and National Israel with each other and with our Redeemer. Boaz portrays the willingness of Christ to extend His virtue over a woman that has a "Nearer Kinsman" than he is to her. We will look at this nearer kinsman in another chapter.

Ephesians 2:12-13 *"That at that time ye were without Christ, being aliens from the commonwealth of Israel, and strangers from the covenants of promise, having no hope, and without God in the world: [13] But now in Christ Jesus ye who sometimes were far off are made nigh by the blood of Christ."*

As a Moabite by birth, Ruth was separated from the hope that only comes from having a relationship with God. However, her marriage to Boaz would change that and secure for her a place within National Israel, and in the Promise that God made to Abraham. Likewise, the Blood of Christ has made the Church His beloved. (See Romans 9:25.)

Ruth 4:11 *"And all the people that were in the gate, and the elders, said, We are witnesses. The LORD make the woman that is come into thine house like Rachel and like Leah, which two did build the house of Israel: and do thou worthily in Ephratah, and be famous in Beth-lehem: [12] And let thy house be like the house of Pharez, whom Tamar bare unto Judah, of the seed which the LORD shall give thee of this young woman."*

The child born to Ruth and Boaz would be the grandfather of David, King of Israel. The genealogy in Ruth 4:18-22 chronicles the ten generations from Judah, which were prerequisite before a descendant of Judah could legitimately sit as God's regent in Israel. The same requirement precipitated God's choice of a Benjamite as the first King of Israel. (See 1 Samuel 8:5-7.)

Jonathan & David

1 Samuel 18:3-4 *"Then Jonathan and David made a covenant, because he loved him as his own soul. [4] And Jonathan stripped himself of the robe that was upon him, and gave it to David, and his garments, even to his sword, and to his bow, and to his girdle."*

In these two covenants (Ruth/Boaz and Jonathan/David), we turn our focus to the "Covering". Garments, as a representation, are a major theme throughout the Word of God. In 2 Samuel 12 we read how King David, after committing adultery with Bathsheba and being found out, fasted and lay upon the earth. But when he arose and came into the house of the Lord to worship he *"...washed and anointed himself, and **changed his apparel**,"*. In Genesis 41:14, when Joseph was called up out of the dungeon to stand before Pharaoh, the Scripture says that *"...**he changed his raiment**,"*.

Most of us can quite easily relate our selection of clothes or apparel with our mood or countenance. We see the outside of our person imaging and reflecting the inside of our person. Or perhaps in an official capacity, we see garments reflecting an authority or position or status. This is the case with a judge or king or, in sports, a referee.

In Exodus 22:6 the raiment or "robe" is actually being given as a pledge for a business transaction. (See also Deuteronomy 24:10-13,17; Proverbs 20:16.) This is very similar to the way we would use a handshake today in personal dealings or agreements. Or, our signature would be offered in more legalistic agreements.

A similar exchange took place in Genesis 38:18, when Tamar asked of Judah a pledge of his signet (his seal, perhaps a ring), staff and bracelets. All of these were very personal items that conveyed Judah's individual personality and identity. In that era, it was common for shepherds to carve into their staff the notable events of their lives. Maybe they would record battles they had fought in, territorial acquisitions, the size of their herds, or their social status within their own family or community. In the shepherd's mind, whatever distinguished him in life would have adorned his most personal and important tool. The shepherd's staff was literally a representation of himself.

This is a fact not lost on Almighty God when He told Moses at the Burning Bush, "cast it on the ground." We have all heard the story of Moses' staff becoming a serpent. (See Exodus 4:2-4.) God didn't make a mistake when He told Moses to, "...*take it by the tail*" when he picked it back up. The picture painted is one of Moses leaning on himself as he entered into God's presence, but realizing as he leaves God's presence that all that he is rightly amounts to nothing in God's sight. Too bad we all don't realize the "we don't impress God" idea for ourselves.

In the dispensations of time prior to the death of Jesus Christ on the Cross, it was expected that if a man died childless, then his brother would take the widow of his brother as his own wife, "to raise up seed" to his brother. (See Deuteronomy 25:5-10; Matthew 22:24; Mark 12:19; Luke 20:28.) More often than not, the laws of a land are from the collective expectation of the people. When Judah failed to give his younger son to Tamar as expected by the law, she took the matter into her own hands.

Genesis 38:24-26 "*And it came to pass about three months after, that it was told Judah, saying, Tamar thy daughter in law hath played the harlot; and also, behold, she is with child by whoredom. And Judah said, Bring her forth, and let her be burnt. *[25]* When she was brought forth, she sent to her father in law, saying, By the man, whose these are, am I with child: and she said, Discern, I pray thee, whose are these,* **the signet, and bracelets, and staff.** *[26] And Judah acknowledged them, and said, She hath been more righteous than I; because that I gave her not to Shelah my son. And he knew her again no more.*"

Just as the "tokens" of a damsel's virginity were to be presented in the damsel's defense under the Law of Moses, Tamar presents the "witnesses" of her agreement with Judah as her defense. This is a right use of the witnesses, considering that the Seed of Promise would pass from Judah to Tamar. Besides Mary, the Mother of Jesus, Tamar is one of only three named women in the genealogy of Jesus; a fourth is referenced but not named.

In the covenant between Jonathan and David there are significant implications for our relationship with Jesus Christ. Jonathan was the Son of King Saul. We will discuss this relationship further under "Law and Grace," but suffice it here to say that Jonathan's robe represented his royalty and his authority to act on behalf of the King and of the state. The sword and bow specified this authority. The girdle was the belt that the weapons hung on. It also may have served to carry the keys to the armories, garrisons, storehouses, stables, gates, prisons and other essentials necessary to operate a kingdom. The belt would also have borne the armor that covered the loins, another reference to the seed.

So in the Scriptural use of covenant, the exchange of garments or robes would be symbolic of trading places with or investing virtue upon, and/or becoming one with another person. This is often why we see a groom place his coat upon his new bride after the vows are spoken in a marriage ceremony. There are still expectations of covenant built into society and humanity by our Loving Creator that we often don't even recognize.

Of most importance, we note that the Kingdom which Jonathan was rightful heir to would now pass from a Benjamite (Rachael) to David of the tribe of Judah (Leah). The transition didn't just happen by a Royal Decree from Heaven, or by the prophecy of the patriarchs, but by the action of covenant.

God & Man(Kind)

This is the New Covenant. It is also called the New Testament. It is the covenant that was mediated by Jesus Christ on behalf of all of humanity, or more specifically that is, "whosoever will." It is necessary for me to restate that the Scriptures listed here are not to be considered as exhaustive or all inclusive. The Witness of God said in **Psalms 40:7**: *"Then said I, Lo, I come: in the volume of the book it is written of me,"* (See also Hebrews 10:7.) To know or partake of every detail, every jot, every tittle, every promise, every hope, or every gift, then you must interact personally and intimately with Jesus Christ, the Author and Finisher of your faith, in His written Word. There are no shortcuts with God. The Scriptures listed here are intended simply as an introduction to the principals of covenant and are for your convenience of reference and study.

Hebrews 8:13 *"In that he saith, A new covenant, he hath made the first old. Now that which decayeth and waxeth old is ready to vanish away."*

Hebrews 7:12 *"For the priesthood being changed, there is made of necessity a change also of the law."*

John 3:16-18 (Terms) *"For God so loved the world, that he gave his only begotten Son, that whosoever **believeth** in him should not perish, but have everlasting life. [17] For God sent not his Son into the world to condemn the* world; but that the world through him might be saved. *[18] He that believeth on him is not condemned: but he that believeth not is condemned already, because he hath not believed in the name of the only begotten Son of God."*

Rom 10:9-11 (Terms) *"That if thou shalt confess with thy mouth the Lord Jesus, and shalt **believe in thine heart** that God hath raised him from the dead, thou shalt be saved. [10] For with the heart man **believeth unto righteousness**; and with the mouth confession is made unto salvation. [11] For the scripture saith, Whosoever **believeth on him** shall not be ashamed."*

Rom 10:13 (Terms) *"For whosoever shall call upon the name of the Lord shall be saved."*

John 5:24 (Terms) *"Verily, verily, I say unto you, He that heareth my word, and **believeth on him that sent me**, hath everlasting life, and shall not come into condemnation; but is passed from death unto life."*

John 6:40 (Terms) *"And this is the will of him that sent me, that every one which seeth the Son, and **believeth on him**, may have everlasting life: and I will raise him up at the last day."*

John 1:12 (Terms) *"But as many as received him, to them gave he power to become the sons of God, even to them that **believe on his name**:"*

John 8:24 (Terms) *"I said therefore unto you, that ye shall die in your sins: for if ye **believe not** that I am he, **ye shall die in your sins**."*

Rev 19:7-8 (Exchange) *"Let us be glad and rejoice, and give honour to him: for the marriage of the Lamb is come, and his wife hath made herself ready. [8] And to her was granted that she should be arrayed in fine linen, clean and white: for the fine linen is the righteousness of saints."*

2 Cor 5:21 (Exchange) *"For he hath made him to be sin for us, who knew no sin; that we might be made the righteousness of God in him."*

Isa 53:12 (Exchange) *"...and he bare the sin of many,"*

1 Pet 2:24 (Exchange) *"Who his own self bare our sins in his own body on the tree, that we, being dead to sins, should live unto righteousness:"*

Isa 61:10 (Exchange) *"I will greatly rejoice in the LORD, my soul shall be joyful in my God; for he hath clothed me with the garments of salvation, he hath covered me with the robe of righteousness, as a bridegroom decketh himself with ornaments, and as a bride adorneth herself with her jewels."*

2 Chr 6:41 (Exchange) *"...let thy priests, O LORD God, be clothed with salvation,"*

Rom 13:14 (Exchange) *"But put ye on the Lord Jesus Christ, and make not provision for the flesh, to fulfil the lusts thereof."*

Gal 2:20-21 (Exchange) *"I am crucified with Christ: nevertheless I live; yet not I, but Christ liveth in me: and the life which I now live in the flesh I live by the faith of the Son of God, who loved me, and gave himself for me. 21 I do not frustrate the grace of God: for if righteousness come by the law, then Christ is dead in vain."*

John 1:29 (Sacrifice) *"The next day John seeth Jesus coming unto him, and saith, Behold the Lamb of God, which taketh away the sin of the world."*

Luke 23:33-34 (Sacrifice) *"And when they were come to the place, which is called Calvary, there they crucified him, and the malefactors, one on the right hand, and the other on the left. 34 Then said Jesus, Father, forgive them; for they know not what they do. And they parted his raiment, and cast lots."*

Eph 5:2 (Sacrifice) *"And walk in love, as Christ also hath loved us, and hath given himself for us an offering and a sacrifice to God for a sweet smelling savour."*

John 6:51 (Sacrifice) *"I am the living bread which came down from heaven: if any man eat of this bread, he shall live for ever: and the bread that I will give is my flesh, which I will give for the life of the world."* John1:14 *"And the Word was made flesh, and dwelt among us,"*

Luke 22:19-20 (Sacrifice/Witness) *"And he took bread, and gave thanks, and brake it, and gave unto them, saying, This is my body which is given for you: **this do in remembrance of me.** 20 Likewise also the cup after supper, saying, This cup is the new testament in my blood, which is shed for you."* (Communion is a memorial meal.)

Luke 24:38-39 (Witness) *"And he said unto them, Why are ye troubled? and why do thoughts arise in your hearts? 39 Behold my hands and my feet, that it is I myself: handle me, and see; for a spirit hath not flesh and bones, as ye see me have. 40 And when he had thus spoken, he shewed them his hands and his feet."* (These wounds serve as a scar or mark in the flesh.)

Heb 11:1 (Witness) *"Now faith is the substance of things hoped for, the **evidence** of things not seen."*

Heb 10:15-17 (Witness) *"Whereof the Holy Ghost also is a witness to us: for after that he had said before, [16] This is the covenant that I will make with them after those days, saith the Lord, I will put my laws into their hearts, and in their minds will I write them; [17] And their sins and iniquities will I remember no more."* (See also Jeremiah 31:31-34.)

2

Applied Precepts

God's Covering

Since our tendency is to view things from a personal perspective, it is probably not yet fully understood what God is speaking in Scripture pertaining to the exchange of raiment. After all, how do we see virtue or righteousness or sin?

Psalm 104:1-2 *"Bless the LORD, O my soul. O LORD my God, thou art very great; thou art clothed with honour and majesty. ² Who coverest thyself with light as with a garment:..."*

Job 40:10 *"Deck thyself now with majesty and excellency; and array thyself with **glory** and beauty."*

Job 40:14 *"Then will I also confess unto thee that thine own right hand can save thee."*

It is almost incomprehensible to imagine what the shepherds saw the night that our Savior entered this physical realm we call the world. As we read the account in Luke 2:9-14, we are given a glimpse into the heavenly worship service. Just as the Glory of God commanded the preeminence in the midst of God-manifestations during the era of the Old Testament, the awe inspiring, all powerful, overwhelming majesty of God's Glory was given the preeminence, as the angelic host announced the birth of God's Salvation to the shepherds. **Luke 2:9** *"And, lo, the angel of the Lord came upon them, and the **glory of the Lord** shone round about them: and they were sore afraid."* The word "sore" in this verse is from the Greek "Megas" or "Megistos" and it simply means that the shepherds could not be more afraid. This was not just a right reaction on the shepherd's part, as if by choice or by reverence. The shepherds literally experienced an input overload. Their bodies (and ours) were not capable of interaction with the divine manifestation of God's Person.

Oh yes, **The Holy Spirit is the Glory of God**. He is the third Person of the Holy Trinity.

Ezekiel 1:26-28 *"And above the firmament that was over their heads was the likeness of a throne, as the appearance of a sapphire stone: and upon the* *likeness of the throne was the likeness as the appearance of a man above upon it. [27] And I saw as the colour of amber, as the appearance of fire round about within it, from the appearance of his loins even upward, and from the appearance of his loins even downward, I saw as it were the appearance of fire, and it had brightness round about. [28] As the appearance of the bow that is in the cloud in the day of rain, so was the appearance of the brightness round about.* **This was the appearance of the likeness of the glory of the LORD.** *And when I saw it, I fell upon my face, and I heard a voice of one that spake."* (See also Ezekiel 8:1-4.)

When we look at the presence of the Holy Ghost in our lives today, we see His manifestations in both the gifts of the Spirit and the fruit of the Spirit. The gifts of the Spirit can be found in Romans 12 and 1st Corinthians chapters 12 and 13. The fruit of the Spirit is listed as such in Galatians 5.

The presence of the Holy Ghost is portrayed by the gifts in Genesis 24:53. This story is of Abraham (a representation of God the Father) sending his servant (a representation of the Holy Spirit) to "take" a wife for Isaac (a representation of Jesus).

Genesis 24:53 *"And the servant brought forth jewels of silver, and jewels of gold, and raiment, and gave them to Rebekah: he gave also to her brother and to her mother precious things."*

In verse 22 of this same chapter, the servant gave to Rebekah a golden earring and two bracelets for her hands. These gifts of gold and jewels represent the gifts of the Spirit given to the Bride of Christ.

As we will see when we look closer into the heavenly worship of God, there is a dynamic and continual investing of virtue when jewels and raiment are given in covenant. In the earthly realm they are symbolic in saying, "you are my chosen" or "my presence is conveyed through you." In the Spirit realm the gifts and raiment are not symbolic, but are literal manifestations of God Himself. Today the gifts of the Spirit are alive and working in the Body of Christ to show forth His presence upon His Bride. These gifts/manifestations of God are more real than the air we breathe and the ground we stand upon. Whereas the gifts of God are eternal in nature, the ground and air are only temporary!

Consider this passage of Scripture, as we ponder the greatness of God's Glory. **2 Peter 3:10-13** *"But the day of the Lord will come as a thief in the night; in the which the heavens shall pass away with a great noise, and the elements shall melt with fervent heat, the earth also and the works that are therein shall be burned up. [11] Seeing then that all these things shall be dissolved, what manner of persons ought ye to be in all holy conversation and godliness,*

¹² Looking for and hasting unto the coming of the day of God, wherein the heavens being on fire shall be dissolved, and the elements shall melt with fervent heat? ¹³ Nevertheless we, according to his promise, look for new heavens and a new earth, wherein dwelleth righteousness."

The Holy Spirit of God is implicit in performing the Word of God. In John 6:63, Jesus says His Word is Spirit. The same Holy Spirit that performed "In the beginning" will also perform the melting with fervent heat. To put this "melting" in proper perspective, a snowflake passing through our sun's core would offer more resistance to melting than would our universe at the presence of God's Glory! This is the power the shepherds experienced as the supernatural briefly interrupted the natural.

His presence is also established in **Galatians 5:22-23**: *"But the fruit of the Spirit is love, joy, peace, longsuffering, gentleness, goodness, faith, ²³ Meekness, temperance: against such there is no law."*

Let's relate for a moment to the plight of the lost, and how unsatisfying life actually is for them. The lost live in a realm where life consumes death and death consumes life. It's a cruel perpetuity that assigns little to no significance or meaning to the lives of the servants that sustain it. For the most part, we suffer circumstance beyond our capability and then strive to insulate our loved ones from it. In the end, we only hope against reality to have made a difference. **Proverbs 30:15** *"The horseleach hath two daughters, crying, Give, give. There are three things that are never satisfied, yea, four things say not, It is enough: ¹⁶ The grave; and the barren womb; the earth that is not filled with water; and the fire that saith not, It is enough."* But the cycle itself continues: taunting, unrelenting, unaffected by our efforts, it jeers gleefully as it exercises dominion over its subjects. This is the plight of the lost and hopeless.

It's no wonder that God has put the witness of eternity into every man's heart. The yearning for a different existence calls us to seek something outside of ourselves. We come to know that the paradigm of this existence cannot be altered from within. If every human that ever lived willed it and worked toward it in perfect unison and harmony, we still could not change it. It requires something external, something larger than fallen creation, to translate us into a new paradigm.

Looking back at my own situation, I remember being in desire for something to satisfy my reason for being. I was hungry for truth. Though it had been offered to me in word, I didn't notice the appeal of it until the truth was manifest in the fruit of the Spirit. That manifestation was in the person of a man, a friend that I worked with. He never mentioned Jesus verbally to me, but I saw in him great joy and gentleness and faith. Today he is still a very close friend and confidant.

Think of how a buffet of all manner of fruit would be enticing to someone who is starving. They have that longing in their soul for sustenance: the craving that says, "Ummm, I need that!" At first, we may not see the immediate connection to covenant or the importance of bearing fruit, until we recognize that the "**seed**" is in the fruit. It is the seed that holds the promise for the next life! The Holy Ghost works implicitly through the fruit of the Spirit to bring orthodoxy into orthopraxy. James said it this way: *"...faith without works is dead also."* In our common vernacular we say that "Right thinking produces right living." Right thinking is only produced by faith, the seed of God in us. The fruit of the Spirit is the nature of God imparted to us by His Holy Ghost, and that presence adorns the person of every Christian that walks in the Spirit. (See Galatians 5:22-26.) Literally, He is, within us, the invitation to the lost to *"...taste and see that the LORD is good."*

This is the "Covering" that God gave to us. It is His person. It is His Righteousness and His Majesty. If we could see past our flesh, we would see the "Robe of Righteousness" that covers the soul of every born-again believer.

The seed also carries an immunity of sorts. **Galatians 5:23** *"...against such there is no law."* This is a reference to the Law of Moses. The majority of the Book of Galatians is a contrast between the two "gospels." We will proceed to contrast the two covenants after we take a closer look at the covering we placed upon Jesus.

The Covering of Man

2 Corinthians 5:21 *"For he hath made him to be sin for us, who knew no sin; that we might be made the righteousness of God in him."*

God manifests His presence through the virtue of faith in both the gifts of the Spirit and the fruit of the Spirit. Faith is the only manifestation to appear in both groups. Moreover, in **Hebrews 11:6** God tells us that: *"...without faith it is impossible to please him:"* That is, it's impossible to please God without faith.

As the Scriptures define faith and sin, we don't have to look far, either in Scripture or in this present world, to see how faithlessness rears itself. Whether in speech, deed, attitude, or doctrine, the effects of faithlessness are inescapable.

Romans 14:23 *"...for whatsoever is not of faith is sin."*

For some people this creates a very broad picture of sin; for others it tends to narrow the view. With differences in denomination and theology within the

Body of Christ, this seems to be the 800 pound gorilla in the room. What is faith? What is sin? Diligence will require several sections as we answer this subject adequately. But don't worry, God didn't call me to make speculation about things He has already determined. He has only one standard for right and wrong.

Just as there are many aspects of God, there are also many aspects or manifestations of evil, or of the Devil. We also know, through reading God's Word, that God has categorized evil spirits into several different types. Each type has a different manifestation and they are named according to their manifestation or ministry. Each demonic spirit serves a different aspect within the whole. In order to thoroughly discover the nature of the adversary, and of sin, we will begin again at the covenant of Jacob and Esau.

Genesis 25:22-26 *"And the children struggled together within her; and she said, If it be so, why am I thus? And she went to inquire of the LORD. [23] And the LORD said unto her, Two nations are in thy womb, and two manner of people shall be separated from thy bowels; and the one people shall be stronger than the other people; and the elder shall serve the younger. [24] And when her days to be delivered were fulfilled, behold, there were twins in her womb. [25] And the first came out red, all over **like an hairy garment**; and they called his name Esau. [26] And after that came his brother out, and his hand took hold on Esau's heel; and his name was called Jacob: and Isaac was threescore years old when she bare them."*

This passage of Scripture pertains to Rebekah, the wife of Isaac, and the events that would befall her and her offspring. Since God has spoken in future terms concerning His answer to Rebekah, we know this event, as well as the lives of Jacob and Esau, to be prophetic. I would restate here that Biblical allegory is a real life event or person or thing that represents another larger idea, concept, or event.

But there is more than allegory going on here. In Genesis 25:30 we are told that his name was called "Edom," referring to Esau. In the Hebrew language, the name Edom comes from the root word for "red," just as "Adam" does.

Genesis 3:1 *"Now the serpent was more subtil than any beast of the field which the LORD God had made."* In Genesis 27:35 we read concerning Jacob that he came with "subtility" and took Esau's blessing. In **Genesis 27:36** Esau said: *"... Is not he rightly named Jacob? for he hath supplanted me these two times:"* The name "Jacob" means "supplanter" or "deceiver."

Now we begin to see that the lives and events portrayed in Jacob and Esau are not just prophetic; they are also revelatory. They are revelatory in the sense that they represent what happened between Adam and Satan in the Garden of Eden.

If we continue to compare the covenant of Edom and The Supplanter with the covenant of Adam and The Deceiver, we notice a bite of food involved. Adam ate of the fruit and Edom ate the lentils. The same act led to the loss of the birthright for both Edom and Adam.

Finally, in comparing the two events, the heel is mentioned. At their birth, Jacob's hand took hold of Esau's heel, and in **Genesis 3:15** God said to the serpent: *"...thou shalt bruise his heel."*

(At this point in the teaching, I would normally field questions from a class. But since the setting doesn't permit that, I will simply refer you to the source. The event is found in Genesis, chapter 25, and reads through chapter 28. There is no substitute for reading your Bible and prayer. In fact, reading your Bible is the listening part of prayer. Perhaps the greatest benefit to reading your Bible prayerfully is that you learn to discern God's voice to you personally.)

I often hear preaching or teaching on how deceptive Jacob was to ask Esau to trade his birthright for a bowl of food. But God summarizes His view of the whole deal in **Genesis 25:34**: *"...thus Esau despised his birthright."* We should ponder this verse, "Thus Esau despised his birthright." How much higher we must exalt ourselves to take all of our Father's possessions, and all of His authority, and all of His virtue, which is conveyed through the seed, and reduce it to a bite of food.

The birthright represents our Father's very person. Thus Esau despised his Father!

What a tragedy! Esau held within him all the promises God had given to Abraham. Esau could have been one of the greatest types or representations of Christ in all of Scripture. He was destined to become a representation of the second Adam spoken of by the Apostle Paul in 1 Corinthians 15:45. Instead, by his own values and subsequent choice, he has become one of the most sinister representations of evil in all of the Word of God. We will look at this representation further in the "Prototype Relevance" section of this book.

So, the covenant and the events in the lives of Jacob and Esau look both forward and backward. Before we can move into the prophetic aspects of these Scriptures, we first must go back and look at another aspect of the covenant in the Fall of Man.

Satan's (Un)Covering

Genesis 2:25 *"And they were both naked, the man and his wife, and were not ashamed."*

Here I would ask you to remember how the Scripture calls attention to the fact that Esau was covered and Jacob was not. At this point, I want to refer you to 1 Corinthians 11:15. We will come back to it later in the study.

In any study of Scripture we find that "shame" and "covering" are synonymous. For example:

1. **Job 8:22** *"They that hate thee shall be **clothed** with **shame;**"*

2. **Isa 20:4** *"So shall the king of Assyria lead away the Egyptians prisoners, and the Ethiopians captives, young and old, **naked** and barefoot, even with their **buttocks uncovered**, to the **shame** of Egypt."*

3. **Rev 3:18** *"I counsel thee to buy of me gold tried in the fire, that thou mayest be rich; and white raiment, that thou mayest be clothed, and that the **shame** of thy **nakedness** do not appear;..."*

4. **Rev 16:15** *"Behold, I come as a thief. Blessed is he that watcheth, and keepeth his garments, lest he walk **naked**, and they see his **shame.**"*

5. See also 2 Samuel 6:20; Proverbs 12:16; Hebrews 12:2 and many others. About 25% of all Scriptures that mention shame also refer to some type of covering or nakedness.

6. In the English language the word "embarrass" is a synonym for shame and literally means to "make bare the buttock." **2 Samuel 10:4-5** *"Wherefore Hanun took David's servants, and shaved off the one half of their beards, and **cut off their garments in the middle, even to their buttocks**, and sent them away. [5] When they told it unto David, he sent to meet them, because the men were **greatly ashamed**: and the king said, Tarry at Jericho until your beards be grown, and then return."*

Because the Bible links nakedness so consistently with shame, I refer to shame as the "Uncovering."

But **Genesis 2:25** says: *"And they were both naked, the man and his wife, and were **not ashamed.**"* From this verse and from Genesis 3:6-7, we assume that Adam's innocence made him vulnerable to influence or coercion. In modern circles of sophistry, the self-acclaimed masters of enlightenment have used the words "ignorant" and "automaton" to describe Adam in his original state of being. And why not? After all, our only example of human innocence is in babies; and they are susceptible to influence and coercion. But this isn't the picture that diligent study of the Scripture develops. As we have just shown from the list above, nakedness and shame are one and the same. The phrase "not ashamed" in Genesis 2:25 is Bible-speak for "not without covering." In other words, Adam and Eve <u>were</u> naked but they <u>were not</u> without covering prior to the Fall of Man in the Garden of Eden.

They were covered with the Glory of God. I say this because the Scripture says they were made in His image. **Psalms 104:1-2** *"Bless the LORD, O my soul. O LORD my God, thou art very great; thou art clothed with honour and majesty.* [2] *Who coverest thyself with light as with a garment:"* Adam could not bear the image of God without the Glory of God! The Glory of God was more tangible as a covering to Adam than the skins he would eventually come to know. The Glory that covered Adam and Eve was the living preeminent Holy Spirit of God. It was His presence that designated Adam as a subordinate Trinity and also as Regent of the physical realm. Both the Trinity and Regency are aspects of God's image. Adam was created to bear God's Glory and he radiated that Glory as light; just as God Himself is covered with light. The Glory of God covered Adam and Eve the same way He covered the face of Moses in Exodus 34:29-35. (See also 2 Corinthians 3:7.) **Mark 9:3** says, speaking of Jesus: *"And his raiment became shining, exceeding white as snow; so as no fuller on earth can white them."*

This is hardly the picture of an ignorant automaton. The idea proposed by sophists that Adam was less than Regal or less than fully cognizant or was somehow limited in his faculties stems from their own faulty "image" of God. From their own flawed condition comes the natural outworking to assign flawed characteristics to the image of God. Because they hold God Himself in contempt, they also hold His image in contempt. But, we know it's absurd for them to think that Almighty God, whose Majesty and Grandeur and Holiness the universe itself can not contain, would create a hapless dimwit and then say, "This is who I am. Rule my physical creation in my stead." (See 1 Kings 8:27; 2 Chronicles 2:6, 6:18.) To look upon Adam was to see the image of God!

But, then it happened. **Genesis 3:6** *"...she took of the fruit thereof, and did eat, and gave also unto her husband with her; and he did eat.* [7] *And the eyes of them both were opened, and they **knew** that they were naked; and they sewed fig leaves together, and made themselves aprons."*

It wasn't that Adam and Eve were blind to something that had been there all along. They were not ignorant of their own person. In the Biblical use of words, "to know or knew" means "to be intimate with" or "to partake of." (See Genesis 4:1, 4:17, 4:25, 19:5-8; Matthew 1:25; Philippians 3:10.) What happened was that Adam and Eve literally partook of shame and nakedness.

When they partook of the forbidden fruit, they entered into covenant with Satan. They became something they had not been before. They took on Satan's nature. They put on Satan's robe! **Job 26:6** *"Hell is naked before him, and destruction hath no covering."*

So, the covenant between Adam and the Deceiver was established. We will never escape the laws and precepts of covenant as an institution. But it is through covenant that God will bear witness of His plan of Salvation until the end. We do, however, have the power to choose our covenant partner: either the Deceiver, or The Way, The Truth, and The Life.

A closer look at the covering the Deceiver has placed on humanity reveals much about his nature and his tactics.

Isaiah 14:12-14 *"How art thou fallen from heaven, O Lucifer, son of the morning! how art thou cut down to the ground, which didst weaken the nations! [13] For thou hast said in thine heart, I will ascend into heaven, I will exalt my throne above the stars of God: I will sit also upon the mount of the congregation, in the sides of the north: [14] I will ascend above the heights of the clouds; I will be like the most High."*

If the definition of pride is to exalt one's self, then the words of Lucifer certainly epitomize this definition. Jesus taught us the quickest way to see into the heart is to hear the words that come from it.

Matthew 12:34 *"...for out of the abundance of the heart the mouth speaketh."* Pride is the nature of Satan. Please note the five references to "I" in Isaiah 14:12-14; we will see it again.

Proverbs 11:2 *"When pride cometh, then cometh shame:"*

Shame is the inevitable conclusion of pride. Shame is the "uncovering" of Satan. It is his robe from God's point of view. Pride is the resultant manifestation of Satan's futile attempt to imitate God's Robe. The words "unfathomable" and "immeasurable" come to my mind as I contemplate the vanity of Satan thinking he could be like God. Let's begin our look at the covering of pride through the dialog between God and Job.

Job 41:1-34 *"Canst thou draw out leviathan with an hook? or his tongue with a cord which thou lettest down? [2] Canst thou put an hook into his nose? or bore his jaw through with a thorn? [3] Will he make many supplications unto thee? will he speak soft words unto thee? [4] Will he make a covenant with thee? wilt thou take him for a servant for ever? [5] Wilt thou play with him as with a bird? or wilt thou bind him for thy maidens? [6] Shall the companions make a banquet of him? shall they part him among the merchants? [7] Canst thou fill his* skin with barbed irons? or his head with fish spears? *[8]* Lay thine hand upon him, remember the battle, do no more. *[9]* Behold, the hope of him is in vain: shall not one be cast down even at the sight of him? *[10]* None is so fierce that dare stir him up: who then is able to stand before me? *[11]* Who hath prevented me, that I should repay him? whatsoever is under the whole heaven is mine. *[12]* I will not conceal his parts, nor his power, nor his comely proportion. *[13]* Who can discover the face of his garment? or who can come to him with his double bridle? *[14]* Who can open the doors of his face? his teeth are terrible round about. *[15]* **His scales are his pride**, shut up together as with a close seal. *[16]* One is so near to another, that no air can come between them. *[17]* They are joined one to another, they stick together, that they cannot be sundered. *[18]* By his neesings a light doth shine, and his eyes are like the eyelids of the morning. *[19]* Out of his mouth go burning lamps, and sparks of fire leap out. *[20]* Out of his nostrils goeth smoke, as out of a seething pot or caldron. *[21]* His breath kindleth coals, and a flame goeth out of his mouth. *[22]* In his neck remaineth strength, and sorrow is turned into joy before him. *[23]* The flakes of his flesh are joined together: they are firm in themselves; they cannot be moved. *[24]* His heart is as firm as a stone; yea, as hard as a piece of the nether millstone. *[25]* When he raiseth up himself, the mighty are afraid: by reason of breakings they purify themselves. *[26]* The sword of him that layeth at him cannot hold: the spear, the dart, nor the habergeon. *[27]* He esteemeth iron as straw, and brass as rotten wood. *[28]* The arrow cannot make him flee: slingstones are turned with him into stubble. *[29]* Darts are counted as stubble: he laugheth at the shaking of a spear. *[30]* Sharp stones are under him: he spreadeth sharp pointed things upon the mire. *[31]* He maketh the deep to boil like a pot: he maketh the sea like a pot of ointment. *[32]* He maketh a path to shine after him; one would think the deep to be hoary. *[33]* Upon earth there is not his like, who is made without fear. *[34]* **He beholdeth all high things: he is a king over all the children of pride.** "

There is no shortage of speculation among theologians as to the being of "Leviathan", which is why I commonly teach new converts or beginners in theology to avoid commentary. The natural response to that statement is, "How am I supposed to learn?" My preferred method of study is to let the Bible define and reveal itself. We are not in this effort alone.

1 Corinthians 2:13 *"Which things also we speak, not in the words which man's wisdom teacheth, but which the Holy Ghost teacheth;"*

1 John 2:27 *"But the anointing which ye have received of him abideth in you, and ye need not that any man teach you: but as the same anointing* *teacheth you of all things, and is truth, and is no lie, and even as it hath taught you, ye shall abide in him."*

Remember that Jesus said His Word is Spirit. When we seek God prayerfully in His Word, it is His pleasure to reveal not just Himself, but also the fullness of our inheritance to us. Understanding God's Word is part of our inheritance, and it is His Spirit that places the Word of God in our lives according to the plan that God has for us individually. How we interact with God's Word and God's calling upon our lives determines the depth of knowledge we will receive from God's Word. But if we are dismissive of God's intentions after He has revealed His Word to us, then we should expect our own understanding to suffer. (See Psalms 119:97-104; James 1:5-8.) If we seek the counsel of God's written Word we will learn to hear God's voice. If we seek the counsel of men (commentary) we will learn to hear the voice of men. (See Galatians 1:15-18.)

In **Genesis 1:28** God gave to Adam dominion *"...over the fish of the sea, and over the fowl of the air, and over every living thing that moveth upon the earth."* If we fast-forward about four thousand years, James writes: *"For every kind of beasts, and of birds, **and of serpents**, and of things in the sea, **is tamed, and hath been tamed of mankind:"** (James 3:7).* Since there are no contradictions in Scripture, we rightly surmise that "Leviathan" is not an earthly animal. What God showed Job was the Dragon himself.

Revelation 12:9 *"...**that old serpent**, called the Devil, and Satan."* This is why God depicts him as a ruler over man and not as one ruled by man.

In **Job 41:34** God says: *"...he is a king over all the children of pride."* It is noteworthy to point out that the Dragon, Adam, and Edom were all red and all fell from a prominent position. (See Revelation 12:3.)

If we continue in Job 41 to compare the descriptive verses with the attributes of a/the Dragon we find:

verse 19 *"Out of his mouth go burning lamps, and sparks of fire leap out."*

verse 20 *"Out of his nostrils goeth smoke,..."*

verse 21 *"His breath kindleth coals, and a flame goeth out of his mouth."*

verse 10 *"None is so fierce that dare stir him up:"*

verse 22 He rejoices in sorrow.

verse 24 *"His heart is as firm as a stone; yea, as hard as a piece of the nether millstone."*

verse 27 *"He esteemeth iron as straw, and brass as rotten wood."* In Bible-speak, iron and brass are symbols of war and judgment, respectively. But, in verse 15 we once again focus on the covering. The Scripture reads: **Job 41:15**

"His scales are his pride, shut up together as with a close seal." This does not mean that he is proud of his scales. It does mean that his pride is likened to scales; it is his covering!

Pvb 11:2 *"When pride cometh, then cometh shame: but with the lowly is wisdom."*

How many ways could we go if we wanted to study the doors opened by pride? Pride is the foundation of jealousy and envy. Jealousy and envy lead to covetousness. The New Testament teaches that covetousness is idolatry. (See Ephesians 5:5; Colossians 3:5.) Arrogance and haughtiness are synonymous with pride; the latter is the assignment given to a whole class of demon spirits. Vanity comes to my mind as a description of pride as "the great big lie". Then there is the treachery and deceit that come as the self-exalted one strives to maintain their superlative status. Pride has been devastating to mankind ever since Adam lost the Glory of God and tried to cover himself. In hindsight, I see the gross insufficiency in my own past, as I tried to cover myself and find something so simple as a place to fit in.

A partial explanation of pride would be to exalt one's self or magnify one's self. It has nothing to do with the joy we have in others...unless we are going to take credit for their accomplishments.

Isaiah 14:12-14, as we have read, gives us the outward working of pride. But we must look at Ezekiel 28 to find the origin and conception of pride. Ezekiel 28 is the tangible manifestation of Isaiah 14:12-14. **Ezekiel 28:13-15,17** *"Thou hast been in Eden the garden of God; every precious stone was thy covering, the sardius, topaz, and the diamond, the beryl, the onyx, and the jasper, the sapphire, the emerald, and the carbuncle, and gold: the workmanship of thy tabrets and of thy pipes was prepared in thee in the day that thou wast created.* [14] ***Thou art the anointed cherub that covereth; and I have set thee so****: thou wast upon the holy mountain of God; thou hast walked up and down in the midst of the stones of fire.* [15] *Thou wast perfect in thy ways from the day that thou wast created, till iniquity was found in thee."* [17] *"Thine heart was lifted up because of thy beauty, thou hast corrupted thy wisdom by reason of thy brightness:"*

The Heavenly Worship of God

Ezekiel 28 paints the picture of the Angelic worship service of God and the use of God's anointing, or covering. The word "anoint" means "to rub or smear" and can also mean "unction." Taken together, we see God covering someone with Himself. As I studied the great diversity of jewels that covered

Lucifer, I learned that most, if not all, of these stones are **translucent**, even the gold. **Revelation 21:18** *"...and the city was pure gold, like unto clear glass."*

In Hebrew the name "Lucifer" comes from the words indicating "clear" or "brightness." Today, we know Lucifer as "the Light Bearer." Not only was Lucifer the light bearer, but he was also the chief musician during the corporate worship. Pipes and tabrets are wind and percussion instruments.

To understand the mechanics of this scenario, focus for a moment on the jewels covering Lucifer. Add now the Glory of God, manifesting as light, emanating and flowing down from the Throne of God, as the anointing onto Lucifer. Here, through the jewels, Lucifer was literally covered with the presence of God. His job was to magnify God as the light passed from jewel to jewel. This is similar to the way a magnifying glass would work.

Lucifer could even discern or separate the light, by manipulating the jewels, to focus on a particular aspect of God. We have an example of this in the natural realm, as water separates light to produce a rainbow. Likewise, the water of the Word separates and manifests the seven-fold ministry of the Holy Ghost. (See Ephesians 5:26; Revelation 1:4, 3:1.) Lucifer could even magnify God as a whole and focus on a singular aspect of God simultaneously. Further, he could direct the **outflow** of the anointing into different parts of the assembly of angels as initiated by the Holy Spirit, or rather, The Glory.

The jewels covering Lucifer also made him invisible. Consider placing mirrors around an object- say, for example a tree- and locating the mirrors at the proper angles to allow us to see clearly anything beyond the tree without seeing the tree. From here, the Presence and Glory of God would flow into the body (assembly) of angels. The angels are referenced individually as "stones of fire" in Ezekiel 28:14. The Glory of God would then be magnified again in each individual angel before being surrendered up (corporately) and received back at the Throne of God. **1 Peter 2:5** *"Ye also, as lively stones, are built up a spiritual house, an holy priesthood, to offer up spiritual sacrifices, acceptable to God by Jesus Christ."*

"What's up with all this magnifying?" some would ask. It is necessary because "No man hath seen God at any time." If God didn't use the magnifying process but allowed His Glory to flow in His fullness, then all of creation, both physical and spiritual, would instantly be consumed!

Just as in the beginning there were two lights in heaven, the relationship between the sun and the moon reflect the relationship between God and Lucifer. Since Lucifer was once covered with life, it is conceivable that the moon also bore life at/prior to the fall of Lucifer. This concept applies to any physical heavenly body that represents a spiritual being, whether fallen or not.

The Fall of Lucifer

Proverbs 16:18 *"Pride goeth before destruction, and an haughty spirit before a fall."*

In **Ezekiel 28:17** we have read: *"Thine heart was lifted up because of thy beauty, thou hast corrupted thy wisdom by reason of thy brightness:"* Lucifer magnified himself because of and through the Anointing. The Anointing did not lead Lucifer to fall, but because he had it, he perverted and abused it.

Consider again "by reason of thy brightness." And now, as Lucifer stood in the presence of God, in the midst of the Glory and the Anointing, as the Archangel of Worship, he manipulated the jewels and the light to imitate or impersonate God Himself! The angels in the assembly no longer saw God through the pulpit. They actually saw two Gods. They saw God on the Throne, and God in the pulpit as an exact image of God on the Throne.

2 Thessalonians 2:3-4,9 *"Let no man deceive you by any means: for that day shall not come, except there come a falling away first, and that man of sin be revealed, the son of perdition; ⁴ Who opposeth and exalteth himself above all that is called God, or that is worshipped; so that he as God sitteth in the temple of God, shewing himself that he is God." "Even him, whose coming is after the working of Satan with all power and signs and lying wonders,"*

2 Corinthians 11:14-15 *"And no marvel; for Satan himself is transformed into an angel of light. ¹⁵ Therefore it is no great thing if his ministers also be transformed as the ministers of righteousness; whose end shall be according to their works."*

If we continue to look at pride as a covering, we must realize as we see the jewels that there is no beauty in them of themselves. To be blunt, try looking at a jewel in the dark! The jewel is simply the mechanism to convey the beauty found in the light. The same principal applies to Lucifer, here and forever after, "Satan."

And now, as Satan stood in the midst of the temple, usurping and abusing the authority of God in(vested) in him, he led the third part of the angels to worship himself. As Satan attempted to intercept the **inflow** of God's magnified Glory, he was immediately struck down. (See Isaiah 42:8.)

Luke 10:18 *"And he said unto them, I beheld Satan as lightning fall from heaven."*

Revelation 12:4 *"And his tail drew the third part of the stars of heaven, and did cast them to the earth:"*

Job 41:32 *"He maketh a path to shine after him;"*

There is a similar principal of the Anointing found in **Acts 5:15:** *"...that at the least the shadow of Peter passing by might overshadow some of them."* The "shadow of Peter" is the same waning Glory that God showed Moses when He put Moses in the cleft of the rock to show Moses His "back parts". (See Exodus 33:18-23.) This is the same Glory that filled the temple in Exodus 40:34-38. The Glory of God is the "The Cloud By Day" and "The Fire By Night" and that Glory of God now adorns His Bride. (Read "Church.")

So now, we see the birth of pride (self-exaltation) into the creation through the heart of Lucifer. And with it came all manner of self-centeredness: self-righteousness, self-justification, self-gratification, self-sufficiency, and so on, and so on, and so on. And thus, when man put on Satan's robe in the Garden of Eden, man also became his own idolatrous god! This is the covering we placed upon Jesus.

A Layman's Study...

3

The Knowledge of Good and Evil

From here we would slip back into the Garden of Eden. Knowing the modus operandi of the "old serpent" to deceive through subtlety and to appear as an angel of light, the question is asked, "Do you want to be like God?" **Genesis 3:5** *"For God doth know that in the day ye eat thereof, then your eyes shall be opened, and ye shall be as gods, knowing good and evil."* This is the word of Satan who also said in **Genesis 3:4**: *"...Ye shall not surely die:"*

Contrary to what many people suppose, God was not trying to withhold some good thing from man in the knowledge of good and evil. I know, I know: to an enlightened culture such as we are today, it sounds naive to think that humanity could reach informed decisions without knowing good and evil. As we let the Scriptures play out, we will see that the knowledge of good and evil was and is not in man's best interest. **Psalms 84:11** *"For the LORD God is a sun and shield: the LORD will give grace and glory: no good thing will he withhold from them that walk uprightly."*

When Eve believed the word of Satan over the Word of God, evil was conceived within her. Satan had planted his seed of unbelief and death. (See Genesis 3:15.) In **Genesis 3:6**, when Eve saw that it was *"...a tree to be desired to make one wise, she took of the fruit thereof."* I had to study a bit to see what wisdom Eve saw in the tree. I am of a firm conviction that there is never wisdom in disobedience to God's Word. I find that sin ushers in spiritual deafness and blindness. A prime example of this would be Judas dipping his bread into the sop and asking, "Is it I?"

James 1:14-15 *"But every man is tempted, when he is drawn away of his own lust, and enticed. [15] Then when lust hath conceived, it bringeth forth sin: and sin, when it is finished, bringeth forth death."*

As I looked over the Scriptural use of "wise" in the Old Testament, I found a word in the Hebrew language of very similar pronunciation (a homonym) meaning "to miscarry." The connection is developed in the New Testament. **James 3:15,17** *"This wisdom descendeth not from above, but is earthly, sensual, devilish." "But the wisdom that is from above is first pure, then peaceable, gentle, and easy to be intreated, full of mercy and good fruits, without partiality, and without hypocrisy."*

1 Corinthians 1:20-21 *"Where is the wise? where is the scribe? where is the disputer of this world? hath not God made foolish the wisdom of this world? [21] For after that in the wisdom of God the world by wisdom knew not God, it pleased God by the foolishness of preaching to save them that believe."*

My point in reprinting these two passages from the New Testament is to show the two types of wisdom and their contentious nature toward each other. We will integrate these thoughts in our understanding of what the knowledge of good and evil really is, as we move through this chapter.

As we have focused a great deal on the covenant principals, I have placed emphasis on those aspects that relate to this study in particular. We will continue to use these aspects to address the relationship of faith and works in the life of the believer and nonbeliever.

Romans 7:7 *"...I had not known sin, but by the law: for I had not known lust, except the law had said, Thou shalt not covet."*

When I was first born again and beginning to place the Word of God in my life, I erroneously took the position that, prior to the Fall of man, Adam and Eve could have done many of the things we now know to be sin and it would not have been sinful for them. After all, the Apostle Paul says in **Romans 7:8**: *"...For without the law sin was dead."*

As God has placed His Word in my life, I recognize that Adam and Eve would not have done anything like the filth and perversity we commonly see throughout the world today. This is because those things would have been **contrary to their nature.** Satan knew that for him to strike a death-blow to mankind he would first have to change our nature.

It is also erroneous to believe that to know God or how good he is, you must know the devil or how bad he is. This concept stems from our fallen nature.

Romans 7:11 *"For sin, taking occasion by the commandment, deceived me, and by it slew me."*

Isaiah 59:2 *"But your iniquities have separated between you and your God, and your sins have hid his face from you, that he will not hear."*

Please allow me an example: Do you have children? If you do, have you ever given them to someone so that they could be mistreated or abused simply to teach them how good you are to them?

Certainly you would never do such a thing! Neither has God done this thing with us. God was content for His children to love Him in innocence, just as you and I are content for our children to love us in innocence. So, knowing or

64

partaking of evil cannot bring us to know God in part or in whole; rather, it separates us from God.

1 Corinthians 2:11-14 *"For what man knoweth the things of a man, save the spirit of man which is in him? even so the things of God knoweth no man, but the Spirit of God. [12] Now we have received, not the spirit of the world, but the spirit which is of God; that we might know the things that are freely given to us of God. [13] Which things also we speak, not in the words which man's wisdom teacheth, but which the Holy Ghost teacheth; comparing spiritual things with spiritual. [14] But the natural man receiveth not the things of the Spirit of God: for they are foolishness unto him: neither can he know them, because they are spiritually discerned."*

These verses stand in direct contrast to man's use of the knowledge of good and evil. Neither disobedience to God's Word nor man's wisdom through the knowledge of good and evil could bring us to know God or to be like God. Jesus said in **Matthew 5:8**: *"Blessed are the pure in heart: for they shall see God."*

The Two Operating Systems

Isaiah 54:1 *"Sing, O barren, thou that didst not bear; break forth into singing, and cry aloud, thou that didst not travail with child: for more are the children of the desolate than the children of the married wife, saith the LORD."*

Many years ago, I was listening to a Christian radio broadcast and the host told the story of a highway intersection in Europe. I will have to apologize for not being able to remember the particulars of when and where I was when I heard it, and who the host was, but that is often the nature of oral teaching. I don't think its happenstance that words spoken do not and should not magnify ministers or ministries, but rather should produce a desired effect in the hearer towards magnifying the Lord Jesus Christ.

The story goes that over time multiple roads came to intersect each other at the same isolated place. With frequent accidents, this particular intersection proved to be dangerous enough that the authorities took notice and began to place traffic signs as needed. Well, that's a right response, we think. But that action didn't help; actually, the accidents became more frequent. So, again the authorities assessed the situation and placed more stringent instructions and signage for navigating this complex intersection. And again the number of accidents increased. They began to call for more experts to help fix their dilemma. They went through the process of evaluation, re-evaluation, and administration again and again only to find that with each effort the condition at the intersection only got worse; people were dying and property was being destroyed. Their efforts continued on and on, always with the same outcome; lives were being lost.

Then, in desperation the decision was made to take down all the signs except for one. Each road got its own "stop" sign at the intersection. The accidents virtually went away.

A closer look at the knowledge of good and evil will reveal much about our distorted view of God. There are, in fact, two views of the knowledge of good and evil. If we discuss man's view first, we find a pattern of attributes arranged categorically on a **vertical scale**. The attributes most offensive to God would be placed at the lower or least honorable positions. The devil would reign at the bottom. Likewise, the attributes most pleasing to God would be placed in the positions we esteem to be the greatest. And God would reign at the top. Out of these attributes would come our actions or inactions. Thus, we have the knowledge of good and evil. It almost resembles a model of evolution, only spiritual.

However, we are presented with the question, "How or who or what determines which attributes are more pleasing to God?" **AMBUSH!** This is an ambush. It is a diversion intended to put our eyes off of God and onto ourselves. This vertical scale is a tactic that has worked to keep people from finding their way back to God. The questions of where vice and virtue appear on the scale wrongly validate the scale in the eyes of those trying to answer the question. To answer the question rightly <u>requires a different scale</u>. Let me tell you about three travelers and a riddle:

Three travelers stopped at a motel to purchase a room for the night. The manager said the room would cost thirty dollars. So, each man paid ten dollars and they went to the room. Later, the manager realized he should have charged only twenty-five dollars for the room. To repay the men, the manager sent a bellhop with five one-dollar bills to give to the men. The young bellhop, not knowing how to divide the five dollars between three men, gave each man a dollar and put two dollars in his own pocket. Since each man got a dollar back, the men effectively paid nine dollars each. If you multiply the nine dollars by the three men you get twenty-seven dollars. Add the two dollars the bellhop put in his pocket and you get twenty-nine dollars. Where is the other dollar?

I don't want to get bogged down or side tracked, so I will be very blunt in explaining this riddle. All the information is there. But, if you make the wrong assumptions, or choose the wrong scale you will never find your dollar.

Likewise, the problem occurs when man attempts to discern the attributes of goodness (God) without the Holy Spirit. <u>The knowledge of good and evil is a fictitious or faulty scale that cannot lead us to God!</u>

Matthew 19:17 *"Why callest thou me good? there is none good but one, that is, God:.."*

Do you remember Eve's motive for partaking of the fruit of the tree of the knowledge of good and evil? She wanted to be like God. Remember also the words of Lucifer in Isaiah 14, *"I will be like the most high."* Just as Lucifer, who was created to lead worship, manipulated his covering to exalt his own self, Eve, yielding to the desire to exalt her own self, ate of the fruit. And what happened? She made herself a covering. **Genesis 3:7** *"...and they sewed fig leaves together, and made themselves aprons."* The covering was a covering of her/their works. **Genesis 2:15** *"And the LORD God took the man, and put him into the garden of Eden to dress it and to keep it."* Though Adam and Eve partook of the fruit for different reasons, the end result was the same. (See 1 Timothy 2:14.) Pride had entered into humanity and they immediately began to cover themselves.

Isaiah 59:6 *"...neither shall they cover themselves with their works: their works are works of iniquity,"* (See also Job 31:33.)

The Scriptures tell us that God desires, "a peculiar people, zealous of good works"; of this there is no debate.

Titus 3:8 *"This is a faithful saying, and these things I will that thou affirm constantly, that they which have believed in God might be careful to maintain good works. These things are good and profitable unto men."*

Ephesians 2:10 *"For we are his workmanship, created in Christ Jesus unto good works, which God hath before ordained that we should walk in them."*

God desires that good works would flow through humanity. But God is repelled by those that cover themselves with their good works.

1 Peter 5:5-6 *"Likewise, ye younger, submit yourselves unto the elder. Yea, all of you be subject one to another, and **be clothed with humility: for God resisteth the proud, and giveth grace to the humble.** [6] Humble yourselves therefore under the mighty hand of God, that he may exalt you in due time:"*

Romans 13:12 *"...let us therefore cast off the works of darkness,"*

Romans 13:14 *"But put ye on the Lord Jesus Christ, and make not provision for the flesh, to fulfil the lusts thereof."*

Very few people cover themselves with their failures or faults or vices or sins. These are the things that we hide from sight. The "works of darkness" mentioned by the Apostle Paul in Romans 13:12 are our good works that we proudly display for all to see. They are as uniquely tailored to suit us as our own personality.

God wasn't happy when He found Adam and Eve wearing fig leaves. The immediate result was an animal or two would have to die. The first sacrifice in the Scripture is a foreshadow of the Lamb of God that would take "our sins in his own body on the tree." The act of sacrificing the animals, by God, speaks that our efforts to cover ourselves only equal insufficiency. In modern jargon, the fig leaf has become synonymous with the word "religion." The Holy Scriptures support, or may even be the source of the synonymy, as six out of the seven appearances of the word "religion" in the New Testament refer to a religion other than Christianity. Likewise, when I survey the religions of the world I don't find any other except Christianity that allows for God to make the way for us; and He did that through the death of His only begotten Son. All other religions in the world require their adherents to achieve or to earn favor from their god.

If it is true that the pride of man manifests itself in good works, then it is also true that man magnifies himself by these same good works. Consider the teaching of Jesus in **Luke 18:9-14**: *"And he spake this parable unto certain which trusted in themselves that they were righteous, and despised others: [10] Two men went up into the temple to pray; the one a Pharisee, and the other a publican. [11] The Pharisee stood and prayed thus with himself, God, I thank thee, that I am not as other men are, extortioners, unjust, adulterers, or even as this publican. [12] I fast twice in the week, I give tithes of all that I possess. [13] And the publican, standing afar off, would not lift up so much as his eyes unto heaven, but smote upon his breast, saying, God be merciful to me a sinner. [14] I tell you, this man went down to his house justified rather than the other: for every one that exalteth himself shall be abased; and he that humbleth himself shall be exalted."* The pattern of using five "I"s from Lucifer's declaration in Isaiah 14 is also found in the Pharisee's oration. The Pharisees were the spiritual leaders of Israel at that time and they exercised the authority of Moses. (See Matthew 23:2.)

So man's view or use of the knowledge of good and evil became the scale by which men justify themselves and condemn others. It is based on works, good and bad, or the lack thereof. Just as the Pharisee thought he could come before God and present to Him his good works, the knowledge of good and evil literally became the doorway of pan-deism, meaning "many ways to God."

While the world flaunts their opinion that their good works will merit favor with God, our Lord Jesus said otherwise! **John 14:6** *"Jesus saith unto him, I am the way, the truth, and the life: no man cometh unto the Father, but by me."*

This brings us to God's view of the knowledge of good and evil. To state it more accurately, we refer to it as God's view of man's use of the knowledge of good and evil. Here is where motive comes in. The question isn't as much what or which one, but rather, why. Since pride leads men to justify themselves by their good works, and since Jesus said we cannot come to God that way, we realize that the knowledge of good and evil is vanity when used for this purpose. Since we now understand that all of our good works are equally ineffective at bringing us into God's presence, we may now do as God does and put them in places of equal stature. That placement would be side by side on a **horizontal scale**.

In same fashion, but by contrast to the vertical scale, **we now find the devil at both ends of the scale.** That's right. God is not on this scale!

If you have read your New Testament you will recall the words of the Apostle Paul in **Romans 7:13:** *"...But sin, that it might appear sin, working death in me by that which is good; that sin by the commandment might become exceeding sinful.".* The pattern is evident. We see Satan deceiving the angels by use of the anointing. Then deceiving Eve through that same subtility, leading her to be more like God. And then finally through pride, he has led mankind to trust in his own ability to keep God's Law or Word, which is our light. (See Psalm 119:105; Proverbs 6:23.)

2 Corinthians 11:13-15 *"For such are false apostles, deceitful workers, transforming themselves into the apostles of Christ. [14] And no marvel; for Satan himself is transformed into an angel of light. [15] Therefore it is no great thing if his ministers also be transformed as the ministers of righteousness; whose end shall be according to their works."*

So, in God's view of man's use of the knowledge of good and evil, where is God? We find God separately, "dwelling in the light which no man can approach unto." God dwells in a place called "purity."

Titus 1:15-16 *"Unto the pure all things are pure: but unto them that are defiled and unbelieving is nothing pure; but even their mind and conscience is defiled. [16] They profess that they know God; but in works they deny him, being abominable, and disobedient, and unto every good work reprobate."*

God is not on any scale! Nothing compares to God! Nothing compares with God! How can the finite compare with the infinite? It doesn't!

If man's use of the knowledge of good and evil were true, then sin and goodness would be interdependent by reason of degree. That is, the placement of one on the scale would depend on the placement of the other. Even more, the very existence of one would depend on the existence of the other. By this implication you could have degrees of goodness but no purity, or no absolutes.

Let me give you an example. If you were to slide a needle down a ruler, and each time you moved it you only went half way to the end, would you ever reach the end?

No!

Likewise, purity cannot be obtained if the knowledge of good and evil defines sin and goodness. But God is pure and absolute. He is completely independent. Moreover, God and His Goodness existed in eternity-past long before evil was conceived in the heart of Lucifer. God and His Goodness existed in eternity-past long before Lucifer was even created.

So, to even see God, we must not look through the eyes of the knowledge of good and evil but through purity itself; but purity has another name.

Matthew 5:8 *"Blessed are the pure in heart: for they shall see God."*

John 12:44-46 *"Jesus cried and said, He that **believeth** on me, **believeth** not on me, but on him that sent me. [45] **And he that seeth me seeth him that sent me.** [46] I am come a light into the world, that whosoever **believeth** on me should not abide in darkness."*

Acts 15:8-11 *"And God, which knoweth the hearts, bare them witness, giving them the Holy Ghost, even as he did unto us; [9] And put no difference between us and them, **purifying their hearts by faith.** [10] Now therefore why tempt ye God, to put a yoke upon the neck of the disciples, which neither our fathers nor we were able to bear? [11] But we believe that through the grace of the Lord Jesus Christ we shall be saved, even as they."*

Acts 15 is the record of the council where the Apostles determined that we are not saved by the works of the law, but by faith. The yoke mentioned in verse 10 is the Law of Moses. Faith and works are the two standards that men use to define sin. They are the two opposing operating systems at war within humanity. Faith and works are the two opposing natures within the life of the believer. We are given insight into their natures as the two opposing operating systems are personified in the antagonistic relationships of Sarah & Hagar, Rachael & Leah, Hannah & Peninnah, and also Boaz and the nearer kinsman.

In the New Testament, the very popular story of the woman with an issue of blood is also an allegory representing these two operating systems. In the story we are first introduced to Jairus (Greek rendering of the Hebrew name Jair, meaning, "the enlightener") and his daughter who was sick. The Scripture tells us the maid was about **twelve** years old. As Jesus was on His way to heal the maid, He encounters the woman with an issue of blood. She had been sick for **twelve** years, all-the-while spending all that she had on physicians. Now that we are looking for allegory and representations, we can identify the sick virgin maid that was near death as the operating system of "Faith." The elder diseased woman who had looked to the physicians for her help (probably priests), we identify with National Israel, and she represents the "Law of Works." In Biblical gematria, the number **twelve** represents governmental perfection. Each of these two women was governed by and represents a different operating system. In the symbology of this event, both the innocent and the legalist are healed in Jesus Christ! (See Matthew 9:18-26; Mark 5:22-43; Luke 8:41-56.)

These two operating systems are also personified in the two women found in the book of Proverbs and in the book of The Revelation. In Proverbs the two women are the Virtuous Woman and the Harlot. They are called Wisdom and the Strange Woman; and these two women are portrayed as competing for the same man. In The Revelation the two women are the Woman Clothed With the Sun and the Great Whore. (See Revelation 17 through 22.)

From Sarah & Hagar in the book of Genesis all the way through to Babylon & New Jerusalem in the book of Revelation, God gives us a composite view of the two contrary and often opposing operating systems that vie for preeminence within humanity and within the individual. Each example within the composite adds insight into the separate natures of the Law of Moses and the Law of Christ.

The tale or tally of this motif is found in **Galatians 4.**

Galations 4:21-31: *"Tell me, ye that desire to be under the law, do ye not hear the law? [22] For it is written, that Abraham had two sons, the one by a bondmaid, the other by a freewoman. [23] But he who was of the __bondwoman__ was born after the flesh; but he of the __freewoman__ was by promise. [24] Which things are an allegory: __for these are the two covenants__; the one from the mount Sinai, which gendereth to bondage, which is Agar __(Hagar)__. [25] For this Agar is mount Sinai in Arabia, and answereth to Jerusalem which now is, and is in bondage with her children. [26] But Jerusalem which is above is free, which is the mother of us all __(Sarah)__. [27] **For it is written, Rejoice, thou barren that bearest not; break forth and cry, thou that travailest not: for the desolate hath many more children than she which hath an husband.** [28] Now we, brethren, as Isaac was, are the children of promise. [29] But as then he that was* *born after the flesh persecuted him that was born after the Spirit, even so it is now. [30] Nevertheless what saith the scripture? Cast out the bondwoman and her son: for the son of the bondwoman shall not be heir with the son of the freewoman. [31] So then, brethren, we are not children of the bondwoman, but of the free."* **(Words added in parentheses are mine. DP)**

As it was revealed in the Law of Moses, the nearest kinsman had a responsibility to perform the duty of a husband to a deceased brother's wife. Although this law predates Levi, this law is known as the Levirate Law. (See Deuteronomy 25:5-10.) When Boaz acknowledged to Ruth that there was another kinsman nearer to her, he was actually saying that there was another kinsman with a nature nearer to her nature. That is, the nearer kinsman to Ruth already shared a nature with her. If we parallel the story of redemption found in Ruth with the broader context of humanity's redemption, we easily identify the nearer kinsman to humanity as the Law of Moses; which law could not redeem us, even though we may find it agreeable with us. Therefore, the virtue of the Law of Moses is based in the knowledge of good and evil and not faith! (See Galatians 3:12.) As a gentile bride, Ruth embodied this nature. But, the Promise of Redemption, through Abraham, came before the Law of Works and Boaz carried this Promise within him. The divine nature imparted by Jesus Christ to His Bride is the same nature that Boaz would impart to Ruth. (See 2 Peter 1:4; 2 Corinthians 7:1.) The Scriptures testify of Jesus Christ, and the Levirate Law is fulfilled in Him.

Luke 16:8 *"And the lord commended the unjust steward, because he had done wisely: for the children of this world are in their generation wiser than the children of light."*

This verse appears to contradict other aforementioned Scriptures that affirm the supremacy of the Heavenly wisdom over the earthly wisdom... but it does not contradict. <u>This verse means that the lost or worldly people know how to be lost better than saved or Spiritual people know how to be Spiritual.</u> In other words, for our current condition, the fallen nature is still our primary nature. While we as Christians have a new nature the new nature is still somewhat a "second nature" and must be nurtured daily if it is to become our primary operating system or nature.

Did God Create Evil?

The short answer is no. Aaah, but books aren't written on short answers. Books are for detailing minutia and for presenting the mundane as critical. And rightly so, because the devil is still in the details. As I prepared to rewrite this book, one of the Scriptures that the Lord impressed upon me was **Daniel 6:4-5:** *"Then the presidents and princes sought to find occasion against Daniel concerning the kingdom; but they could find none occasion nor fault; forasmuch as he was faithful, neither was there any error or fault found in him. ⁵ Then said these men, We shall not find any occasion against this Daniel, except we find it against him concerning the law of his God."* This is the same thing that Satan did with Adam in the Garden of Eden. (God *"called their name Adam,"* [**Genesis 5:2**].) The one rule that God gave to man was the one thing that Satan used to corrupt man's relationship with God.

Now that we are on this side of the Fall of Adam, and now that our understanding has been skewed, we tend to warp the meaning of the Scriptures so that we are more comfortable with what we interpret them to say. Even the New Testament says that the Gospel of Jesus Christ is offensive. (See Romans 9:33; 1 Peter 2:8.) Nobody likes to hear, "You're not good enough to get to heaven on your own." But that is what the Gospel implies. That's what everything in the Bible implies. Would God send His Son to take our sin into His own body if we were good enough to get to heaven on our own merit?

The Scriptures are commonly twisted and bent and reshaped by us anywhere they meet something errant in our person that we want to hold on to. It's our pride that prevents us from receiving the simple truth of God's Word.

Proverbs 11:2 *"When pride cometh, then cometh shame: but with the lowly is wisdom."*

The nature of sophistry is that it is the wisdom that comes from the knowledge of good and evil. Because it looks like God, it has not only found agreement with but has flourished within organized religion. Organized religion is responsible for propagating almost all of the more prolific elements of Biblical false doctrine that permeate our societies today. It is Isaiah 45:7 that bears an excessive amount of this abuse pertaining to the knowledge of good and evil.

Isaiah 45:7 *"I form the light, and create darkness: I make peace, and create evil: I the LORD do all these things."*

The Hebrew word translated as "evil" in Isaiah 45:7 has many different applications. The word "evil" is used in Job 42 to mean "adversity." In Genesis 37:20 the same word "evil" means "grievous or harmful or hurtful." In Proverbs 13:21 evil is the "trouble" that pursues sinners. This is the same application of the word when God told David, *"Thus saith the LORD, Behold, I will **raise up evil** against thee out of thine own house, and I will take thy wives* *before thine eyes, and give them unto thy neighbour, and he shall lie with thy wives in the sight of this sun."* In this application it is the consequence of David's transgression. Adam, King David, national Israel, and Babylon all authored the evil that God would "raise up" as a consequence to their own actions. This is the essence of "eye for an eye." This is also the apparent sense of the word "evil" in Isaiah 45:7, as God explains His sovereignty to Cyrus. King Cyrus, by conquest, would become the successor to the Babylonian Kingdom of Nebuchadnezzar, which executed God's judgment (evil) upon the nation of Israel. King Cyrus would become a representation of successive eras of gentile control of Israel. The introduction by God of Himself to Cyrus in Isaiah 45:1-8 is no less than a mandate to the nations that would soon come to effect Israel's existence to consider Him as the Great Dread Sovereign, with which they would have to give account.

It's a far cry for me to find the meaning of "moral corruption" in the context of Isaiah 45:7, when Isaiah 45:8 calls for righteousness as the result of Cyrus' regency. When the world speaks of evil today it is usually an inference to moral corruption: filth, perversity, debauchery, etc. By implication, they assume that God created the knowledge of good and moral corruption and then told Adam not to partake of it. This is a wrong implication and a wrong assumption. The evil that God created is the adverse consequences of sin, and not moral corruption as an alternative to God.

Why Did God Create the Knowledge of Good and Evil?

Let's first establish that Adam and Eve had choice before they fell into sin. They were not mindless automatons, but from the creation were free moral agents. The fact that they fell into sin proves they had freedom of choice. The choice was they could obey God's Word and remain in God or disobey God's Word and turn from God. If the choosing to disobey is the turning from God, what then would they have turned to? In the context of "adverse consequences," God did not create "evil" as an alternative or as a choice. But rather, it is the answer to a wrong choice.

God framed the consequences of wrong choice within the knowledge of good and evil as an operating system. The knowledge of good and evil is a default setting for the offenders (humanity). It was not offered as an alternative to God, but as a system it was offered to point us back to God.

The Sign of the Serpent

Jeremiah 2:19 *"Thine own wickedness shall correct thee, and thy backslidings shall reprove thee: know therefore and see that it is an evil thing* *and bitter, that thou hast forsaken the LORD thy God, and that my fear is not in thee, saith the Lord GOD of hosts."*

It is in this application that God links the knowledge of good and evil to the Law of Moses. When Moses interacted with God at the Burning Bush, he basically asked God for a sign because he knew the Egyptians would not believe that he spoke for God. **Exodus 4:2-3** *"And the LORD said unto him, What is that in thine hand? And he said, A rod. [3] And he said, Cast it on the ground. And he cast it on the ground, and it became a serpent; and Moses fled from before it."* **Exodus 7:10-12** *"And Moses and Aaron went in unto Pharaoh, and they did so as the LORD had commanded: and Aaron cast down his rod before Pharaoh, and before his servants, and it became a serpent. [11] Then Pharaoh also called the wise men and the sorcerers: now the magicians of Egypt, they also did in like manner with their enchantments. [12] For they cast down every man his rod, and they became serpents: **but Aaron's rod swallowed up their rods.**"*

The sign of the serpent in the hands of God's Prophet and in the hands of God's (soon to be) High Priest speaks to God's "in your face" attitude toward Satan and his vicar, Pharaoh. The act, by God, toward Pharaoh with his ministers and counselors and magicians and generals and servants and worshippers in attendance was no less than a "Ha, Ha, and there's nothing you can do about it" announcement of Satan's impending demise; and God did it in Satan's own throne room upon the earth! The Hebrew bondage in Egypt is a microcosm of the world's bondage to Satan in his operating system. Insult upon injury to Pharaoh would be the lingering stench of sheep and slaves in the midst of Pharaoh's I-love-me party. In the face of such humiliation, Pharaoh couldn't help but harden his heart against God. But, it is the utter defenselessness of the king of Egypt to withstand God that resonates today against all of the world's organized attempts to be more like God.

God would further signal the codifying of the knowledge of good and evil into the Law of Moses when the people of Israel sinned by speaking against God and Moses in Numbers 21:4-9.

Numbers 21:6-9 *"And the LORD sent fiery serpents among the people, and they bit the people; and much people of Israel died. [7] Therefore the people came to Moses, and said, We have sinned, for we have spoken against the LORD, and against thee; pray unto the LORD, that he take away the serpents from us. And Moses prayed for the people. [8] And the LORD said unto Moses, Make thee a fiery serpent, and set it upon a pole: and it shall come to pass, that every one that is bitten, when he looketh upon it, shall live. [9] **And Moses made***

a <u>serpent of brass</u>, and put it upon a pole, and it came to pass, that if a serpent had bitten any man, when he beheld the serpent of brass, he lived."

This is the event that Jesus spoke of in **John 3**

John 3:14-16: *"And as Moses lifted up the <u>serpent in the wilderness</u>, even so must the Son of man be lifted up: ¹⁵ That whosoever believeth in him should not perish, but have eternal life. ¹⁶ For God so loved the world, that he gave his only begotten Son, that whosoever believeth in him should not perish, but have everlasting life."*

For humanity, the Cross of Christ is the pivotal point in all of eternity. There are an innumerable amount of prophecies and archetypes and direct references and indirect references and traditions and rituals and ceremonies and ordinances and customs that are all fulfilled in the Cross of Jesus Christ. Historically, the Cross signifies a changing of the times; that is, methods, expectations, understanding, liberties, and authorities would all take on new relevance within the new paradigm. Although thousands of people would die on the Roman cross, under Roman authority, today the Cross is still universally recognized with only the death of the Man Jesus Christ. For the believer, the Cross of Christ represents the passing from death to life. And in all simplicity, when people see the Cross today, it signifies a person's faith in God; and that faith is recognized as an operating system solely associated with Jesus Christ.

So when Jesus elevated the sign of the brazen serpent in the hand of Moses to that of HIS Cross, He was indicating that the operating system that Satan hijacked in the Garden of Eden for humanity's destruction, God had been using for humanity's correction. Again, it is an "in your face" application of God beating Satan at Satan's own game; that game was legalism. Now, at the Cross, the two events would stand as opposing ensigns, each one emblematic of an opposing operating system.

What if, for humanity, there was no reproof or correction from sin? What if God had framed the consequences of wrong choice in terms of automatic total destruction? (See Jeremiah 18:7-11.) At this point in the writing I hope everyone understands there is Heaven to gain and hell to shun! The consequences of our relationship to God the Father and God the Son by God the Holy Ghost amount to eternal life in peace and joy or eternal death in unquenchable fire.

1 John 1:3-4 *"That which we have seen and heard declare we unto you, that ye also may have fellowship with us: and truly our fellowship is with the Father, and with his Son Jesus Christ. ⁴ And these things write we unto you, that your joy may be full."*

Adam was created to operate in God's system called faith. Since faith is presented by the Scriptures as a seed, we understand that Adam would have grown in the knowledge of that system. Adam would have learned to use faith to discern right from wrong. Humanity would have learned how to articulate thoughts and ideas into actions and realities using the operating system of faith. By using the system of faith, we would have been better able to understand the sciences of the created physical realm. The possibilities as we interacted with the created physical realm and with one another would have been limitless if we had continued using faith as our operating system.

But all of that would be derailed before it got a chance to get started. Disobedience brought its own operating system. Disobedience coupled within covenant brought a new master. It was Adam that granted Satan authority to operate as a potentate within God's physical creation; not God. As an operating system, the knowledge of good and evil would skew our discernment of right and wrong. By pride, it would limit our ability to understand and articulate thoughts. Rather than limitless possibilities within creation we became subjects of the creation and aligned ourselves with death. (See Genesis 2:17.)

The example of the highway intersection in Europe is a good example of the collapse of expectation that happens when the operating system of faith is replaced with the operating system of law. Laws and rules cause in us a readiness to rely on laws and rules, but faith causes in us a readiness to care for the well-being of others and to expect a good outcome for every situation. All laws found in Scripture are either faith based or work based.

Galatians 5:6 *"For in Jesus Christ neither circumcision availeth any thing, nor uncircumcision; but faith which worketh by love."* **Galatians 3:12** *"And the law is not of faith:.."*

Through the Scriptures, we have seen and will see the contentious nature of these two operating systems within humanity as they are perfected in the Law of Moses and in the Law of Christ. Inasmuch as I like to think that, because I am a Christian the fight is over, the reality is the fight has just begun. As faith has been birthed within me by the death, burial, and resurrection of Jesus Christ, both operating systems now vie for the preeminence within my being. **Matthew 10:16** *"...be ye therefore wise as serpents, and harmless as doves."*

I am comforted by the fact that nowhere in the Scriptures does God say, "Choose evil." Today, being inherently evil, the only choice for humanity is, "Will we be restored to righteousness by the Blood of Jesus?"

Summary

If we were to review and summarize briefly what we have covered thus far, we would state that Satan has shown a pattern of using the good of God to work evil and death. But we also see that God, being up to the challenge and willing to meet His adversary head on, has chosen to bring good from bad, life from death, and/or life through death.

Hebrews 2:9-10 *"But we see Jesus, who was made a little lower than the angels for the suffering of death, crowned with glory and honour; that he by the grace of God should taste death for every man.* [10] *For it became him, for whom are all things, and by whom are all things, in bringing many sons unto glory, to make the captain of their salvation perfect through sufferings."*

Hebrews 2:14-16 *"Forasmuch then as the children are partakers of flesh and blood, he also himself likewise took part of the same; that through death he might destroy him that had the power of death, that is, the devil;* [15] *And deliver them who through fear of death were all their lifetime subject to bondage.* [16] *For verily he took not on him the nature of angels; but he took on him the seed of Abraham."*

Ever since the Fall of man in the Garden of Eden, covenant has been and is the basis for man's relationship with God. Covenant is the mechanism to convey the seed that changes our nature from corrupt to incorruptible. Just as in marriage, two people die to their individuality and become one flesh; life is passed to and through the seed!

4

Dispensations

When I Was A Child

1 Corinthians 13:11 *"When I was a child, I spake as a child, I understood as a child, I thought as a child: but when I became a man, I put away childish things."*

I'd like to begin the trek into dispensations with a story of my oldest son while he was a toddler. Having our new little son in our lives was a great time for my wife and for me. The experiences of wonderment and joy cannot be over-expressed as each new moment offered its own magical gifts. Interacting with this little person who didn't know malice or greed or envy and was so full of laughter and joy and delight was a gift from God that I will always cherish. The changes that the experience of parenting invoked in me are beyond evaluation in so many aspects of my life. For me, the Love of the Father for His children became tangible when I held my own son.

When my son was about nine months old, he was typically explorative. Most healthy babies do this. They want to crawl about and see and touch. My little speedster was doing this about the house when he began to notice the electrical outlets in the walls. They must have stood out to him like a bull's-eye, since they were all at eye level to a crawling toddler. He would crawl across the floor, and when he got near to something he would stop and raise himself up to interact with this new part of his world. As parents, we had already put those safety plugs in the outlets to prevent any mishaps. But, as Dad, I could see that my son distinguished the safety plug from the outlet, and was not content to leave until he had figured out what that was all about.

So, I picked him up away from the outlet and told him "No!" As expected, we would repeat this process a few times until I felt sure that he understood not to touch the outlets. Now as he wandered about, he would occasion to find himself near enough to an outlet that his curiosity would cause him to reach for the outlet. I knew this was a natural healthy response, from his perspective. My naturally healthy response was to spank the cheek of his backside. And we would repeat this process until he did learn not to touch the outlets.

One day about this same time, my son and I were wrestling on the couch. It was great. He would confidently take on the big guy and didn't pull any punches. We wrestled and wrestled until the big guy got tired. Of course the little dynamo didn't want to stop. I thought if I retreated into the recesses of the couch he would lose interest. Needless to say, he didn't stop. So, I nudged him off the couch. When he hit the floor, I rolled over to look at him with eyebrows raised as if to say, "Had enough yet?"

However, he landed on the floor on all fours and when he looked up, there in front of his face was an electrical outlet. I was staring right at him. As he turned to look up at me with a great big grin, he reached out and put his hand on the outlet and then burst into laughter. It was so funny! I couldn't help but laugh. We laughed a good, long, hard belly laugh together, and I told him as he pulled himself to stand up at the couch, "That's so funny!" The image of joy that my little son had on his face is still in my mind today, as he found a way to triumph. But in the same breath, I also told him, "Now I have to whip you." Our laughter was only fleeting. He wept, and along with the moderate dose of pain, I made sure, verbally, that he understood that he could not touch the outlets. He knew exactly why he got the spanking. Of course it broke my heart. Holding him until he finished crying allowed me to hide my own tears from him, as I didn't want to cast any doubt in him about the rule and the correction. I still weep today when I think about that incident, but I don't regret my actions. You see, a few days later, my wife and my son were at my grandmother's house, and my son was once again exploring his new domain. Her electrical outlets are also at eye level to a toddler, but she doesn't use safety covers. My wife said that he happened upon an outlet, and when he saw it, without hesitation began to say, "*Da, Da, Da, Da*," as he promptly crawled away from the outlet.

Yes, it's a nice story, full of meaning and significance; but don't get ahead of me, because I have not yet made my point. Here is the point. Today my son is a healthy young adult. And, as is often the case with young adults, he teaches me about technology and electronics. Today, I don't mind asking him to "Hook this up for your old dad." As an adult, he is at liberty to plug in whatever he needs to plug in.

Hebrews 7:12 *"For the priesthood being changed, there is made of necessity a change also of the law."*

One of the hardest concepts for human beings to grasp is how God can change the law or the rules and still maintain consistent standards of righteous conduct for His people. The differing dispensations establish the proper context for the changes in His rules. The pattern of changes in dispensations, that is from one dispensation to the next, is the pattern of a loving Father as

He guides His child through the changing stages of maturity. God has dealt with the world as with a child that matures through these stages of the growth process.

Before we go further, it is of the utmost importance to remember that God does not change. His character or His nature does not change. God does not waver between opinions, He does not debate, and He is not ever confused as to the essence of a matter. He sees everything, both spiritual and physical, with perfect clarity, and then calls it for what it is. God is never duplicitous, but He always exhibits the perfect integrity that He requires from all those that bear His name. His Name is "Holy"!

From the Scriptures, the dispensations show us how God does change the methods that He uses to interact with humanity. And although it's not a product of dispensationalism, God does change His course of action based on how we respond to Him. We have already referenced this from Jeremiah 18:7-11. But as with any valid application of any doctrine from the Scriptures, there also arises imitation, misunderstanding, and misapplication of the dispensational model. While there is no shortage of ideas surrounding the study of dispensationalism, it is my intention to focus solely on what the Scriptures say of the subject. Again, if you want to know everybody's opinion, read the commentaries. If you want to know what the Scriptures say, read your Bible.

Colossians 1:25-26 *"Whereof I am made a minister, according to the* **dispensation of God** *which is given to me for you, to fulfil the word of God;* *26 Even the mystery which hath been hid from* **ages and from generations**, *but now is made manifest to his saints:"*

Ephesians 1:10 *"That in the* **dispensation of the fulness of times** *he might gather together in one all things in Christ, both which are in heaven, and which are on earth; even in him:"*

Ephesians 3:2-5 *"If ye have heard of the* **dispensation of the grace of God** *which is given me to you-ward: 3 How that by revelation he made known unto me the mystery; (as I wrote afore in few words, 4 Whereby, when ye read, ye may understand my knowledge in the mystery of Christ) 5* **Which in other ages** **was not made known unto the sons of men, as it is now revealed** *unto his holy apostles and prophets by the Spirit;"*

There are seven distinct successive ages or dispensations found in the Scriptures:

1. Innocence

2. Sin-Conscience

3. Human Government

4. Promise

5. Law

6. Grace

7. Kingdom

In a closer look at the various ages, I would begin with the fourth dispensation. It is unique in that it is the only dispensation that the Scriptures give us the exact number of years the dispensation would cover.

Galatians 3:15-19 *"Brethren, I speak after the manner of men; Though it be but a man's covenant, yet if it be confirmed, no man disannulleth, or addeth thereto. [16] Now to Abraham and his seed were the promises made. He saith not, And to seeds, as of many; but as of one, And to thy seed, which is Christ.* [17] **And this I say, that the covenant, that was confirmed before of God in Christ, the law, which was <u>four hundred and thirty years after</u>, cannot disannul, that it should make the promise of none effect.** [18] *For if the inheritance be of the law, it is no more of promise: but God gave it to Abraham by promise.* [19] *Wherefore then serveth the law? It was added because of transgressions, till the seed should come to whom the promise was made; and it was ordained by angels in the hand of a mediator."*

The Apostle Paul says clearly that the Law of Moses came 430 years after the covenant God made with Abraham. As a tangent, I would offer to correct a pervasive misunderstanding of the Scriptures by the Church: The Children of Israel were not in Egypt for 430 years. The Scripture above is the first and greatest evidence of the misunderstanding: it reads the law came 430 years after the promise. **Genesis 15:13** *"And he said unto Abram, Know of a surety that thy seed shall be a stranger in a land that is not theirs, and shall serve them; and they shall afflict them four hundred years;"* We have read this verse, and in human simplicity have applied this to mean Egypt only; after all, Acts 7:6 counts this as fulfilled from Exodus 12:40.

Acts 7:6 *"And God spake on this wise, That his seed should sojourn in a strange land; and that they should bring them into bondage, and entreat them evil four hundred years."*

Exodus 12:40 *"Now the sojourning of the children of Israel, who dwelt in Egypt, was four hundred and thirty years."*

But look also at:

Hebrews 11:9 *"By faith he <u>sojourned</u> <u>in the land of promise</u>, as in a strange country, dwelling in tabernacles with Isaac and Jacob, <u>the heirs with him of the same promise</u>:"*

Hebrews 11:13 *"These all died in faith, <u>__not having received the promises__</u>, but having seen them afar off, and were persuaded of them, and embraced them, and confessed that they were strangers and pilgrims on the earth."*

The sojourning of Abraham and his children was in the land of Canaan and in the land of Egypt. They were in Egypt only about half of that time. As a Pharisee, the Apostle Paul would have memorized the five books of the Pentateuch from his youth. He further would have been more than familiar with the extra-biblical writings of Moses, Enoch, Jasher, Ezra, Solomon, and so on. Yes, Moses wrote books that are not included in the Bible. Yes, some of these writings are inspired; and yes, the Bible is complete without them. While many of the ancient historical writings of the Hebrews, and before the Hebrews, contain inspired writing, they do not add anything to God's Plan of Salvation. They can be instrumental in providing context to our Holy Scriptures; the Apostle to the Gentiles would have been more than adept at applying this to our Canon.

In this particular instance, I would be remiss to neglect mention of the Septuagint. The Septuagint is a translation of the Hebrew Scriptures into the Greek language by the Hebrew scholars about two and a half centuries before Christ. It would have been a prominent source of study for the Greek-speaking peoples of Israel during the time of Christ and of the Apostle Paul. A well translated version of the Septuagint into English is a must have for any serious student of the Scriptures. My Septuagint is a translation by Sir Lancelot C. L. Brenton, 1851, and translates Exodus 12:40 "And the sojourning of the children of Israel, while they sojourned in the land of Egypt and the land of Chanaan, was four hundred and thirty years."*

Since the translation known as "The Septuagint" was by the Hebrew scribes, of the Hebrew Scriptures, and largely for Hebrew readers, it passes muster of **Romans 3:2**: *"...unto them were committed the oracles of God."* By this standard, the Septuagint is suitable as a reference when forming doctrine from our Canon. (Please note the difference between translations & historical texts against commentaries.)

The Relationship Between Covenants and Dispensations

In that the fourth dispensation is delineated by Scriptures as being 430 years, we can properly assign the end of the third dispensation and the beginning of the fifth dispensation appropriately. Galatians 3:19 refers to the covenant that God made with Abraham, the covenant that God made with the nation of Israel, and also the covenant that God made with "Whosoever Will" through Jesus Christ, which is the fulfillment of God's covenant with Abraham. The pattern that emerges is one where covenants are used to separate dispensations.

The seven ages as delineated by five covenants:

1. The Age of Innocence

2. The covenant God made with Adam ushers in the Age of Sin-Conscience.

3. The covenant God made with Noah ushers in the Age of Human Government.

4. The covenant God made with Abraham ushers in the Age of Promise.

5. The covenant God made with Israel ushers in the Age of Law.

6. The covenant God made with "Whosoever Will" ushers in the Age of Grace.

7. The Kingdom Age

We will discuss the absence of covenants in the first and last ages in another chapter. Properly stated, a covenant begins each new dispensation. Following is a brief statement on each dispensation:

The period of **Innocence** began at creation and ended with the Fall of Adam. This is the shortest-timed of all dispensations. It was the period when Adam began his relationship with the Father in innocence, but it ended when he began to view God through a different perspective: sin.

The period of **Sin-Conscience** follows and covers the time from God's covenant with Adam and the expulsion of man from the Garden of Eden to the Flood of Noah and the ensuing covenant. In the physical, it is a period when we deal with our children over faults, but we recognize that they lack understanding. **Genesis 6:5** *"And GOD saw that the wickedness of man was great in the earth, and that every imagination of the thoughts of his heart was only evil continually."*

The period of **Human Government** is from the Covenant of God with Noah to the giving of the Promise to Abraham. In the human realm, it is a period when young adults are forced to apply the rules and precepts, knowing that consequences are real and have lasting effects. During this period in Scripture, we read of the authority and influence of kingdoms. **Genesis 10:32** *"These are the families of the sons of Noah, after their generations, in their nations: and by these were the nations divided in the earth after the flood."*

The period of the **Promise** is from the giving of the Promise by God to Abraham to the giving of the Law at Mt. Sinai. It is well defined by the Scriptures in Galatians 3:17-19. During this time we read in Scripture of the difficulties of the Hebrews in obtaining the Promise. **Genesis 12:1-3** *"Now the LORD had said unto Abram, Get thee out of thy country, and from thy kindred, and from thy father's house, unto a land that I will shew thee: ² And I will make of thee a great nation, and I will bless thee, and make thy name great; and thou shalt be a blessing: ³ And I will bless them that bless thee, and curse him that curseth thee: and in thee shall all families of the earth be blessed."*

The period of **Law** is from the giving of the Law at Mt. Sinai to the crucifixion of Christ at Mt. Calvary. The Law is said in Galatians 3:17-19 to be temporary and was added, in my words, "to keep man on track to receive the promise." **Galatians 3:19** *"Wherefore then serveth the law? It was added because of transgressions, till the seed should come to whom the promise was made;..."* It is representative of a time in a young adult's life when they are capable of applying concepts of higher learning and reasoning to more abstract knowledge.

Galatians 3:24 *"Wherefore the law was our schoolmaster to bring us unto Christ, that we might be justified by faith. ²⁵ **But after that faith is come, we are no longer under a schoolmaster**. ²⁶ For ye are all the children of God by faith in Christ Jesus."*

Also the Apostle Paul likens the <u>transition of dispensations to a growing adolescent in **Galatians 4.**</u>

Galatians 4:1-5: *"Now I say, That the heir, as long as he is a child, differeth nothing from a servant, though he be lord of all; ² But is under tutors and governors until the time appointed of the father. ³ Even so we, when we were children, were in bondage under the elements of the world: ⁴ <u>But when the fulness of the time was come</u>, God sent forth his Son, made of a woman, made* *under the law, ⁵ To redeem them that were under the law, that we might receive the adoption of sons."* (See also Proverbs 17:2.)

The period of **Grace** is from the crucifixion of Jesus to the rapture of the Church. It is a time in the physical of the fullness of God's promise. During this time, we know and understand the precepts of God and apply them to our own benefit. During this period in life, as adults, we reap the benefits of God in abundance. God gave instruction to the Hebrews while in the wilderness to pick two days worth of manna on the sixth day; once in the Promised Land, the sixth year, God provided to the Hebrews twice the yield of crops so that during the seventh year they would rest. With the number "six" in the Scriptures initially representing a double portion or a double blessing, the sixth dispensation reflects the time in an adult's life when they come into their period of greatest earnings and abundance. **John 10:10** *"I am come that they might have life, and that they might have it more abundantly."*

The period of the **Kingdom** begins at the rapture of the Church and lasts for a thousand years.

2 Peter 3:8 *"But, beloved, be not ignorant of this one thing, that one day is with the Lord as a thousand years, and a thousand years as one day."*

Prophetically, it is the seventh "day" of creation. It is the time when the Christian gets his/her glorified body: no more to be subjected to hunger, cold, sickness, tiredness, etc. In the physical, as witnessed in traditional Christian nations, it is the time of rest (retirement).

Again pertaining to the time between the Law and the Kingdom (3 dispensations), the Apostle Paul writes in **1 Corinthians 13:9**: *"For we know in part, and we prophesy in part. ¹⁰ But when that which is perfect is come, then that which is in part shall be done away. ¹¹ When I was a child, I spake as a child, I understood as a child, I thought as a child: but when I became a man, I put away childish things. ¹² For now we see through a glass, darkly; but then face to face: now I know in part; but then shall I know even as also I am known."*

1 John 3:2 *"Beloved, now are we the sons of God, and it doth not yet appear what we shall be: but we know that, when he shall appear, we shall be like him; for we shall see him as he is."*

"That which is perfect" is a reference to the Kingdom Age, when Jesus comes again and begins His one-thousand year reign upon the earth. (See Revelation 20:2-7.)

I have purposely kept my comments brief on the characteristics of the individual dispensations. It is my trust that as you read God's Word and interact with Him, He will fill in the blanks for you. While the study of the dispensations would fill volumes of books, my hope is that I have given enough of an introduction on the subject to provoke you to further study of the Scriptures.

In summary, I would say that each successive age or dispensation is initiated by a covenant that governs man's relationship with God **for that age**. Some of the rules we learned as children stay with us for life, and some of the rules quickly pass with age. How laughable (sad) would it be for a grown man to say, "I can't plug that in; Dad won't let me." It is equally laughable for an adult to say, "No rule applies to me."

Bibliography:

* The Researcher's Library of Ancient Texts, Volume III, The Septuagint, Translation by Sir Lancelot C. L. Brenton, 1851

Defense / Crane, Mo. 65633 / Copyright 2012 Thomas Horn / ISBN 13: 978-0-9856045-4-7

A Layman's Study...

5

Law and Grace

A Divided Trinity

Romans 13:1-14 *"Let every soul be subject unto the higher powers. For there is no power but of God: the powers that be are ordained of God. [2] Whosoever therefore resisteth the power, resisteth the ordinance of God: and they that resist shall receive to themselves damnation. [3] For rulers are not a terror to good works, but to the evil. Wilt thou then not be afraid of the power? do that which is good, and thou shalt have praise of the same: [4] For he is the minister of God to thee for good. But if thou do that which is evil, be afraid; for he beareth not the sword in vain: for he is the minister of God, a revenger to execute wrath upon him that doeth evil. [5] Wherefore ye must needs be subject, not only for wrath, but also for conscience sake. [6] For for this cause pay ye tribute also: for they are God's ministers, attending continually upon this very thing. [7] Render therefore to all their dues: tribute to whom tribute is due; custom to whom custom; fear to whom fear; honour to whom honour. [8] Owe no man any thing, but to love one another: for he that loveth another hath fulfilled the law. [9] For this, Thou shalt not commit adultery, Thou shalt not kill, Thou shalt not steal, Thou shalt not bear false witness, Thou shalt not covet; and if there be any other commandment, it is briefly comprehended in this saying, namely, Thou shalt love thy neighbour as thyself. [10] Love worketh no ill to his neighbour: therefore love is the fulfilling of the law. [11] And that, knowing the time, that now it is high time to awake out of sleep: for now is our salvation nearer than when we believed. [12] The night is far spent, the day is at hand: let us therefore cast off the works of darkness, and let us put on the armour of light. [13] Let us walk honestly, as in the day; not in rioting and drunkenness, not in chambering and wantonness, not in strife and envying. [14] But put ye on the Lord Jesus Christ, and make not provision for the flesh, to fulfil the lusts thereof."*

As we begin to look at the law in Scripture we find three distinct divisions, or more accurately three realms. The first realm of law is the rule of man, then the Law of Moses, and finally the Law of Christ. Please note, this is not necessarily a chronological listing; and I will refer to the rule of man as, "Caesar".

Today, we seldom equate or think of the Scriptures as the "go to" reference for matters of jurisprudence. Especially in an age when mankind tends to see itself as enlightened apart from the Scriptures, the "civilizing" effect of a codified legal system often becomes the lens of the blinders. Notwithstanding the misapplication of God's intent, the authority of man to rule is established and validated by God in numerous Scriptures. A partial list may include: Deut 28; Dan 4:25, 5:18-21; Matt 17:27, 22:17-21; John 19:11; Rom 13; 1 Tim 2:1-3; 1 Pet 2:13-15.

Proverbs 29:2 *"When the righteous are in authority, the people rejoice: but when the wicked beareth rule, the people mourn."*

I would also restate what has already been written in these pages: God used a Babylonian King to bring judgment upon His wayward people, and then used a Persian King to restore them to their homeland. Further validation of this delegation of authority to "Caesar" is found in the examples of Joseph, the son of Jacob, and Daniel the Prophet. Both of these men were descendants of Abraham and heir to the Promises. Both men represent the Spiritual aspects of faith. Both men faced similar oppositions in their lives. Each man was thrust center stage into the political arena of the dominant world power of his day. Yet, neither man reached the highest position of authority in his respective kingdom: Joseph in Egypt, nor Daniel in Babylon. Each man was held by God to the position of second in command under the king.

We are all very familiar with the form of governance known as "Caesar." It is external, physical, brutal, and even overbearing, if not downright oppressive. Yet, it is entirely necessary.

The other two forms of governance operate internally by the covenant process. Although all three operate in different realms, they all set the standards of conduct for their realm, respectively. In other words, they have different jurisdictions. Romans chapter 13 includes all three realms and tells us to submit to the higher powers. Romans 13 also tells us that in all three realms, "...he that loveth another hath fulfilled the law."

If we look at the Law of Moses and it says to do "this," and then we look at the Law of Christ and it says to do "that," then the two laws appear to be contradictory. But from the dispensational viewpoint, we can see that there are no contradictions in the Scriptures. Each covenant provides the laws that fulfill God's intentions for that age. They establish His Kingdom majestically, systematically, practically, and mercifully; and we don't mix the terms of one covenant with the terms of another covenant.

I will say here, in all sensitivity, that even though the terms of the covenant of Moses are no longer binding, they are, *"...profitable for doctrine, for reproof,* for correction, for instruction in righteousness:" (**2 Timothy 3:16**). We will continue to affirm this principle as the Scriptures bear witness.

Ephesians 2:15 *"Having abolished in his flesh the enmity, even the law of commandments contained in ordinances; for to make in himself of twain one new man, so making peace;"*

Why has God divided the law into three realms?

Romans 8:7 *"Because the carnal mind is enmity against God: for it is not subject to the law of God, neither indeed can be."*

Let that verse sink in for a minute. How can something not be subject to the law of God? Before we move into just what the carnal mind is subject to, let me first say that man himself operates in all three realms. The three realms are **Spirit, soul**, and **body**! The mind, will, and emotions constitute the soul.

Matthew 3:16-17 *"And Jesus, when he was baptized, went up straightway out of the water: and, lo, the heavens were opened unto him, and he saw the Spirit of God descending like a dove, and lighting upon him: [17] And lo a voice from heaven, saying, This is my beloved Son, in whom I am well pleased."*

God is a Trinity. Just as man was made in the image of God, man also was created as a trinity. The Apostle Paul states as much in **1 Thessalonians 5:23**: *"And the very God of peace sanctify you wholly; and I pray God your whole spirit and soul and body be preserved blameless unto the coming of our Lord Jesus Christ."* But on the day that man rebelled against God in the Garden of Eden to magnify himself, he broke God's one law by partaking of the forbidden fruit and death entered into humanity. The word "division" comes from two base words. "Di" means two, twain, or to separate, and "vi" means life. Therefore, it is as God had said to Adam, "...in the day that thou eatest thereof thou shalt surely die." Adam died Spiritually... instantly. The Glory of God was gone. Adam went from being a Spirit that had a soul and lived in a body to being a body and a soul united within an evil framework. **No longer a trinity, mankind found itself in a "<u>biune</u>" condition after the Fall of Adam.**

Enter Melchisedec

Hebrews 7:4 *"Now consider how great this man was, unto whom even the patriarch Abraham gave the tenth of the spoils."*

I want to start right off by saying that Melchisedec was a man! He was not a pre-incarnate Christ. He was not some otherworldly immortal being. Forget all the fantastical hype that you may have heard of him. The Scriptures report him to be a MAN!

So let's look at him from the Scriptures.

Hebrews 7:1-4 *"For this Melchisedec, king of Salem, priest of the most high God, who met Abraham returning from the slaughter of the kings, and blessed him; ² To whom also Abraham gave a tenth part of all; first being by interpretation King of righteousness, and after that also King of Salem, which is, King of peace; ³ Without father, without mother, without descent, having neither beginning of days, nor end of life; but made like unto the Son of God; abideth a priest continually. ⁴ Now consider how great this man was, unto whom even the patriarch Abraham gave the tenth of the spoils."*

The writer of Hebrews, most likely the Apostle Paul, recounts here the interaction between Melchisedec and Abraham from Genesis 14:18-20. What he says in the Letter to the Hebrews is basically what is said in Genesis, but with some explanation. The Hebrew audience to which the letter was written would have had an understanding of the interaction between Melchisedec and Abraham, and would also have known about the man himself. But being separated from that culture by both time and distance, as westerners, we don't have the proper context to reference the man adequately.

To remedy this problem I will begin with the fact that Melchisedec is not his name. "Melchisedec" is a proper title. It's very similar to the way us commoners would address the President of the United States as "Mr. President," if we were going to speak to him personally. As commoners, we don't have the privilege to call the President by his name. Whether we like him or not, whether we agree with him or not, we have reverence for the office that bestows upon the President both authority and responsibility above and beyond every other American citizen. As citizens we are subject to a government over which the President presides. I said it's similar because The Melchisedec would have been born into his position, and as King he would have commanded much more reverence from his subjects. We will discuss Melchisedec's birth name in another chapter.

The designator, "King of Salem" we are told in verse 2 means "King of peace", but it is given to him because he is the King of Jerusalem; the Hebrew word for "peace" being "shalom/salem". The Hebrew word "Melek" means "King". The Hebrew word "Tsedek" means "Righteous". From Melek Tsedek, or as it's transliterated, Melchisedec, comes "King of Righteousness". Where **Hebrews 7:2** says: *"...first being by interpretation King of righteousness, and after that also King of Salem, which is, King of peace;"* we are given, by the King James interpreters, the interpretation of his proper title. In our modern, western mentality we would say, "The Melchisedec" when we refer to him or speak about him. I personally don't have a problem interpreting his name to mean "The Righteous King of Peace," knowing that his office represents the ministry of The Lord Jesus Christ. I do transliterate, with all reverence, as "The Melek Tsedek."

Hebrews 7:3 *"Without father, without mother, without descent, having neither beginning of days, nor end of life; but made like unto the Son of God; abideth a priest continually."*

This phrase from verse 3 is a reference to the "order" of the Melek Tsedek. Because it was a father/son order, there was no need for genealogy. This was in contrast to the Levitical Priesthood which required proof of ancestry to hold office as priest, seeing that they were many cousins. (See 1 Chronicles 24.) While the translation appears to suggest that The Melek Tsedek would live forever, it is actually referring to his office. Since it was a father/son order, there was never a time without a king/priest; when the father died the son automatically became the new one. There was no need for rituals of consecration or ceremony; the office continued without vacancy.

If we fulfill verse 4 and consider how great was the man "Melchisedec," then we would need to read the rest of the chapter. For brevity's sake, suffice it here to say that the rest of the chapter details how The Melek Tsedek was greater than Abraham. Therefore, as a priesthood, the order of Melek Tsedek would represent the Priesthood of The Lord Jesus Christ; that Priesthood would be greater than the Levitical Priesthood which came after Abraham. In other words, the ministry of Melchisedec represents the Ministry of Jesus Christ.

I want to quantify what has just been said in the above explanation of Melek Tsedek: If you still think he was a pre-incarnate Christ, that's OK. If you believe he was immortal, that's OK too. What is important at this point in the study is that Melek Tsedek was a Priest and a King; of that there is no doubt. It is written in Hebrews 7:1 and Genesis 14:18 that he was a king and a priest. The significance of this fact is that a **priest governs the inward workings of a man** and a **king governs the outward workings of a man.** In that both ministries are combined in a single man, it is a ministry suitable for a **<u>biune</u>** people.

It is no accident or coincidence that Melchisedec appears in the Scriptures between the third and fourth dispensation of time. His ministry covers the second, third, and fourth dispensations and is given to a biune people. At that time, all people were biune, that being soul and flesh united. This would be the case until the fifth dispensation of time, when God would do something different. When God made the Covenant of Law with the Nation of Israel, He provided a priesthood for the people, but no king. God intended for Himself to be their King.

If you have read your Bible, then you remember how the people in **1 Samuel 8:5** said to the Prophet and Judge of Israel, Samuel, *"Behold, thou art old, and thy sons walk not in thy ways: now make us a king to judge us like all the nations."* And God responded in **1 Samuel 8:7**: *"Hearken unto the voice of the people in all that they say unto thee: **for they have not rejected thee, but they have rejected me, that I should not reign over them.**"* **v9** *"Now therefore hearken unto their voice: howbeit yet protest solemnly unto them, and shew them the manner of the king that shall reign over them."* **v19-22** ***"Nevertheless the people refused to obey the voice of Samuel; and they said, Nay; but we will have a king over us;*** *[20] That we also may be like all the nations; and that our king may judge us, and go out before us, and fight our battles. [21] And Samuel heard all the words of the people, and he rehearsed them in the ears of the LORD. [22] And the LORD said to Samuel, Hearken unto their voice, **and make them a king...**"*.

It is a sad note in the annals of Israeli history but it doesn't change the fact that the Kingdom and Priesthood were deliberately separated by God under the Law of Moses. Why would God do this?

Ps 19:7 *"The law of the LORD is perfect, converting the soul:.."*

Only the Blood of Jesus can restore the soul of man to a righteous relationship with God our Father. The general sense of the word "converting" in this Psalm of David is one of "causing to repent". Specifically it is often used to mean "to return to the starting point" or "to return home". The soul is made of our mind, will, and emotions; it is conditioned by the ceremonies and the rituals and the mandates of the Law to become a servant of the Spirit. When we were in a biune state of being, our souls were suitable servants of the flesh, a condition that God neither created nor accepts. The Law of Moses converts, through process, the soul of man to become a servant of the Spirit.

Moses alluded to the duality of the ministry of the Levitical Priesthood when he blessed the Levites before his death.

Deuteronomy 33:10 *"They shall teach **Jacob** thy judgments, and **Israel** thy law:.."*

Jacob was the pre-covenant name for Israel. The name, as it's used here, is consistent with the original meaning of "deceiver" and "supplanter," and is a reference to the pre-covenant "carnal" man. Likewise, the name "Israel" is a reference to the post-covenant "Spirit" man. Hence, the Apostle Paul writes of this duality in **Romans 8:6**: *"For to be carnally minded is death; but to be spiritually minded is life and peace. ⁷ Because the carnal mind is enmity against God: for it is not subject to the law of God, neither indeed can be."* The Spiritual man gets the laws and the carnal man gets the judgments.

The Law of Moses, as our schoolmaster, was preparatory in nature. It separated the carnal aspects of my soul from the spiritual aspects of my soul, but it lacked the unction to make me "perfect," or rather "complete," or rather "whole." **Hebrews 10:1-3** *"For the law having a shadow of good things to come, and not the very image of the things, can never with those sacrifices which they offered year by year continually make the comers thereunto perfect. ² For then would they not have ceased to be offered? because that the worshippers once purged should have had no more conscience of sins. ³ But in those sacrifices there is a remembrance again made of sins every year."* (To be "perfect" in the Biblical use of the words means to be complete. As a Christian, I still retain a flawed nature. But the remedy for my flaws and failures also resides within me. His name is Jesus. Therefore, in Him I am complete or rather, "perfected.")

Do we remember with our mind or our Spirit? We remember with our mind. Likewise, I look in retrospect at my own conversion, and afterward and I see that many of the issues that I battled with were largely matters of habit. Even though the Law was our schoolmaster to bring us to Christ, had Jesus not changed our/my nature, and my desires with it, the changing of habits and/or rituals and ceremonies would have done nothing to reconcile me to God.

2 Peter 1:4 *"Whereby are given unto us exceeding great and precious promises: that **by these** ye might be partakers of the divine nature, having escaped the corruption that is in the world through lust."*

The Law left me incomplete. The Law left me divided within myself.

Romans 7:22-25 *"For I delight in the law of God after the inward man: ²³ But I see another law in my members, warring against the law of my mind, and bringing me into captivity to the law of sin which is in my members. ²⁴ O wretched man that I am! who shall deliver me from the body of this death? ²⁵ I thank God through Jesus Christ our Lord. So then with the mind I myself serve the law of God; but with the flesh the law of sin."* **The Law of Moses left me as a <u>dichotomy</u>, that is a soul and flesh divided!**

2 Corinthians 5:17 *"Therefore if any man be in Christ, he is a new creature: old things are passed away; behold, all things are become new."*

As anyone that has experienced the New Birth in Christ is more than happy to attest, there is nothing like it. The joy and peace that replace the guilt and shame of sin is indescribable. Knowing that we are accepted by God on behalf of Jesus Christ gives us that rest and peace that surpasses all understanding. Knowing that we have been cleansed of all our sins motivates us with new purposes in Christ. We are given new hopes and dreams knowing the Love of God that He freely gives to His children. That love also assures us that He will not withhold any good gift from us. We become lighthearted as we cast all our cares upon Him. We gain insight into heavenly wisdom and heavenly protocols, and so on and so on.

But if we ask the same person to describe the new creature, we would probably get about three sheets of blank paper as a response. Maybe we would get a few, "Sorry, I don't understand the question" responses. Or a right response would typically be, "I have no idea...but let me tell you about the experience!"

The new creature we become when we enter into covenant with the Lord Jesus Christ is a "trichotomy." Literally Jesus imparts His nature to us. That nature is The Holy Ghost. Jesus Christ becomes the Lover of our soul and covers our inner man with Himself. His Spirit is joined to our soul, but our flesh is contrary to the Spirit. I would love to be able to report to you that the Trinity of Man has been restored, but the truth is, we're not there yet.

Romans 8:9 *"..Now if any man have not the Spirit of Christ, he is none of his."*

Our body, meaning our flesh and blood and bone and organs, etc., collectively has its own nature. This is what the Scripture refers to as our "flesh". Whereas we were primarily Spirit when God created us, we became primarily fleshly when we were corrupted in the Garden of Eden. At that time, the flesh of man took on Satan's nature of self-exaltation, and that nature still resides within the body of the born-again believer **after** we receive Jesus Christ as our Savior. This is why the Apostle Paul said in **1 Corinthians 15:31**: *"I protest by your rejoicing which I have in Christ Jesus our Lord, **I die daily**."* Jesus said it this way in **Luke 9:23**: *"...If any man will come after me, let him deny himself, and **take up his cross daily**, and follow me. [24] For whosoever will save his life shall lose it: but whosoever will lose his life for my sake, the same shall save it. [25] For what is a man advantaged, if he gain the whole world, and lose himself, or be cast away?"* The cross is where we crucify our flesh. But it is not a onetime event. As long as we live in this body, we will have to regularly contend with our fleshly nature. We will have to strive against, *"...the lust of the flesh, the lust of the eye, and the pride of life"* daily. There is only one prescription given by our Great Physician: the Cross of Christ will defeat the nature of the flesh if we apply it faithfully. We will have to do this daily until we get our glorified body! **Philippians 3:21** *"Who shall change our vile body, that it may be fashioned like unto his glorious body, according to the working whereby he is able even to subdue all things unto himself."*

Saul, Jonathan, and David

James 4:1 *"From whence come wars and fightings among you? come they not hence, even of your lusts that **war in your members**?"*

If we look deeper into the division of man and how there is actually a war within the person, then we can properly relate or parallel the natures of the flesh, soul, and Spirit with the persons of Saul, Jonathan, and David, respectively.

Saul was the first King of Israel. Jonathan was his offspring and heir to the throne. David was not from Saul's lineage but would ascend to the throne after the fall of King Saul. In the position and in the relationship these three men had with each other and with God, we find an accurate representation of the three-part being of the born-again believer.

King Saul, the person, shows a distinct correlation to fallen man in that he was first, he was anointed or covered, he had the preeminent position within the kingdom, and he fell through disobedience. As the Holy Spirit illuminates the Scriptures, we are able to relate the patterns of Saul with the flesh.

As we have begun to see, there is an obvious contrast between the flesh and the Spirit. The contrast is so definite that to study it out completely, we would have to reread and refer to the Bible as a whole. We would have to mention every aspect of the one, and thereby, the other, as well. In the use of the word "anti or ante," we understand that it not only means "against, oppose, or before," but also means "to be in direct contrast with." It's almost like a twin, but the second is the exact opposite of the first.

The primary distinction between Saul and David was that Saul disobeyed God's commands, but David trusted God in every way. With a casual glance, this does not look like an exact opposite, but as we apply the Scriptures personally, we learn that trust placed in the Lord produces obedience to the Lord!

1 Samuel 28:16-18 *"Then said Samuel, Wherefore then dost thou ask of me, seeing the LORD is departed from thee, and is become thine enemy?* [17] *And the LORD hath done to him, as he spake by me: **for the LORD hath rent the***

kingdom out of thine hand, and given it to thy neighbour, even to David:
¹⁸ Because thou obeyedst not the voice of the LORD,..."

In 1 Samuel 13:14, we read that God sought a man after His own heart; which man we know to be David. Suffice it here to say that David, a man not of Saul's lineage or offspring, chosen by God, represents the Spirit. David was under obedience to Saul but he was not of Saul. This relationship is evidenced further in **Hebrews 5:6** where God said, speaking of Jesus: *"Thou art a priest for ever after the order of Melchisedec."*

Heb 7:11-12 *"If therefore perfection were by the Levitical priesthood, (for under it the people received the law,) what further need was there that another priest should rise after the order of Melchisedec, and not be called after the order of Aaron? ¹² For the priesthood being changed, there is made of necessity a change also of the law."*

Although Jesus changed the Law, He came into the picture under the Law. His purpose was *"to redeem them that were under the law,.."* (**Galatians 4:5**).

In summary, David was under Saul but not of Saul, and by the Hand of God, David replaced Saul as King. Likewise, Jesus came into this world under the Law but not of the Law, and by the Hand of God, Jesus would replace Aaron as our Great High Priest.

Now we come to Jonathan, the man in the middle and a representation of our soul, being in direct kinship and subservient to (that is, desiring to please) our flesh. Seeing that Saul fathered Jonathan, he would have mentored and shaped Jonathan's character more than any other man. Saul and Jonathan would share a nature that had been written into their DNA by generations that came before them. Saul was all Jonathan knew and aspired to be...that is, until David came on the scene.

It is a beautiful illustration in 1 Samuel 17 how the lad, David, would refuse to wear the King's armor. The armor of King Saul wasn't just a representation of Saul. It was a repository of Saul's trust in himself; it was his outer man; it was his covering, almost like scales. Perhaps this is beginning to sound familiar. After David killed Goliath, the man of war, Jonathan and David made a covenant.

1 Samuel 18:1-4 *"And it came to pass, when he had made an end of speaking unto Saul, that the soul of Jonathan was knit with the soul of David, and Jonathan loved him as his own soul. ² And Saul took him that day, and would let him go no more home to his father's house. ³ Then Jonathan and David made a covenant, because he loved him as his own soul. ⁴ And Jonathan* stripped himself of the robe that was upon him, and gave it to David, and his garments, even to his sword, and to his bow, and to his girdle."

I thank God for that Spirit Man, Jesus Christ. He is fully man and fully God. He came into my life to defeat the champion of my enemy; the enemy that kept me in both fear and hopelessness. And Jesus gave me hope and faith and direction, bound up in His own Heavenly Nature, that I should "...walk not after the flesh, but after the Spirit." in righteousness.

The War Within Begins

1 Samuel 19:1 "And Saul spake to Jonathan his son, and to all his servants, that they should kill David."

1 Samuel 19:2 "But Jonathan Saul's son delighted much in David:..."

There is no doubt that Jonathan was torn between the love for his father and the love for David. (See Matthew 10:37-38.) This is a hard place for anyone to be. Yet, we are all in this exact predicament; we desire to please God, and we desire to please our flesh. If we continue to read the account from Scripture, we find a second covenant between Jonathan and David. It is in this covenant, after Jonathan is required to choose, that Jonathan secures for his house (seed) the kindness of David. (See 1 Samuel 20:11-17.)

1 Sam 20:30-34 "Then Saul's anger was kindled against Jonathan, and he said unto him, Thou son of the perverse rebellious woman, do not I know that thou hast chosen the son of Jesse to thine own confusion, and unto the confusion of thy mother's nakedness? [31] For as long as the son of Jesse liveth upon the ground, thou shalt not be established, nor thy kingdom. Wherefore now send and fetch him unto me, for he shall surely die. [32] And Jonathan answered Saul his father, and said unto him, Wherefore shall he be slain? what hath he done? [33] And Saul cast a javelin at him to smite him: whereby Jonathan knew that it was determined of his father to slay David. [34] So Jonathan arose from the table in fierce anger, and did eat no meat the second day of the month: for he was grieved for David, because his father had done him shame."

Remember, we are relating the lives of Saul, Jonathan, and David to our flesh, soul, and Spirit, respectively. Because of Saul's disobedience, God Himself would depose Saul from the Throne of Israel. The principal that looms in this setting is that "The seed brings forth after its kind." For this reason, Jonathan (our soul) also would be removed from any right he had to reign in the kingdom. Saul knew this. (See John 3:30.) After the death of Saul and

Jonathan, David laments and says in **2 Samuel 1:23**: *"Saul and Jonathan were lovely and pleasant in their lives, and in their death **they were not divided:.."***

Just as Jonathan was pulled in two directions within himself, man also faces this same war. Joshua, another representation of the Spirit Man, said in **Joshua 24:15**: *"..choose you this day whom ye will serve;.."*

The Appeal

The question arises: what do we do when our leaders, whether family, civic, or spiritual, are in the wrong? If we use the folly of Saul toward David as an example, we find Jonathan asking, *"...what hath he done?"* (**1 Samuel 20:32**).

1 Samuel 19:4-5 *"And Jonathan spake good of David unto Saul his father, and said unto him, Let not the king sin against his servant, against David; because he hath not sinned against thee, and because his works have been to thee-ward very good:* [5] *For he did put his life in his hand, and slew the Philistine, and the LORD wrought a great salvation for all Israel: thou sawest it, and didst rejoice: wherefore then wilt thou sin against innocent blood, to slay David without a cause?"*

Jonathan makes his first appeal to his own father, who is obviously in the wrong. In his appeal Jonathan mentions "sin" three times as well as "innocent blood". Although Jonathan is commanded under the Law of Moses to honor his father, Jonathan rightly invokes the Law of Moses as an appeal. At that time, it was the Law of Moses that defined both sin and innocent blood. So, to escape one law or power we are drawn to a higher law or power; this is the nature of the appeal. Jesus referred to this idea in **Mark 2:23-28**: *"And it came to pass, that he went through the corn fields on the sabbath day; and his disciples began, as they went, to pluck the ears of corn.* [24] *And the Pharisees said unto him, Behold, why do they on the sabbath day that which is not lawful?* [25] *And he said unto them, Have ye never read what David did, when he had need, and was an hungred, he, and they that were with him?* [26] *How he went into the house of God in the days of Abiathar the high priest, and did eat the shewbread, which is not lawful to eat but for the priests, and gave also to them which were with him?* [27] *And he said unto them, The sabbath was made for man, and not man for the sabbath:* [28] *Therefore the Son of man is Lord also of the sabbath."* (See also Matthew 12:1-8; Luke 6:1-5.)

There are several "priestly" aspects to King David's ministry. But I am constrained here to focus on this one point: David was able to do that which was not lawful because David was operating under a higher law!

The Bible, as a whole, establishes reciprocity as a precept. In the Old Testament we find "eye for an eye", and many examples of it. In the New testament we find **Galatians 6:7**: *"Be not deceived; God is not mocked: for whatsoever a man soweth, that shall he also reap."* These verses, along with many others, establish reciprocity as an operating principal within the Kingdom of God.

But the same Bible in the New Testament declares in **Matthew 5:39**: *"But I say unto you, That ye resist not evil: but whosoever shall smite thee on thy right cheek, turn to him the other also."* **Romans 12:21** *"Be not overcome of evil, but overcome evil with good."*

Love is God's highest law! Even faith works by love. (See Galatians 5:6.) We can escape reciprocity only through a higher law! Love is God's highest law!

Jonathan found a limited success in his appeal to his father.

1 Samuel 19:6 *"And Saul hearkened unto the voice of Jonathan: and Saul sware, As the LORD liveth, he shall not be slain."* Jonathan's success is limited, because in verse 9 of the same chapter that evil spirit is once again working in King Saul, and he tries again to kill David. Some appeals are not going to be successful. Even the Apostle Paul, though he was in God's perfect will, appealed unto Caesar and was ultimately beheaded. (See Acts 25:11.) In the example of the Apostle Paul's appeal, I must believe God's will prevailed. God's itinerary is oftentimes very different than ours. **Philippians 4:22** *"All the saints salute you, chiefly they that are of Caesar's household."*

So what do we do when our leaders are wrong? The one thing we can do in any situation like this is to seek God's will. Pray! We should make our appeal to God! As Christians we have the promise of God in **1 John 5:14-15**: *"And this is the confidence that we have in him, that, if we ask any thing according to his will, he heareth us: *[15]* And if we know that he hear us, whatsoever we ask, we know that we have the petitions that we desired of him."*

James 5:16 *"The effectual fervent prayer of a righteous man availeth much."*

Surrender to God is our ultimate appeal.

Jonathan had obviously purposed in his heart not to harm David; he was already in covenant with him. Would Jonathan have resisted his father, the King, with force? It's only my opinion, but I think not.

The Legal Precedent of Acts Chapter 4

In Acts 4, we read how the rulers, elders, scribes, and the High Priest and his kindred were gathered together to examine Peter and John concerning a miracle done in the name and power of Jesus Christ. After examining them, the council commanded Peter and John, contrary to the commandment of Christ, *"not to speak at all nor to teach in the name of Jesus."*

Acts 4:19 *"But Peter and John answered and said unto them, Whether it be right in the sight of God to hearken unto you more than unto God, judge ye."* While most people stop right here when trying to answer the rules and regulations of government that are too often contrary to the Gospel of Jesus Christ, the Apostles did not stop here but followed through with an appeal to God. They would have been wrong to do otherwise.

Acts 4:23-31 *"And being let go, they went to their own company, and reported all that the chief priests and elders had said unto them. ²⁴ And when they heard that, they lifted up their voice to God with one accord, and said, Lord, thou art God, which hast made heaven, and earth, and the sea, and all that in them is: ²⁵ Who by the mouth of thy servant David hast said, Why did the heathen rage, and the people imagine vain things? ²⁶ The kings of the earth stood up, and the rulers were gathered together against the Lord, and against his Christ. ²⁷ For of a truth against thy holy child Jesus, whom thou hast anointed, both Herod, and Pontius Pilate, with the Gentiles, and the people of Israel, were gathered together, ²⁸ For to do whatsoever thy hand and thy counsel determined before to be done. ²⁹ And now, Lord, behold their threatenings: and grant unto thy servants, that with all boldness they may speak thy word, ³⁰ By stretching forth thine hand to heal; and that signs and wonders may be done by the name of thy holy child Jesus. ³¹ And when they had prayed, the place was shaken where they were assembled together; and they were all filled with the Holy Ghost, and they spake the word of God with boldness."*

Verse 24 begins the Apostles' appeal to God and verse 31 is God's judgment in the matter. The Apostles appealed to God first, before resuming their ministry. Today this act stands as a precedent to operating in Kingdom authority. It is OK to disagree in principal with civil authorities, but to operate contrary to their authority requires a mandate from Heaven. It is incumbent upon ministers and their ministries to know that God has ordained secular governments, and that He has retained and affirmed His Supremacy in meting out the laws and their respective realms in perfect judgment.

As an example of this, Acts 4:27 references the powers that be. Pontius Pilate and Herod were both representatives of "Caesar." While Pilate was purely civil or secular, Herod was more closely related to the Jews and to their mindset. Herod was a religious interface between Caesar and the Hebrews of that day. As you read your Bible, please notice who was in authority between Pilate and Herod; it was Pilate. At best, Herod could only serve Pilate's desire as Herod ruled in Israel. We will see this relationship between Pilate and Herod again, as it has prophetic implications for the hour in which we now live. (See Luke 23:7.)

Summary

So we assert that the procession of dispensations parallels the changing stages of man's being. As **biune** and corrupt, we were governed by a combined king/priest. When God began to separate our being, He gave us new laws and the priesthood was separated from the kingdom; we were left as a **dichotomy**. After this stage, mankind was ready to receive the Messiah of God. Jesus imparted (and still imparts) the Holy Spirit to all that call upon His name; and we became a **trichotomy**. But God is not finished yet.

Mankind went from one law in the Garden of Eden to a period of judgments in the next three succeeding dispensations to six hundred-thirteen laws in the fifth dispensation back to one law in the current sixth dispensation. **Romans 5:14** says: *"Nevertheless death reigned from Adam to Moses,..."* (The second thru fourth dispensation). They got judgment but no law, just as my son got striped from time to time before he understood words. The Great Flood of Noah and the dispersion of man at the Tower of Babel are examples of judgment during these dispensations. Of the fifth dispensation the Apostle Paul writes in **Romans 5:20**: *"Moreover the law entered, that the offence might abound.* ***But where sin abounded, grace did much more abound:"*** It is almost universally accepted in theology that the number five is representative of God's grace, and here it is rightly applied to the fifth dispensation. Moving into the sixth dispensation, we are restored to God's singular highest law: love! And that, with a double portion!

1 John 4:10 *"Herein is love, not that we loved God, but that he loved us, and sent his Son to be the propitiation for our sins. [11] Beloved, if God so loved us, we ought also to love one another. [12] No man hath seen God at any time. If we love one another, God dwelleth in us, and his love is perfected in us. [13] Hereby know we that we dwell in him, and he in us, because he hath given us of his Spirit."*

We learn from the appeal process that we always appeal to a higher law. Spiritual laws are higher than both fleshly (biune) and soulish (dichotomy) laws. If we are going to appeal to God's higher laws, I think in all fairness God will expect us to walk in them. We don't get to receive God's forgiveness and then not forgive others. (See Matthew 18:23-35.) By the same standard, if we break God's Spiritual laws then we break God's highest laws; and yes, the consequences also are greater. Whether we are applying God's love toward us or our love toward others, love as defined by God must be the basis of our actions and intentions.

Law In/And The Church

Galatians 4:1 *"Now I say, That the heir, as long as he is a child, differeth nothing from a servant, though he be lord of all; ² But is under tutors and governors until the time appointed of the father."*

Now that we are in the Dispensation of Grace, and now that we have moved into the trichotomy stage of being, with all of its dogmas and catechisms, theologies, revelations and new insights, with gimmicks and methods and both subtle and not so subtle expectations of conformity, we as Christians are confronted with the daunting question of "What is the truth?" And, with every possible conflicting answer being offered by the Church, it's a wonder the Church maintains even a semblance of a monolithic or unified body. While we consider the discombobulated, confused, and varied nature of the Church today, we are tempted to throw up our hands in utter surrender and think, "Who can fix this?"

My response is "All is well! This is by design." What we are witnessing when we see all the divisions within the Body of Christ is the Great Physician performing surgery on His child named "Humanity" (Adam).

Hebrews 4:12 *"For the word of God is quick, and powerful, and sharper than any twoedged sword, piercing even to the dividing asunder of soul and spirit, and of the joints and marrow, and is a discerner of the thoughts and intents of the heart."*

In large part, the Word that God uses to divide asunder is what I refer to as "dispensational holdovers." I would define that to mean "Precepts or intentions of God handed down through tradition or specified in His Word to one dispensation, but that have been held onto and carried into successive dispensations." In the broader general context, dispensational holdovers lack any authority over the general population. (There is one great exception. I will not discuss it in this book.) Contrariwise, in the specific or individual context, adherents to a system of belief lack any unction to escape the dispensational holdover unless they escape by a right application of God's Word.

All is well when God uses dispensational holdovers, but that doesn't mean that Satan doesn't corrupt the intent of God's Word when his ministers of righteousness imitate the ministry within the Church. We are not to be ignorant of his devices. Some dispensational holdovers are used by God to teach carnal Christians the precepts and foundations of Faith. Some of the same dispensational holdovers are applied corruptly by Satan to reinforce self-righteousness within carnal Christians.

Often laws pertaining to clean and unclean animals eaten as foods are invoked by Christians, unwittingly, as dispensational holdovers. The vast majority of Christians don't have a problem with eating pork. But for the Christians that have a problem with eating pork, nothing we can say will deter their abstinence. Often, they insist that the rest of us must be out of step with God's will. Or maybe we just haven't read the Bible enough to know what God wants. But, if they are to be liberated from the Old Covenant ordinance it must be a work of the Holy Spirit; and it usually involves the New Covenant Word of God. As the Apostle Paul says, *"...for the letter killeth, but the spirit giveth life."* (**2 Corinthians 3:6**).

I can personally attest to the binding authority of the holdover in my own life. When I first got saved, I became convinced that I was supposed to keep the Sabbath as a day of rest. I read it in the Bible and nobody was going to convince me otherwise. When I learned that the Sabbath Day was actually Saturday, I was convinced that I was supposed to keep Sabbath on Saturday. As I got stricter and stricter about what I thought I could and couldn't do on the Sabbath, the Holy Ghost began to deal with me about my motives for keeping the Sabbath in the first place. As I read the New Testament Scriptures that label the Law of Moses as a yoke of bondage (See Galatians 5:1; Acts 15:10.) I realized that I had been trying to keep the Sabbath to show God how good and committed I was, which is an obvious perversion of God's intention. Ultimately, it was the Holy Ghost and the Word of God that delivered me from the dispensational holdover, for nowhere in the New Testament or Dispensation of Grace do the Scriptures that govern us say, "Remember the Sabbath day, to keep it holy." However, the whole process of being bound by God's Word and then being delivered by God's Word had the effect of separating my carnal nature from my Spiritual nature. God made me aware of the imitating tendency of my own pride, literally fulfilling Romans 3:20. Today I am constantly assessing and reassessing my own motives as I submit to the Word of God, to prayer for myself, and to those people God has placed over me in the Lord. Thank You, Jesus!

Jeremiah 31:22 *"How long wilt thou go about, O thou backsliding daughter? for the LORD hath created a new thing in the earth, A woman shall compass a man."*

The dispensational effect is evidenced in the macro from a historical context, as an over-arching theme for that particular age, but in the micro from a here-and-now context as an over-arching theme for the individual. I laugh as I write this, because the very attack that Satan pressed against God's law to divide man in the Garden of Eden is the very method that God would use to restore fallen man to his former state of Glory! The six hundred and thirteen laws God instituted at Mt. Sinai would divide the flesh from the soul, and prepare the soul to serve the Spirit.

Romans 3:31 *"Do we then make void the law through faith? God forbid: yea, we establish the law."*

The Apostle Paul, writing in Romans, begins to contrast law and faith: specifically, the righteousness which is of the law, and the righteousness which is by faith.

Romans 3:21-22 *"But now the righteousness of God without the law is manifested, being witnessed by the law and the prophets; ²² Even the righteousness of God which is by faith of Jesus Christ unto all and upon all them that believe: for there is no difference:"*

This verse is in contrast to **Deuteronomy 6:25**: *"And it shall be our righteousness, if we observe to do all these commandments before the LORD our God, as he hath commanded us."*

The righteousness which is by faith is God's righteousness, meaning His character or nature or virtue. This is the same righteousness which is imputed or given to all that believe in Jesus Christ as their personal Lord and Savior. This is the exchange according to **2 Corinthians 5:21**: *"For he hath made him to be sin for us, who knew no sin; that we might be made the righteousness of God in him."* The righteousness of God that He imputes to us is not dependant on the law; that righteousness and the faith which it comes through existed long before the law was given, in the person of God Himself.

Hebrews chapter 11 contains 40 verses that are basically in chronological order. Faith is the theme of this chapter. Verse 3 takes us all the way back to "In the beginning," and verse 40 includes us. The period of the law doesn't even begin until verse 30 and concludes in verse 39; and of these verses, verse 31 pertains to Rahab, who wasn't even under the law at that time.

Abel, Abraham, Noah, Daniel, and Job are all <u>declared to be righteous</u> according to Scripture. (This is a partial list only.) Four of these men lived prior to the Law of Moses:

Abel	Matt 23:35
Abraham	Gen 15:6; Rom 4:3; Gal 3:6
Noah	Gen 7:1; Ezek 14:14
Job	Job 1:1; Ezek 14:14

Romans 3:10 *"As it is written, There is none righteous, no, not one:"*

If the Scriptures proclaim **_none_** to be righteous, then how do the Scriptures proclaim **_some_** to be righteous?

Isaiah 64:6 *"But we are all as an unclean thing, and all our righteousnesses are as filthy rags;"*

Our righteousness (self-righteousness) is equated by God in Isaiah 64:6 with the death of the seed. Our righteousness is based on works, that faulty standard! "Filthy rags" is a reference to a woman's soiled menstrual cloth now worn in décor. Hebrews chapter 11 shows us that faith in God has always been God's standard for imputing **God's Righteousness** to us. The Scriptures do agree; they are consistent!

Galatians 3:19 *"Wherefore then serveth the law? It was added because of transgressions, till the seed should come to whom the promise was made; and it was ordained by angels in the hand of a mediator."*

Do you notice how the law came because of transgressions in Galatians 3:19? Well, a careful student of the Word might ask, "What about **1 John 3:4**: *'Whosoever committeth sin transgresseth also the law: for sin is the transgression of the law.'*?" The Apostle Paul says the law came because of transgressions and the Apostle John says sins are a transgression of the law; so, which came first, the law or the transgression? **Because there could be no transgressions against the law until after the law was given, we know the transgressions spoken of in Galatians 3:19 were transgressions against faith.** After the law was given, transgressions were still against faith. Only now transgressors had the law to deal with also. The law was intended by God to preserve our faith, even in the Garden of Eden. The law is a faith preserver!

Romans 3:31 *"Do we then make void the law through faith? God forbid: yea, we establish the law."*

So, how do we establish the law? We do not consciously go about trying to establish the law. We couldn't do it if we tried. We can't establish the number of hairs on our head, let alone the virtues and precepts of God. The law is established through faith, and that is a work God does through us.

Galatians 5:6 *"For in Jesus Christ neither circumcision availeth any thing, nor uncircumcision; but faith which worketh by love."* Our lot is to obey. It is faith that does the work!

The Law is Good

What then is the proper relationship between law and grace? Is there a place for law within the Church? As long as man is divided between Spirit, soul, and flesh, there will be differences in law and it's administrations, especially in different Churches.

Let me further complicate the matter. Every Church (local congregation) does not have the same ministry or calling. This is true even of different congregations within the same denomination. For example, one Church may have a large youth ministry. Another Church may focus on prison ministries. Yet another may be called to reach shut-ins or the homeless through benevolence or resource giving.

As each local congregation fulfills its calling and direction, there are three basic administrations that it will operate in. They are word ministries, worship ministries, and war ministries. When we refer to war ministries, we are referring to Spiritual warfare and this ministry is accomplished by prayer. To examine each ministry, or combination of ministries, would be too extensive for this study. Such an examination would probably be too extensive for any study to form definitive conclusions. (See Luke 17:20.) But, these three ministries are the same three ministries that we find in the Spiritual realm, and they are characterized by the archangels Gabriel, Lucifer, and Michael. (If there are other angels characterizing a specific ministry, they are not validated by Canon of Scripture.)

To further categorize ministry callings and operations would require a study into the seven administrations of the Holy Spirit at the corporate level. (See Psalms 133:1-2; Revelation 1:4,12,20, 5:6.) Finally, we would move into the different operations of the Holy Spirit at the individual level. (See Romans 12:3-8; 1 Corinthians 12:4-30.)

Now let me back up and regroup. The Scriptures do show a pattern of placement of law within the body of Christ. Take, for example, a Church with a large youth ministry and a zeal to make new converts. The majority of this congregation could very well be comprised of what Scripture calls "babes in Christ." This is the ministry that could be characterized by dynamic worship (Psalms 8:2) and teaching and preaching super or ultra-conservatism, meaning law.

1 Corinthians 3:1 *"And I, brethren, could not speak unto you as unto spiritual, but as unto carnal, even as unto babes in Christ. ² I have fed you with milk, and not with meat: for hitherto ye were not able to bear it, neither yet now are ye able. ³ For ye are yet carnal:..."* In the New Testament, the word "carnal" refers both to immature Christians and to commandments and ordinances. (See Hebrews 7:16, 9:10.)

Galatians 4:1 *"Now I say, That the heir, as long as he is a child, differeth nothing from a servant, though he be lord of all; ² But is under tutors and governors until the time appointed of the father."*

The contrast in Galatians 4:1 is between the heir and the servant. Christ is sometimes referred to as a servant, but Moses is always referred to as a servant. The heir (Son) is used almost exclusively to designate Christ. (See Hebrews 3:3-6.)

Proverbs 17:2 *"A wise servant shall have rule over a son that causeth shame, and shall have part of the inheritance among the brethren."*

Specifically or in the macro, this verse is a reference to the authority vested in Moses over the nation of Israel. Generally or in the micro, it can refer to any and all that have come to Jesus Christ for their salvation, but have not yet learned to operate in faith. Young Christians often don't realize or respond to God's call to Holiness or Sanctification, which is the outworking of faith. (See Hebrews 12.)

Galatians 4:2 *"But is under tutors and governors until the time appointed of the father."*

God the Father sanctions and moderates the virtue of law within the Body of Christ. He knows that the seed may take longer to grow in some cases and He has every intention to preserve the good work He has begun in us. The law is still a faith preserver.

As a faith preserver, The Law of Moses had many provisions or ordinances bound up within it that dealt with the fleshly nature of man. That is, they held in check the fleshly nature of man as God's desire is actually to destroy that nature altogether. Conversely, our fleshly nature does please God,..... when it is burnt in judgment as a sweet smelling savor! **Isaiah 53:10** *"...it pleased the Lord to bruise Him;"* **Ephesians 5:2** *"...and hath given himself for us an offering and a sacrifice to God for a sweetsmelling savour."*

As we submitted to the law, we found our flesh growing weaker until we came to Christ, our Great High Priest, who dealt with our flesh mercifully and in finality. To sacrifice an animal at the altar required care and precision. The incision to the animal's jugular vein had to ensure a swift, painless death. If an animal experienced fear or stress during the sacrifice, then poisons would have been released into its body, thus contaminating the sacrifice. To minimize the likelihood of stress, the animal was to feel love through the whole process. Kosher was to be more than the cut of meat or the type of animal, but also involved the manner of care for the animal during its life and the sacrificial ritual or method of death.

When God said "eye for an eye," He mercifully limited our punishment to the crime. The concept of eye for an eye alone would be an ample deterrent to prevent transgressions against the law, but at the same time God made a reflection of the crime in the punishment. Because the punishment reflected the crime, we were to see ourselves. The law, as our accuser, forced us to look at our own depravity. **John 5:45** *"Do not think that I will accuse you to the Father: there is one that accuseth you, even Moses, in whom ye trust."* (See also Romans 3:19.)

God gave us the law for our own good and for the establishment of His Kingdom and principals. The Apostle Paul wrote in **Romans 7:14**: *"For we know that the law is spiritual: but I am carnal, sold under sin."* Throughout the Word of God, we find God giving good things to man, some material and some abstract, and then man turning or perverting the natural use of the gift to suit his own selfish desire. This has also been the case with both law and grace.

For example, the Apostle Paul writes in **1 Timothy 5:23**: *"...use a little wine for thy stomach's sake and thine often infirmities."* But in **Proverbs 20:1** we are warned that, *"Wine is a mocker, strong drink is raging: and whosoever is deceived thereby is not wise."* And again in 1 Corinthians 6:10, "drunkards" shall not inherit the kingdom of God. So, while many of God's precepts are absolute, "thou shalt not" others are governed by faith and should follow God's intent for the gift.

I know of Churches that use wine with communion; and there is nothing wrong with this practice of itself. But, it is more important to remember that many people struggle with alcoholism. To have love and compassion on a weaker brother or sister, love says it is good to substitute wine with grape juice when partaking of communion. It is only when we seek to be justified somehow by partaking of communion, or any other rite, that we begin to observe stricter and stricter rules concerning the use of the same.

Likewise, there is a debate between those that believe communion represents the body of Christ and those that believe communion becomes the body of Christ. Who is right? Remember the ambush in the knowledge of good and evil? If anyone is willing to argue for or against a doctrine he will surely do it with Scripture. But, Jesus didn't say when you do this you will be justified. He did say, *"...this do in remembrance of me."* (**Luke 22:19**).

Communion comes from what we call "the Last Supper". It was actually part of the Passover observance. Jesus also said in **Luke 22:19**: *"This is my body which is given for you:"* When God brought His people out of Egypt, He instructed them how to take a lamb, kill it, roast it, eat it, and to apply the blood. Then in **Exodus 12:14,** God said: *"And this day shall be unto you for **a memorial**; and ye shall keep it a feast to the LORD throughout your generations; ye shall keep it a feast by an ordinance for ever."* Look at the relationship: "a memorial" / "this do in remembrance." If Jesus said, *"...this do in remembrance of me"* does it constitute a New Testament law? Sure it does, but it is for our benefit and not for our justification. The primary purpose for the memorial in covenant is that it brings our mind and our eyes back to God. Specifically, the memorial bears witness to our covenant with God. This is a great benefit when circumstances arise that may cause us to doubt if God still cares for us. (See Genesis 28:18-22, 35:1.)

Galatians 2:16 *"Knowing that a man is not justified by the works of the law, but by the faith of Jesus Christ, even we have believed in Jesus Christ, that we might be justified by the faith of Christ, and not by the works of the law: for by the works of the law shall no flesh be justified."*

This same principal applies to water baptism or any other New Testament rite established by God.

Romans 5:1 *"Therefore being justified by faith, we have peace with God through our Lord Jesus Christ:"*

In comparing the two covenants further, as an element, both covenants agree in establishing a meal as a memorial. The fundamental of "covering" is not in agreement between the two covenants. On the one hand, we have from the Law of Moses, **Deuteronomy 6:25**: *"And it shall be our righteousness, if we observe to do all these commandments before the LORD our God, as he hath commanded us."* Then, on the other hand, we have from the New Testament,

Revelation 19:8: *"And to her was granted that she should be arrayed in fine linen, clean and white: for the fine linen is the righteousness of saints."* Because each covenant stands alone, each covenant offers its own covering. From the comparison, the righteousness we could not earn under the Law of Moses became a gift in the Law of Christ. (See Acts 15:8-11.)

Matthew 9:16-17 *"No man putteth a piece of new cloth unto an old garment, for that which is put in to fill it up taketh from the garment, and the rent is made worse. ¹⁷ Neither do men put new wine into old bottles: else the bottles break, and the wine runneth out, and the bottles perish: but they put new wine into new bottles, and both are preserved."*

In those days, "bottles" were made of skins. Wine is a representation of the Holy Spirit. The skins had to be renewed with oil to prevent them from bursting. Oil also is a representation of the Holy Spirit. Jesus is saying He didn't come to patch up an old covering or to put His Spirit into old and dry vessels. He came to renew the vessels and restore the Holy Spirit.

The Apostle Paul also contrasts the two covenants in the book of Galatians, calling the Law of Moses *"...another Gospel:"* (**Galatians 1:6**). The student of gematria would find a glaring indictment of the Law of Moses in the letter to the Galatians in that the Apostle references "works of the law" six times. The seventh time it is mentioned it reads "works of the flesh." This would link the operating system of the law with the nature of the operator.

The Contrast

John 1:17 *"For the law was given by Moses, but grace and truth came by Jesus Christ."*

These are fitting Scriptures to begin a contrast of law and grace. In fact, a large portion of the New Testament is a direct contrast to the Law of Moses. A fourth grader once wrote a dissertation in which he explained the relationship between law and grace. He wrote, "The Old Testament is the New Testament concealed and the New Testament is the Old Testament revealed." ...and then he was immediately promoted to be the Head of the Church. Of course, I am being sarcastic here. But the cliché that continues to circulate through the Church evidences the ease in which Christians agree with sophistic train of thought, or nursery rhymes.

I admit that contrasting two opposing operating systems is no small task, but the Lord Jesus Himself invited us to look into the matter when He began His New Testament teaching with five recorded sayings of, "Ye have heard that it was said by them of old time" and, "But I say unto you."

I am sensitive to those who say, "Jesus didn't come to destroy the law." There are a couple of Scriptures that people erroneously cleave to as they attempt to combine the two covenants. The first is **Matthew 5:17-18**: *"Think not that I am come to destroy the law, or the prophets: I am not come to destroy, but to fulfil. ¹⁸ For verily I say unto you, Till heaven and earth pass, one jot or one tittle shall in no wise pass from the law, till all be fulfilled."* Here I would ask as a rebuff, "Did Jesus fulfill the law?" Or "Are we waiting for someone else to fulfill the law?" Of course, Jesus fulfilled the law.

Colossians 2:14 *"Blotting out the handwriting of ordinances that was against us, which was contrary to us, and took it out of the way, nailing it to his cross;"* Think of it this way: God took the fullness of the law, in the person of Jesus Christ, and nailed it to the cross. **Ephesians 2:15** *"Having abolished **in his flesh** the enmity, **even the law of commandments contained in ordinances;** for to make in himself of twain one new man, so making peace;"*

The second set of Scriptures that people use to cleave to the law is **Matthew 19:16-19**: *"And, behold, one came and said unto him, Good Master, what good thing shall I do, that I may have eternal life? ¹⁷ And he said unto him, Why callest thou me good? there is none good but one, that is, God: but if thou wilt enter into life, keep the commandments. ¹⁸ He saith unto him, Which? Jesus said, Thou shalt do no murder, Thou shalt not commit adultery, Thou shalt not steal, Thou shalt not bear false witness, ¹⁹ Honour thy father and thy mother: and, Thou shalt <u>love</u> thy neighbour as thyself."*

The thought in these verses is that Jesus validates the Ten Commandments as binding in the New Testament. But, a review of the Ten Commandments will point out that "love" is not mentioned as a commandment in the Ten Commandments. (See Exodus 20; Deuteronomy 5.) In the Ten Commandments, love is only mentioned in an explanatory role. However, the commands to love thy neighbor and to love the Lord thy God were commanded under the law. (See Leviticus 19:18; Deuteronomy 6:5.) Therefore, when Jesus told this **young** man to love his neighbor as himself, He was validating the whole law and not just part of it. As we have already pointed out, Jesus was under the whole law and never said anything to contradict the authority of the law. (See Galatians 4:4.)

Here the question arises: are the Ten Commandments binding according to the New Covenant? Of the original Ten Commandments, only nine are found in the New Covenant. The Sabbath has changed, but not in the way that you probably think!

All of the Jewish Holy Days represent some aspect of Jesus Christ. For example: The Passover and "Behold the Lamb"; the First-fruits of the Barley

Harvest and "Christ the First-fruits"; the Feast of Weeks and "the same is he which baptizeth with the Holy Ghost"; the Day of Atonement and "by whom we have now received the atonement"; the Jubilee and "Stand fast in the liberty wherewith Christ hath made us free"; and so on. Likewise, people hold to the idea that the resurrection is a day yet to come. But Jesus said, "I am the Resurrection." This is the virtue of the New Testament Sabbath also.

Matthew 11:28-30 *"Come unto me, all ye that labour and are heavy laden, and **I will give you rest**. ²⁹ Take my yoke upon you, and learn of me; for I am meek and lowly in heart: and ye shall find **rest unto your souls**. ³⁰ For my yoke is easy, and my burden is light."*

Of the Ten Commandments, the one not found in the New Testament is, *"Remember the sabbath day, to keep it holy."* (**Exodus 20:8**). In the Old Testament, the Sabbath was a day. In the New Testament, the Sabbath is a man; His name is Jesus. The "rest" in the Old Testament that was so elusive to the subjects of the Law of Moses is given inherently when we receive Jesus Christ as Lord and Savior of our lives. From Hebrews 4:9-10, we rightly assign the rest that remains (continuous) as the **rest for our soul**. The weekly Sabbath offered in the "Old Covenant" was a **rest for the flesh**, and it came and went once a week. Just like all of the other "Holy Days" found in the Law of Moses, the Sabbath Day also pointed to a finished work that could only be accomplished by our Lord Jesus Christ.

Galatians 4:24 *"...for these are the two covenants;"*

Hebrews 8:6-13 *"But now hath he obtained a more excellent ministry, by how much also he is the mediator of a better covenant, which was established upon better promises. ⁷ For if that first covenant had been faultless, then should no place have been sought for the second. ⁸ For finding fault with them, he saith, Behold, the days come, saith the Lord, when I will make a new covenant with the house of Israel and with the house of Judah: ⁹ Not according to the covenant that I made with their fathers in the day when I took them by the hand to lead them out of the land of Egypt; because they continued not in my covenant, and I regarded them not, saith the Lord. ¹⁰ For this is the covenant that I will make with the house of Israel after those days, saith the Lord; I will put my laws into their mind, and write them in their hearts: and I will be to them a God, and they shall be to me a people: ¹¹ And they shall not teach every man his neighbour, and every man his brother, saying, Know the Lord: for all shall know me, from the least to the greatest. ¹² For I will be merciful to their unrighteousness, and their sins and their iniquities will I remember no more.*

¹³ In that he saith, A new covenant, he hath made the first old. Now that which decayeth and waxeth old is ready to vanish away."

Galatians 4:21-5:4 *"Tell me, ye that desire to be under the law, do ye not hear the law? ²² For it is written, that Abraham had two sons, the one by a bondmaid, the other by a freewoman. ²³ But he who was of the bondwoman was born after the flesh; but he of the freewoman was by promise. ²⁴ Which things are an allegory: for these are the two covenants; the one from the mount Sinai, which gendereth to bondage, which is Agar. ²⁵ For this Agar is mount Sinai in Arabia, and answereth to Jerusalem which now is, and is in bondage with her children. ²⁶ But Jerusalem which is above is free, which is the mother of us all. ²⁷ For it is written, Rejoice, thou barren that bearest not; break forth and cry, thou that travailest not: for the desolate hath many more children than she which hath an husband. ²⁸ Now we, brethren, as Isaac was, are the children of promise. ²⁹ But as then he that was born after the flesh persecuted him that was born after the Spirit, even so it is now. ³⁰ Nevertheless what saith the scripture? Cast out the bondwoman and her son: for the son of the bondwoman shall not be heir with the son of the freewoman. ³¹ So then, brethren, we are not children of the bondwoman, but of the free. Stand fast therefore in the liberty wherewith Christ hath made us free, and be not entangled again with the yoke of bondage. ² Behold, I Paul say unto you, that if ye be circumcised, Christ shall profit you nothing. ³ For I testify again to every man that is circumcised, that he is a debtor to do the whole law. ⁴ Christ is become of no effect unto you, **whosoever of you are justified by the law; ye are fallen from grace."***

Just as we were instructed in Leviticus 19:19 to not mingle our seed or our covering, the New Testament also holds to this same principal. We cannot mix our covenants!

Let's summarize a bit.

Hebrews 4:12 *"For the word of God is quick, and powerful, and sharper than any twoedged sword, piercing even to the dividing asunder of soul and spirit, and of the joints and marrow, and is a discerner of the thoughts and intents of the heart."*

We have found that man is divided between the Spirit, soul, and flesh. Because the carnal mind is not subject to the law of God, God divided the laws accordingly, with each realm being governed by a different ruler: Christ, Moses, and Caesar. As the first man was earthly, "and afterward that which is spiritual" the covenant of Moses came before the covenant of Christ. The only way to "rightly divide" the Word of God is to divide it where God divides it. **Covenants offer the natural division in the Word of God!**

Galatians 3:24-25 *"Wherefore the law was our schoolmaster to bring us unto Christ, that we might be justified by faith. ²⁵ But after that faith is come, we are no longer under a schoolmaster."*

The laws were given to man by God for our good, but man, being self-centered, has used the laws for self-exaltation; remember Lucifer. Because God had every intention to bring us to Christ, the Law of Moses also contained many provisions to destroy or oppress the fleshly nature of man, without destroying man. Once man was brought or restored into the Spiritual realm through covenant with Jesus Christ, the Old Covenant through Moses was to "vanish away" or that is, to relinquish authority over us. This whole process is partly to show us the nature of man, specifically Christians, as a divided trinity. God revealed this division to us through the covenant process and through the persons of Saul, Jonathan, and David.

Joshua 24:15 *"And if it seem evil unto you to serve the LORD, choose you this day whom ye will serve;"*

Romans 8:6 *"For to be carnally minded is death; but to be spiritually minded is life and peace."*

Psalms 19:7 *"The law of the LORD is perfect, converting the soul:"*

Our mind is part of the soul and our soul will serve either the Spirit or our own flesh. **Matthew 6:24** *"No man can serve two masters: for either he will hate the one, and love the other; or else he will hold to the one, and despise the other. Ye cannot serve God and mammon."* We must choose between the two. We can serve the flesh or we can serve the Spirit. Our flesh has the nature of the Devil. The Spirit is the Nature and Power of God. Just as God never intended for man to live alone within his own soul, He never intended for man to live self-sufficiently within the Law of Moses.

Deuteronomy 9:8-11 *"Also **in Horeb** ye provoked the LORD to wrath, so that the LORD was angry with you to have destroyed you. ⁹ When I was gone up into the mount to receive the tables of stone, even the tables of the covenant which the LORD made with you, then I abode in the mount forty days and forty nights, I neither did eat bread nor drink water: ¹⁰ And the LORD delivered unto me two tables of stone written with the finger of God; and on them was written according to all the words, which the LORD spake with you in the mount out of the midst of the fire in the day of the assembly. ¹¹ And it came* *to pass at the end of forty days and forty nights, that the LORD gave me the two tables of stone, even the tables of the covenant."*

The name "Mount Horeb" is used interchangeably in the Scriptures with "Mount Sinai." Horeb is the name of the mountain that God "cut" the two tablets of stone out of, and on these He wrote the Ten Commandments. The importance of the name "Horeb" is found in its symbolism as it means "to make barren" or "desolate." Specifically, it means to kill by depriving of water. This is the mount from which the Ten Commandments were cut. The Apostle Paul contrasts the covenant of Moses against the covenant with Jesus Christ using this very concept in 2 Corinthians 3.

2 Corinthians 3:6-14 *"Who also hath made us able ministers of the new testament; not of the letter, but of the spirit: for the **letter killeth, but the spirit giveth life.** ⁷ But if the ministration of death, written and engraven in stones, was glorious, so that the children of Israel could not stedfastly behold the face of Moses for the glory of his countenance; which glory was to be **done away**: ⁸ How shall not the ministration of the spirit be rather glorious? ⁹ For if the ministration of condemnation be glory, much more doth the ministration of righteousness exceed in glory. ¹⁰ For even that which was made glorious had no glory in this respect, by reason of the glory that excelleth. ¹¹ For if that which is **done away** was glorious, much more that which remaineth is glorious. ¹² Seeing then that we have such hope, we use great plainness of speech: ¹³ And not as Moses, which put a vail over his face, that the children of Israel could not stedfastly look to the end of that which is **abolished**: ¹⁴ But their minds were blinded: for until this day remaineth the same vail untaken away in the reading of the old testament; which vail is **done away** in Christ."*

What a vivid contrast to the ministry of Jesus Christ.

John 4:14 *"But whosoever drinketh of the water that I shall give him shall never thirst; but the water that I shall give him shall be in him a well of water springing up into everlasting life."*

Revelation 22:1 *"And he shewed me a pure river of water of life, clear as crystal, proceeding out of the throne of God and of the Lamb."* And it is a vivid contrast indeed. Surely no man would choose that slow, agonizing death offered at Mt. Sinai/Horeb over the pure living water of life of Mt. Calvary!

Lest we paint a dark picture of the Law of Moses, it becomes imperative to remember, *"...the law is good, if a man use it lawfully;"* (**1 Timothy 1:8**). All laws in Scripture are either **"work"** based or **"faith"** based. The Law of Moses is the pinnacle of the operating system derived from the knowledge of good and evil, and is based in works. Our greatest and perhaps only example of the law being used lawfully comes from the life and ministry of Jesus Christ Himself.

Jesus never broke a law of God or man. He never spoke against any authority that God had placed over man. This included the authority of His own parents, the Law of Moses, or the rule of Caesar. Had Jesus broken any law, He would have been lawless and disobedient. Had He spoken against the rule of authority, He would have been in rebellion.

All accusations against Jesus pertaining to Him not keeping the Sabbath were based on man's erroneous interpretations of God's law. By the ruling authority's own standard, if a man's sheep fell into a pit on the Sabbath day, it was lawful to lift it out. I submit to you that all things that Jesus did, He did to save us from the pit, Sabbath day or not! Therefore, Jesus only spoke against the Pharisee's perverted use of God's laws.

Moreover, Jesus didn't walk straddling the Law of Moses and the rule of Caesar. But rather, He walked confidently, fully under both. He was able to do this for two reasons that are actually one and the same. First is **1 Timothy 1:9**: *"...the law is not made for a righteous man,"* And second, He had not come to submit to the desires of His own flesh. He had come to please His Heavenly Father. (See also Hebrews 4:15.) **John 8:29** *"...for I do always those things that please him."*

The Transition

In Luke 9:51-56 there is record of an event in the ministry of Jesus where the disciples were offended. The offense is not our focus, but the Lord's response is.

Luke 9:54-55 *"And when his disciples James and John saw this, they said, Lord, wilt thou that we command fire to come down from heaven, and consume them, even as Elias did?* [55] **But he turned, and rebuked them, and said, Ye know not what manner of spirit ye are of."**

The name "Elias" is a New Testament rendering of the name "Elijah." There are types and shadows throughout the Word of God, and here there is an unmistakable correlation between the ministries of Elijah and Elisha with that of John the Baptist and Jesus.

Matthew 11:13 *"For all the prophets and the law prophesied until John."*

In fact, the first direct mention of Elijah in the New Testament comes from Jesus speaking to the multitudes concerning John the Baptist. Jesus said in

Matthew 11:14: *"And if ye will receive it, __this is Elias__, which was for to come."* (Elijah).

Look now at the last three verses from the Old Testament.

Malachi 4:4-6 *"Remember ye the law of Moses my servant, which I commanded unto him in Horeb for all Israel, with the statutes and judgments. ⁵ Behold, I will send you Elijah the prophet before the coming of the great and dreadful day of the LORD: ⁶ And he shall turn the heart of the fathers to the children, and the heart of the children to their fathers, lest I come and smite the earth with a curse."*

As it pertains to this study, Jesus asked in **Matthew 11:8-10** *"But what went ye out for to see? **A man clothed in soft raiment? behold, they that wear soft clothing are in kings' houses.** ⁹ But what went ye out for to see? A prophet? yea, I say unto you, and more than a prophet. ¹⁰ **For this is he, of whom it is written, Behold, I send my messenger before thy face, which shall prepare thy way before thee."***

A man clothed with soft raiment? Both Elijah and John the Baptist wore a "rough garment" woven of wool. Remember in Leviticus 19:19 how we are commanded not to wear a garment mingled of woolen and linen. When we take the Scriptures that pertain to garments or coverings as a whole, we understand they represent and contrast the coverings offered by the Law of Moses (Works) and the Law of Christ (Faith). (See also Deuteronomy 22:9-11.)

A good example of their symbolism is found in **Ezekiel 44:17-18**: *"And it shall come to pass, that when they enter in at the gates of the inner court, they shall be clothed with linen garments; and no wool shall come upon them, whiles they minister in the gates of the inner court, and within. ¹⁸ They shall have linen bonnets upon their heads, and shall have linen breeches upon their loins; **they shall not gird themselves with any thing that causeth sweat."*** Please notice that as the minister of the tabernacle is drawn inward, he is commanded to be clothed with linen garments and not wool. The New Covenant agrees, as it also says that fine linen, clean and white, is the righteousness of saints; and that righteousness is by faith.

Philippians 3:9 *"And be found in him, not having mine own righteousness, which is of the law, but that which is through the faith of Christ, the righteousness which is of God by faith:"* (See also Romans 4:13, 9:30-33; Galatians 2:21.)

It is amazing to me that as prolific as sweat is in life, sweat is only mentioned three times in all of Scripture. I think back to my teenage years and remember when the summers were spent hauling peanut hay in the dusty fields of south Alabama; the sweat seemingly just boiled up out of my skin. I remember the dryness of the dirt as the peanuts were uprooted for harvest, and then the plants were left to dry in the sun until they were ready to be baled. I remember the dust and sweat and dust and sweat with each bale that left me covered in a salty, crusty mud at the end of the day.

In south Georgia, when I enlisted in the Army, I remember the heat and humidity of the summer while we trained in this pit and in that pit. Our bodies would sweat, but the humidity was so high it didn't evaporate. It only took a few minutes in the August heat for our skin to become waterlogged and wrinkled. Later, while still in service, I remember my unit leaving Alaska while it was spitting snow and sleet in the spring time, only to arrive in Thailand to an oppressive 110 degrees F in the shade. Sleeping in our cots at night was like sleeping in a sauna.

We come to think of sweat as so normal that we really don't give it much thought. It's just how it is. I have spent the last twenty years or so as a welder. It was not too bad in the winter, but in the summer I comforted myself pitying the roofers and the guys spreading asphalt, injection molders, press operators, masons, etc.

The first mention of sweat in the Scriptures is when God proclaimed the curses that Adam had invoked upon himself when he sinned in the Garden of Eden. Again, the punishment reflects or mirrors the crime. The last mention of sweat was when Jesus, the second Adam, travailed in prayer in the Garden of Gethsemane.

Luke 22:44 *"...and his sweat was as it were great drops of blood falling down to the ground."* (Perhaps this was the same place.)

And now, in these verses in Ezekiel 44, right in the middle, a priest after the order of Aaron, who could come in and out of the tabernacle, that three part dwelling place of God, was commanded not to gird himself with anything that causes sweat as he came into the presence of God.

No wonder Jesus travailed in prayer! He knew this would be His last opportunity to come into the presence of His Heavenly Father before His death; before He became sin! Jesus knew that it was impossible to come into the presence of our Heavenly Father through the sweat of His brow! He knew that blood was required to come into God's Presence! *"And being in agony he prayed more earnestly:.."* *"And being in agony he prayed more earnestly:.."* *"And being in agony he prayed more earnestly: and his sweat was as it were great drops of blood falling down to the ground."*

Sweat and wool are synonymous with the Law of works. Rest and fine linen are synonymous with the Law of Faith. The transition of authority from Moses to Joshua, and from Elijah to Elisha is synonymous with the transition from John the Baptist to Jesus; they signify the transition from the Law of Moses to the Law of Christ.

Noticeably, in all three examples there is no overlap or mingling of leadership; the former was removed as the latter was established! (See Deuteronomy 34:8-9; 2 Kings 2:11-14; Matthew 14:10; John 3:30.) Take the time to check these references. The Melchisedec was also removed in this same fashion when God established the Law of Moses. (More on this to come.)

What is Faith?

John 3:16 *"For God so loved the world, that he gave his only begotten Son, that whosoever believeth in him should not perish, but have everlasting life."*

Perhaps John 3:16 is the most quoted Scripture in the Bible today, and with good reason. But how many people comprehend what it means to "believe in Him?" To believe in Him means that we trust in His goodness and not our own! It means that our hope for salvation rests in the person of Jesus Christ and His finished work at Calvary, rather than in our own ability to please God. It means so much more than believing that He existed, or even that He died for us. A lot of people will believe that Jesus died for us, but still trust in their own goodness in an effort to merit eternal life. They believe that Jesus died <u>for</u> us, but they don't understand that He died <u>as</u> us. Do you remember the Satanic half-truth in the "Example of Marriage"?

For many people, the concept of faith is almost like some far away indefinable abstract. At best it becomes a collective "belief." What they end up with is faith in "the faith", rather than faith in God. Having faith in God through the Blood of Jesus is a relationship of trust in God's ability and desire to save us. It brings us into His rest so that we can cease from our own works.

You may ask, "What of the Scriptures that say, *'...faith without works is dead'* and *'...show me thy faith without thy works , and I will show thee my faith by my works.'* (**James 2:20,18**); do the Scriptures contradict?" Absolutely not!

The question is why do we do what we do? Do we walk in holiness so that we can be holy? Or, do we walk in holiness because we are holy? The answer is, if we have been washed in the Blood of Jesus Christ then we are holy, and our walk comes from this. (See Revelation 1:5,7:14; Hebrews 9:14-15.) There is a debate today in circles of theology stemming from the Apostle Paul's writings as compared to James' writing. The debate is centered around the relationship between works and grace within the life of the believer. But, the debate itself is completely divergent from the consistent message of the Bible, as Paul writes about works from the pre-salvation context and James writes about works from the post-salvation context. Both writers agree with the consistent teaching of Scripture that God created us "unto good works."

Our actions (works) can exercise our faith or they can destroy our faith. Faith only comes through receiving the Word of God, but faith is exercised by us through our works. This is partially why we must be careful to maintain good works. If our works are not according to faith, what happens? Don't we fall into ideas like, "I wonder if God still loves me?"

In my own experience as a heathen, I was bound by many evils: particularly, covetousness. I was out for number one. Everything I could gain and possess gave me control and identity, or at least, so I thought. I had an insatiable appetite to please me; and the harder I tried, the harder it got. I was looking for more and more, and in more places. But nothing seemed to satisfy me. I slid down into the decadence of sin, deeper and deeper, until God brought me to ask, "Is this all there is? Is this all life is about? Why am I so empty?" After all, I had been taught in school, "There is no God. Man evolved."

I remember the night I walked into my room and picked up a Bible that had been given to me by a company that I worked for; in despair, I said, "God, if you've got something in here for me, I want it." I had previously tried to read the Bible on several occasions, but I would always become lost after one or two verses. I would just put it back down and think, "That sounded good. I wonder what it meant."

But this time, God began to open my eyes to particular Scriptures, and then He led me to others of similar nature. Like many people, I began reading in the book of Revelation. Because my Bible was marked with references, I would bracket back and forth between the Old Testament and the book of Revelation each time a Scripture would interest me.

I didn't know it at the time, but the call to "Repent" is found more times in the book of Revelation than in any other New Testament book. Finally, after being hammered over the course of several days by, "**Repent!**" and judgment to come, I landed in the book of Matthew. I found myself at the Sermon on the Mount and heard the Lord say, "Love your enemies."

Wait a minute! My father was a military man. I grew up reading magazines that glorified war and death. In my home, we practiced with knives and guns and martial arts and tactics. For us it was "eye for an eye" and peace through superior firepower.

But now, there was something on the inside screaming, "**This is it!** This is what you've been looking for!" I reasoned that man doesn't say these things. Love your enemies? This has to be God. Immediately I was convicted of a lifetime of sin and debauchery, guilt and heartache, knowing that I was at fault. I was at fault not only for my own wretchedness, but also for offending a loving, merciful, pure, patient, all seeing, and Holy God.

I fell on my face right there on my living room floor at about two in the morning. I wept and heaved to the point I nearly vomited, knowing my own filth. I asked God to forgive me and almost immediately, event after event began to roll through my mind. One by one I would say, "I'm sorry" and again ask for forgiveness. But the Holy Spirit led me to realize my error through a question:

"How old are you?" He said to me.

"Twenty-eight," I responded.

"Well if you are going to do it this way, you'll be here for another twenty-eight years." I knew then and said, "Lord, I'm sorry for trying to live my life without you." I tell you I got up from that floor "a new creature." There was no one there to lead me in this way or that way, just the Word and the Spirit to lead me in God's way.

I knew I was different! I had hope and joy and a new reason to live and to love. God had changed me by His power and by His presence, and for His own good pleasure. I couldn't help it; the first thing I wanted to do was to take my stuff and sell it. God had freed me from the idolatry of covetousness. And I did just that; I sold and I gave. I hadn't even read about the rich young ruler yet. I was giving because I was going...going to Heaven that is. Nobody had to tell me to do this or that. When God comes in, the reaching out in good works is built in.

So, how we walk comes from who we are, and not the other way around. If who we are comes from how we walk, then our identity is self-centered and wavering and not Christ -centered and eternal. We don't put the cart in front of the horse.

I want to encourage you to examine yourself. Or even better, call on God to examine you. He knows us better than we know ourselves. Ask Him to lead you to, and grant to you repentance. The act of asking for forgiveness can become an empty ritual, just like coming to Church, paying tithes, feeding the hungry, or anything else done of our own self-will can become an empty ritual. If, however, you feel God drawing you, then just ask and receive and believe; nurture that seed of faith that God has placed within you through prayer and confession to God. (See John 6:44.) (We confess our **sins to God**. We confess our **faults to Brothers and Sisters in Christ** that they may pray for us. Each part of the body of Christ supplies what another part lacks. See James 5:16.)

Jesus said in **John 6:29**: *"This is the work of God, that ye believe on him whom he hath sent."* Trusting in Jesus will bring you peace and rest and deliverance from the bondage of religion. He will enable you to do the things that He desires of you, "in Spirit and in Truth."

The night I was saved, I didn't realize that I had entered into covenant with God. Had someone tried to explain this process to me, as a sinner most grievous, I would surely have focused on my end of the deal. Probably, I would have declined. Thank God He made salvation so easy. Jesus did all the work. From a covenant perspective, we literally traded places.

Galatians 2:20 *"I am crucified with Christ: nevertheless I live; yet not I, but Christ liveth in me: and the life which I now live in the flesh I live by the faith of the Son of God, who loved me, and gave himself for me."*

In hindsight, I realize now that as I was going down, I was taking off that robe of pride, that fig leaf of religion. As Jesus passed by, He saw me there naked and "polluted in my own blood." It was then that He covered me with His own robe and entered into covenant with me. (See Ezekiel 16:8.)

But it didn't stop there. The Word of God demands justice as well as mercy. Over and over throughout the Word of God, we are given examples of sin bringing forth death.

Romans 6:23 *"For the wages of sin is death;.."* (See also Hebrews 2:2-3.)

That's when Jesus took my robe upon Himself! You can believe what you will. But, I believe Jesus wasn't even granted a loincloth, as He hung there dying on the cross. Luke 20:11 declares they treated Him shamefully! Shame implies nakedness! Both Isaiah 53 and 1 Peter 2 tell us that He bore our sins on the cross. Jesus didn't just become a sin offering; He literally became sin. Yes, it's a hard thought.

Let me challenge your thinking here. Neither the cross nor physical death was the punishment for sin(s); not for Jesus, or for you and me. If the cross was the punishment for sin, then you and I could face our punishment, die, and then walk justified into Heaven.

Galatians 3:13 *"Christ hath redeemed us from the curse of the law, being made a curse for us: for it is written, Cursed is every one that hangeth on a tree:"*

The cross wasn't a punishment. The cross was a place of meeting! The cross was the only place ordained by God where sin and evil spirits and death could touch God! That is literally what happened at the cross. As Jesus hung there dying, sin crawled up on Him and death stalked closer and closer until sin had finished.

The Psalmist David recorded various aspects of this event prophetically in Psalm 22. We know this Psalm today as the Crucifixion Psalm, but it is actually an image of a sacrificial "Morning Deer." I had an occasion to hear a wounded deer bleat once. I was a young man and very inexperienced. We were hunting near home on this occasion. Routinely, as each day ended we would all wait around an old fence post until all the hunters made it out.

On this particular day, I came out just before dark. It was the time of twilight when everything is grey. Right at sunset but before dark a shot rang out. *Boooomm!* It echoed down the gentle slope and across the creek. The air was still and crisp, as frost blanketed the landscape. The hunter couldn't have been more than a hundred yards from the path. And although I couldn't see him, I could hear the hunter's footsteps across that wooded, now still and silent countryside: *kcht... kcht ...kcht,* slowly, as he approached the deer.

But, in the twilight, the first shot had missed its mark slightly. The hunter approached closer and closer to the wounded deer. Suddenly I could hear the deer begin to thrash about, as it tried frantically to get back up and away! Finally, in despair, as death loomed as a hungry beast in the presence of the hunter, the deer began to bleat and cry out in fear!

Immediately, I was paralyzed with the same fear that had gripped that animal! It sounded just like a man screaming in fear! I had never heard this before. I thought, "My God! He's shot somebody!" My fear turned to terror and confusion as the final shot rang out.

I can't help but remember this event when I read the Word of God. I remember, as Jesus, the Lamb of God, nailed there to the cross, not just for me but as me, looking face to face with death; how He also was given to fear. He too began to bleat and cry out in fear for a savior! Oh yes, He cried in fear for a savior. Look at **Matthew 27:46-47,49**: "*And about the ninth hour Jesus cried with a loud voice, saying, Eli, Eli, lama sabachthani? that is to say, **My God, my God,** why hast thou forsaken me?* [47] *Some of them that stood there, when they heard that, said, **This man calleth for Elias.** 49 The rest said, Let be, **let us see whether Elias will come to save him.**"*

Eloi! (Father help me!) Eloi! (Father send the angels!) Then, after there was no response from Heaven, Jesus asked the question, "Why have you forsaken me?"

Romans 8:32 "*He that spared not his own Son, but delivered him up for us all, how shall he not with him also freely give us all things?*"

Do you know why God had forsaken Him?

John 9:31 *"...God heareth not sinners:"*

I usually hear silence as a response when I teach this. How can I say that about Jesus, you might ask?

2 Corinthians 5:21 *"For he hath made him to be sin for us, who knew no sin; that we might be made the righteousness of God in him."*

You see now that when we entered into covenant with Jesus, He took our place and punishment; He gave us His place and life. He took our covering of nakedness (shame) and sin and pride. He then gave us His covering of righteousness, authority, and Son-ship. It was a family robe!

When Jesus said in the Garden of Gethsemane that He could call more than twelve legions of angels, He was speaking in present tense. (See Matthew 26:53.) Twice in the same verse He declares the tense of the verse. Moreover, in the garden, sin had not yet crawled up onto His body! Jesus did call for the angels to save Him. But the only response from Heaven was laughter. Proverbs 1:26-28 was fulfilled upon Jesus Christ at the Cross of Calvary. **Isaiah 53:10** says: *"...it pleased God to bruise him."* This is because, as Jesus wore our robe of self-righteousness and sin, God didn't see Jesus on the cross. God saw you and me on the cross!

The cross was a terrible place, and a suitable punishment by our standards. But remember, we are fallen. Humanity, as a whole, embraces sin. We cannot go by our standards. The punishment for sin is the second death and not the first.

Revelation 20:14-15 *"And death and hell were cast into the lake of fire. **This is the second death. ¹⁵ And whosoever was not found written in the book of life was cast into the lake of fire.**"*

The first death, our physical death, is a servant, if you will. Though unwilling, the first death bears witness to the second death. How many people, when confronted with the reality of death in another, or perhaps even their own death, have said in their own mind, "I wonder where he went?" Or "I wonder what is on the other side?"

God was so merciful to put man out of the Garden of Eden before He could eat of the Tree of Life. Just think, if man had eaten of the Tree of Life and become immortal while sinful, then Jesus would not have been able to die for us! The second death is the Lake of Fire that burns with brimstone.

Revelation 21:8 *"But the fearful, and unbelieving, and the abominable, and murderers, and whoremongers, and sorcerers, and idolaters, and all liars, shall* have their part in the lake which burneth with fire and brimstone: **which is the second death.** " (See also Micah 7:19.)

This is the final destination for all who die in sin, for all sins, and for the Devil and his angels. (See Matthew 25:41.) **This is the punishment for sin.** This is what Jesus faced as He carried our sin into the heart of the earth. He faced the wrath of God for all humanity; that is for all that enter into covenant with Him. (See Romans 10:13.)

Touch Me Not

I know there are some people who don't believe Jesus burned in hell. Both Abraham and Moses attest that the Lamb would be burnt.

Genesis 22:8 *"And Abraham said, My son, God will provide **himself a lamb** for a **burnt offering**: so they went both of them together."*

Exodus 12:8-9 *And they shall eat the flesh in that night, **roast with fire**, and unleavened bread; and with bitter herbs they shall eat it. [9] Eat not of it raw, nor sodden at all with water, but **roast with fire**; his head with his legs, and with the purtenance thereof.*

Abraham and Moses were not run-of-the-mill, ordinary, minor, etc., but these men by their relationship with God governed entire dispensations. Not to mention, the whole sacrificial system in the Law of Moses was based on burning the sacrifices on the altar. It's OK to not be sure about Jesus burning in hell, but before you argue against the idea, consider the Scriptures that say He did; your argument will be against them.

It was absolutely necessary that Jesus go into hell. As we transferred our sin into Jesus' body through confession to God and repentance, Jesus transferred our sin into the Lake of Fire through touch. It was customary in the Law of Moses for a person to lay their hand on the animal's head while they confessed their sins so as to transfer their sin into the animal. That animal became a substitute for the sinner as a burnt offering on the altar.

I know that Jesus went into that tomb with my sins in His body. But when He came out of the tomb He was clean. (See 1 Peter 2:24; Isaiah 53:12.)

John 20:17 *"Jesus saith unto her, Touch me not; for I am not yet ascended to my Father:"*

These are the words Jesus spoke to Mary Magdalene as she stood outside the sepulcher. It was early on the morning of the Resurrection of Jesus. It is a significant statement, because according to the laws of clean and unclean, if anything unclean had touched Jesus, He would have become unclean.

This was especially true for a Priest. A Priest attempting to come into the Most Holy Place to minister while unclean would have died. The Most Holy Place was God's Throne Room within the tabernacle or temple. **Exodus 28:35, Exodus 28:43, Exodus 30:20, Exodus 30;21, and Leviticus 8:35 all warn the Priest that death awaits any that come into God's presence while unclean.** But we don't forget; the Scriptures bear witness of Him, Jesus Christ.

Hebrews 9:11-12 *"**But Christ being come an high priest of good things to come**, by a greater and more perfect tabernacle, not made with hands, that is to say, not of this building; [12] Neither by the blood of goats and calves, **but by his own blood he entered in once into the holy place**, having obtained eternal redemption for us".*

While the work of covenant was finished at the Cross, the heavenly temple was still unclean from Lucifer's hateful work of rebellion. This is the Holy Place mentioned in Hebrews 9:11-12. Since the Bible is consistent about the fact that our sins went into Jesus' Body on the cross, how then could Jesus approach God the Father without Himself first being cleansed? There are three agents used by God in Scripture to cleanse something of uncleanness; they are water, blood, and fire. When Jesus said in **Mark 14:22**: *"Take, eat: this is my body."* that bread that He gave to the disciples had just come from the oven. If Mary had touched Jesus after His Resurrection and said something like, "Forgive me" Jesus would not have been able to enter the Heavenly Temple.

Hebrews 9:23-28 *"It was therefore necessary that the patterns of things in the heavens should be purified with these; but the heavenly things themselves with better sacrifices than these. [24] **For Christ is not entered into the holy places made with hands, which are the figures of the true; but into heaven itself, now to appear in the presence of God for us**: [25] Nor yet that he should offer himself often, as the high priest entereth into the holy place every year with blood of others; [26] For then must he often have suffered since the foundation of the world: but now once in the end of the world hath he appeared to put away sin by the sacrifice of himself. [27] And as it is appointed unto men once to die, but after this the judgment: [28] So Christ was once offered to **bear the sins of many**; and unto them that look for him shall he appear the second time without sin unto salvation."*

Jesus' Blood covered not only the earthly, but the heavenly also. How great a work was achieved at Calvary we may not fully know until we get to heaven. One thing is certain: the New Covenant instituted at the Cross of Christ satisfied the certain judgment that we were to face, and at the same time granted us mercy that we could be spared from the same.

God is so wonderful! What more could we say about Him that has not already been proclaimed? He alone is worthy of our trust! This is faith!

Proverbs 1:20-33 *"Wisdom crieth without; she uttereth her voice in the streets: [21] She crieth in the chief place of concourse, in the openings of the gates: in the city she uttereth her words, saying, [22] How long, ye simple ones, will ye love simplicity? and the scorners delight in their scorning, and fools hate knowledge? [23] Turn you at my reproof: behold, I will pour out my spirit unto you, I will make known my words unto you. [24] Because I have called, and ye refused; I have stretched out my hand, and no man regarded; [25] But ye have set at nought all my counsel, and would none of my reproof: [26] I also will laugh at your calamity; I will mock when your fear cometh; [27] When your fear cometh as desolation, and your destruction cometh as a whirlwind; when distress and anguish cometh upon you. [28] Then shall they call upon me, **but I will not answer**; they shall seek me early, **but they shall not find me**: [29] For that they hated knowledge, and did not choose the fear of the LORD: [30] They would none of my counsel: they despised all my reproof. [31] Therefore shall they eat of the fruit of their own way, and be filled with their own devices. [32] For the turning away of the simple shall slay them, and the prosperity of fools shall destroy them. [33] **But whoso hearkeneth unto me shall dwell safely, and shall be quiet from fear of evil."***

Today is the day of Salvation. Today is a good day to be saved. Perhaps you think, "I don't feel love for God." That's OK; neither did I. But God loved me... and God loves you. At this point, the beginning of your relationship with God is an invitation by you for God to be God in your life. It may start with "repent" or it may start with a cry for God's help or it may start as a simple prayer of, "God, I want to know you." But however faith begins to grow in your life, it is a work initiated by God that needs to be nurtured by you. Acknowledging God's love for you will always empower you to respond correctly to His prompts.

A Layman's Study...

6

Till Death Do Us Part
Covenant Breakers

The Perfecting of Evil

Every Scripture in the Word of God that links sin and death bears witness to this covenant principal; that is, every covenant established by blood (sacrifice) can only be nullified by blood. Every covenant established on death can only be nullified in death. Covenants established by the shedding of blood require the shedding of blood when the covenant is broken!

Hebrews 8:13 *"In that he saith, A new covenant, he hath made the first old. Now that which decayeth and waxeth old is ready to vanish away."*

As the Law of Moses was established by the shedding of blood, it too would only be nullified by the shedding of blood. At the Cross of Christ, we find that transition taking place lawfully: out with the old, in with the new. At the Cross, this principal is not only reaffirmed, but is validated to the extent that the Son of God Himself died to uphold this concept. **Ephesians 2:15** *"Having abolished in his flesh the enmity, even the law of commandments contained in ordinances; for to make in himself of twain one new man, so making peace;"*

In one fell swoop, Jesus' shed Blood at Calvary abolished the Law of Works (the Old Covenant) in righteousness and established the Law of Christ (the New Covenant) in that same righteousness! The authority that the first man, Adam, gave to Satan to rule in the physical realm has been reclaimed by the man, Jesus Christ, the second Adam. (See 1 Corinthians 15:45.) The operating system of the knowledge of good and evil, codified into the Law of Moses, has now been rendered ineffective in the life of the Spiritual participant.

Of equal importance and related to this principal is the command not to mingle our seed. The death of Jesus ensured that only one covenant was in place at a time. That is, there was no overlap of law and grace. Had there been an overlap a man might be justified for lingering in the valley of decision. We will address this principal one last time shortly, as it relates to the spirit of antichrist.

I could stop right here and justice would have been served in addressing this principal of sin bringing forth death. Just as the other principles of God are affirmed from the one covenant to the next, and from one dispensation to the next, so the relationship between sin and death are inexorably linked in the New Covenant also.

Hebrews 10:26-29 *"For if we sin wilfully after that we have received the knowledge of the truth, there remaineth no more sacrifice for sins, [27] But a certain fearful looking for of judgment and fiery indignation, which shall devour the adversaries. [28] He that despised Moses' law died without mercy under two or three witnesses: [29] Of how much sorer punishment, suppose ye, shall he be thought worthy, who hath trodden under foot the Son of God, and hath counted the blood of the covenant, wherewith he was sanctified, an unholy thing, and hath done despite unto the Spirit of grace?"*

Because we are addressing covenant breakers in this section, it is needful for many people that I discuss the error of the doctrine of unconditional eternal salvation. This is commonly referred to as, "once saved, always saved."

The leadership within the Church that propagates this ideology does so from the doctrinal position that because God knows the future in certainty, we couldn't possibly have a real choice. While we have been affirming in this book the right relationship between man's choice and God's responses, the carnally-minded tend to serve error. After all, the carnal mind draws us into and serves the flesh. To correct this, I would ask, does man define God? Or does God define Himself? This is a prime example of how the knowledge of good and evil distorts our view of God. Can the blind lead the blind; shall they not both fall into the ditch?

The question to ask that brings our eyes back to God is this: Can God know the certain future outcome or decision of any given situation or person and still give us a bonafide choice concerning it in the present? In other words, can God know the future and still give us a choice? And the answer is as absolute as God Himself. Yes!

"But how?" you ask.

Matthew 19:26 *"With men this is impossible; but with God all things are possible."*

God operates above and outside the realm of time and space. The creature was made subject to vanity, not the Creator. Besides, time and space are created components of the physical realm. Our current definition of time is always offered in relation to distance and motion. Because God is omnipresent, He doesn't need time to get from point A to point B. Even though God is a Spirit, He retains sovereignty over every realm that He has created.

This idea of the removal of our right to choice through God being subject to time has also led to the error of "predestination." This doctrinal position assumes that God has chosen some to be saved and some to be cast off, or damned. If this idea were true then we could argue that we were saved because we weren't like them. And our eyes would again be on ourselves. But this isn't true. We are all born in need of a savior. And God has said that as all are born in sin, whosoever will may come to be cleansed by the Blood of Jesus.

If you are having a hard time grasping this concept of our legitimate choice in the context of God fore-knowing the outcome, let me ask you another question. Do you believe that God is a Trinity? The carnal mind would say, "How can one be three and not be divided; especially in a living thing?" 1 John 5:7-8 tells us there is no division in God. But this isn't the point.

This is the point. One idea is readily accepted because it's not too confrontational. The other slaps you in the face and makes you accountable! **Jude 5-6** *"I will therefore put you in remembrance, though ye once knew this, how that the Lord, having saved the people out of the land of Egypt, afterward destroyed them that believed not. ⁶ And the angels which kept not their first estate, but left their own habitation, he hath reserved in everlasting chains under darkness unto the judgment of the great day."*

This idea that we no longer have choice is refuted in over one thousand, five hundred Scriptures containing the word "if." **Romans 6:5** *"For if we have been planted together in the likeness of his death, we shall be also in the likeness of his resurrection:"* **Romans 6:8** *"Now if we be dead with Christ, we believe that we shall also live with him:"* Therefore, if you practice "once saved, always saved" to justify sin or a sinful lifestyle, then you deny the power of the Resurrection and you surely will not partake of it!

Deuteronomy 29:19-20 *"And it come to pass, when he heareth the words of this curse, that he bless himself in his heart, saying, I shall have peace, though I walk in the imagination of mine heart, to add drunkenness to thirst: ²⁰ The LORD will not spare him, but then the anger of the LORD and his jealousy shall smoke against that man, and all the curses that are written in this book shall lie upon him, and the LORD shall blot out his name from under heaven."*

Isaiah 5:13-14 *"Therefore **my people** are gone into captivity, because they have no knowledge: and their honourable men are famished, and their multitude dried up with thirst. ¹⁴ Therefore **hell hath enlarged herself**, and opened her mouth without measure: and their glory, and their multitude, and their pomp, and he that rejoiceth, **shall descend into it**."* (See also Hosea 4:6.)

There is hope! God is near to the brokenhearted. If you are not satisfied with your lifestyle, or if you don't know why there is no peace or rest in your heart, perhaps God is calling you to draw near to Him. **1 John 1:9** *"If we confess our sins, he is faithful and just to forgive us our sins, and to cleanse us from all unrighteousness."* Confess your sins to God in prayer. Acknowledge your total dependence on Him. Trust in the sacrifice of Jesus Christ, and God is happy to remove your sin as far away from you and Him as, "the east is from the west."

On the other hand, if you refuse sound doctrine and repentance and humility, then you reject the message of Jesus Christ. Know surely that you will move farther and farther from God, not just in this life but in eternity as well. **Proverbs 1:23-33** *"Turn you at my reproof: behold, I will pour out my spirit unto you, I will make known my words unto you.* [24] *Because I have called, and ye refused; I have stretched out my hand, and no man regarded;* [25] *But ye have set at nought all my counsel, and would none of my reproof:* [26] *I also will laugh at your calamity; I will mock when your fear cometh;* [27] *When your fear cometh as desolation, and your destruction cometh as a whirlwind; when distress and anguish cometh upon you.* [28] *Then shall they call upon me, but I will not answer; they shall seek me early, but they shall not find me:* [29] *For that they hated knowledge, and did not choose the fear of the LORD:* [30] *They would none of my counsel: they despised all my reproof.* [31] *Therefore shall they eat of the fruit of their own way, and be filled with their own devices.* [32] *For the turning away of the simple shall slay them, and the prosperity of fools shall destroy them.* [33] *But whoso hearkeneth unto me shall dwell safely, and shall be quiet from fear of evil."*

Again, the purpose of this work is to show the relationship of faith, religion, and the Antichrist. The Scripture verses that I provide hereafter are not intended to fuel any debate over the invalidity of unconditional eternal salvation, but are to address the nature and character of the Antichrist.

John 5:14 *"...Behold, thou art made whole: sin no more, lest a worse thing come unto thee."*

2 Peter 2:20-22 *"For if after they have escaped the pollutions of the world through the knowledge of the Lord and Saviour Jesus Christ, they are again entangled therein, and overcome,* **the latter end is worse with them than the beginning.** [21] **For it had been better for them not to have known the way of righteousness, than, after they have known it, to turn from the holy commandment delivered unto them.** [22] *But it is happened unto them according to the true proverb, The dog is turned to his own vomit again; and the sow that was washed to her wallowing in the mire."*

There is an overwhelming consistency within the New Testament proclaiming the danger of drawing near to God, and then turning away from Him. Surely, there was no angel in heaven closer to God than was Lucifer. By his very relationship with God, he was the mediator of God's Glory. Remember how God covered Lucifer with jewels as the mechanism to convey God's presence. (See Ezekiel 28.)

2 Corinthians 11:13-15 *"For such are false apostles, deceitful workers, transforming themselves into the apostles of Christ. [14] And no marvel; for Satan himself is transformed into an angel of light. [15] Therefore it is no great thing if his ministers also be transformed as the ministers of righteousness; whose end shall be according to their works."*

At this point, I want to plant a thought through a question. The gifts are without repentance, but Satan is certainly no longer in God's Presence; where then does he get the light? Light is not self-perpetuating. There must be a source. See from the text how that light and righteousness are synonymous.

The idea of a person coming to faith and then falling into rebellion has been established throughout the Scriptures with examples of both individuals and nations. Nehemiah chapter 9 records at least four times this very thing happening to the Nation of Israel. Verse 29 of the same chapter says that God was trying to bring them again unto His law, yet they dealt proudly. And what happened? Each time, God turned them into the hands of their enemies to be destroyed. (See also Deuteronomy 28:48-50.) This pattern was repeated at the destruction of Jerusalem in AD 70. It has occurred numerous times in various countries throughout history and it will be repeated once more on a much larger scale soon enough.

Matthew 12:43-45 *"When the unclean spirit is gone out of a man, he walketh through dry places, seeking rest, and findeth none. [44] Then he saith, I will return into my house from whence I came out; and when he is come, he findeth it empty, swept, and garnished. [45] Then goeth he, and taketh with himself seven other spirits more wicked than himself, and they enter in and dwell there: and the last state of that man is worse than the first. Even so shall it be also unto this wicked generation."*

Again, the Scripture warns not only of the possibility of turning away, but also of the consequences. Jesus said the unclean spirit would take with him seven other spirits more wicked than himself. Why seven, and not ten or twenty? Why not a "legion?"

Seven is God's number of perfection or completeness. What Jesus is implying is that this person, nation, or generation would be given over totally, wholly, or without reservation to serve the adversary. For example, if Jesus had said that the spirit taketh with him forty other spirits, we would assert that the giving over would only have been probationary. Or, if Jesus had said that he taketh with him eighteen other spirits, we could simply assert that the person was once again in bondage. So in this case of symbolism, less is more. As it pertains to the perfecting of evil, the cycle has now been completed and one would be hard pressed to find a person in worse condition. Falling away is the precedent set by Lucifer/Satan in Heaven, and this is the model for the Antichrist to fulfill in the Earth.

Let me now say that what the Church and the world commonly call "The Antichrist" is not referred to as "The Antichrist" in Scripture. The Scriptural references to antichrist are specifically to the spirit of antichrist and to the ministry of that spirit. What the Scripture does label this person as is "The Man of Sin" or "The Son of Perdition." Both of these labels are found in 2 Thessalonians 2:3 and are one and the same. The primary inference from the Scriptures that the Man of Sin will operate in an anti Christ capacity is from New Testament allegory in Matthew chapter 2 and from prophetic revelations of the Unholy Trinity in Revelation chapters 12 and 13.

The Fullness of Satan

In my study of Scripture, I find at least twelve or thirteen types or classifications of demon spirits. These are designated by sixteen or so different names. For example, what the Apostle Paul refers to as the spirit of slumber in Romans 11:8, the Prophet Isaiah refers to as the spirit of deep sleep in Isaiah 29:10. These two names are very similar and don't present us with any real problem in discerning that they are one and the same.

This isn't the case with other spirits. The name of the spirit designates the ministry of the spirit and not necessarily the individuality of the spirit. For example, God gave apostles, prophets, evangelists, pastors and teachers. There is nothing to prevent a man who has been called and anointed by God to serve as a pastor from operating in a prophetic capacity. Or, a man with an evangelical anointing could serve God's purposes as a teacher.

Likewise, one demon spirit could have multiple ministries or manifestations. This seems to be the case with the spirit of error, the spirit of bondage, and seducing spirits. Their ministry pertains primarily to false doctrine.

The terms "unclean spirit, foul spirit, and evil spirit" in Scripture, are generic terms used to represent, designate, or denote any type of demon spirit. The spirit of the world is not a demon spirit. It is the cumulative outworking of the knowledge of good and evil through the world. (See Ephesians 4:23.) It is a stronghold from which demon spirits are empowered to operate.

What many people classify as the spirit of witchcraft is actually classified by Scripture as the sin of witchcraft. The sin of witchcraft is the product of demon spirits, probably multiple, working in unison through a person or people to achieve a goal through manipulation.

Here is a list of demon spirits and a corresponding reference:

1.	Familiar Spirit	Lev 20:27; Isa 29:4
	Divination	Acts 16:16; 1 Sam 28:8
2.	Jealousy	Num 5:14
3.	Lying	1 King 22:21
4.	Haughty	Pvb 16:18
5.	Perverse	Isa 19:14
6.	Deep Sleep	Isa 29:10
	Slumber	Rom 11:8
7.	Heaviness	Isa 61:3; Isa 29:2
8.	Whoredom	Hos 4:12
9.	Infirmity	Luke 13:11
10.	Fear	2 Tim 1:7
11.	Antichrist	1 John 4:3; 1 John 2:18-**24**
12.	Error	1 John 4:6
	Seducing	1 Tim 4:1
	Bondage	Rom 8:15

This brief section only offers a glimpse at the fullness of Satan. If this offering differs from other studies on demon spirits, please know it is not as important to be able to identify a particular spirit as it is to know that their purpose and intention is to destroy the Kingdom of God. The battle is between God and Satan. Our power over these spirits doesn't come by our understanding of them. But, our empowerment and discernment comes from our relationship with the Lord Jesus Christ through His Holy Ghost.

Before we begin to move into the summation of things discussed, let's look at one last aspect of falling away.

Galatians 5:4 *"Christ is become of no effect unto you, whosoever of you are justified by the law; ye are fallen from grace."* (**Ephesians 2:8** *"For by grace are ye saved through faith;"*)

When I delve into the Word of God that pertains to judgment and condemnation, I always find an unsavory element that causes a repulsive reaction within my being. As I look into the nature of my response, I am convinced that it is a God-centered response. I am comforted to know that I am repelled by the thoughts of sin and the consequences it brings: namely death, judgment, condemnation, shame, suffering, exclusion, etc. I am comforted because I find all of this is contrary to God, also. I am reassured by this witness that God did not create man to operate in sin or it's accompaniments, because God does not desire to operate in these errant perversions. With this thought in mind, I am glad the Word taught in this book is not mine. The Author of the subject matter in this book is Divine and He retains all authority to execute judgment of His Word in perfect righteousness.

Anytime we find words in the Scriptures disagreeable with ourselves, we usually have one of two responses: we turn away from the Word of God or we turn the Word of God to make it more suitable. Both of these responses are natural (carnal) human behavior. But there is a third unnatural response. That third, Spirit-led response is to receive the Word of God as is; knowing that we don't have it all figured out. Yes, we are often uncomfortable with God's Word, but God didn't send His Word to make us comfortable, but rather conformable. In this we give thanks that the Apostles and Prophets did not mince words or pull punches, but were themselves surrendered to the full Word and Spirit of God.

The New Testament draws some distinctions between willful sin and inherent sin, and while time and space do not permit a thorough study of the topic, here I do recommend you to a personal study of the topic. But, from this topic Jesus tells us that whosoever hates his brother without a cause has murdered him in his heart. Likewise, whoever looks upon a woman to lust after her has committed adultery. Therefore, sin is still sin before it is necessarily manifested in our actions. **Hebrews 12:15-16** *"Looking diligently lest any man fail of the grace of God; **lest any root of bitterness springing up trouble you, and thereby many be defiled;** [16] Lest there be any fornicator, or profane person, as Esau, who for one morsel of meat sold his birthright."*

From the New Testament, speaking to those people that have been saved, you don't necessarily have to commit some unclean act to fall from grace. You don't have to become a pervert. It doesn't take stealing, fornication, or lying. All you have to do to fall from grace is trust in your own **GOOD** deeds!

This is what God is speaking of when He commanded us not to mingle our seed. We know that Jesus is the only begotten Son of God. We know that He died for us. We know that He rose again the third day. But then, do we trust that our good deeds will merit favor with God? This will certainly happen through pride when we look at our own good works, rather than looking at God's good works.

See how the Apostle Paul spends much time in the book of Romans, contrasting law and grace. And then in Romans 13:12, he tells us to cast off the works of darkness and let us put on the armor of light. The works of the law were good works, but we were never supposed to cover ourselves with them. Likewise, we can profess to know Jesus and profess salvation, but cover ourselves with our own good works, and the works themselves will actually bear witness that we deny Christ! **John 5:36** *"But I have greater witness than that of John: for the works which the Father hath given me to finish, the same works that I do, bear witness of me, that the Father hath sent me."* For a person to cover themselves with their own good works is a subtle but nonetheless devastating ministry of the spirit of antichrist. (See 1 John 2:22, 4:3; 2 John 7.) **Titus 1:16** *"They profess that they know God; but in works they deny him, being abominable, and disobedient, and unto every good work reprobate."*

Matthew 7:22-23 *"Many will say to me in that day, Lord, Lord, have we not prophesied in thy name? and in thy name have cast out devils? and in thy name done many wonderful works?* [23] *And then will I profess unto them, I never knew you: depart from me, ye that work iniquity."*

Matthew 10:33 *"But whosoever shall deny me before men, him will I also deny before my Father which is in heaven."*

Good works are always works of iniquity when we use them to exalt our own self. Our tendency is to try and help Jesus save us. If we apply our good works toward our effort to merit salvation, then our works prove (that is, they bear witness) that we think that the Blood of Jesus is insufficient for the job. When Jesus says "I never knew you" from Matthew 7:23, He is actually saying I never partook of you, and you haven't partaken of me. If you had, you wouldn't be wearing that robe of self-righteousness. You'd be wearing my robe! Depart from me, ye that work iniquity!

1 Peter 5:5 *"Likewise, ye younger, submit yourselves unto the elder. Yea, all of you be subject one to another, and be clothed with humility: for God resisteth the proud, and giveth grace to the humble."*

The Man of Sin

As a Christian, it is not wise to look to mythology, mysticism, Hollywood, and/or especially other present day religions in an attempt to ascertain just who the Man of Sin will be. Without question, mixing our doctrines will leaven the whole lump. Surely, there are Scriptures in the Bible that reveal clues to this person that have not been addressed in this book. It was never my intention to rehash well-known Scripture simply to fan the fire, stir up debate, or point the finger at who might be the Antichrist. Neither is this book a tool to predict where he will come from geographically. As a matter of fact, I am not at all interested in his ethnicity, race, or national origin. The externals of any man's person are a non-starter when attempting to discern the things of the Spirit.

When I was a new Christian, my Pastor exhorted our congregation to "ask of God" for wisdom. It was just a normal Church service in every aspect, but I responded by asking God what was on my mind. So I said to God, "Who is the Antichrist?" God wanted to make sure that I was able to know this person in great detail, so He responded to my request by holding the mirror in front of my face. As I read the Word of God, He would turn the mirror slightly so that I could see every aspect of this person clearly. Yes, I am telling on myself. With each new revelation came the command, "Repent." As I continued seeking after God and the things of God, I continued growing and learning. God's intended use of His Word is first inward and then outward. Proverbs 16:32 says he is better that rules his own spirit than he that takes a city. I am thankful God doesn't overlook the small for the great, but His design is that the great is made up of the small.

As we move into types and shadows of the Man of Sin, we will continue to look for those attributes that most accurately reflect the nature of Satan. Because a person who has fallen away from faith is particularly suited for this position, we should not look for him to come from another religion. In all probability, he will be a person operating in "the Church," but still operating under the Old Covenant. **1 Corinthians 15:56** *"...the strength of sin is the law."*

Hebrews 2:14 *"...that through death he might destroy him that had the power of death, that is, the devil;"* The devil was never given the power of life and death. His power was in the form of a ministry. He was/is the minister of death, and only death for all of humanity that has not died in Jesus Christ at the cross; remember the exchange. Satan's ministry was/is a ministry of death through the law, and thereby has to have someone to agree. Once there is agreement, death has free reign.

So, this person that I speak of will not be someone who casually attended Church for a while. The Antichrist will be well studied and able to quote Scripture after Scripture, as led by Satan. Because the Man of Sin will be able to perform miracles, it is likely that he will have been familiar with the Pentecostal anointing. (See 2 Thessalonians 2:9; Revelation 13:13-15; Deuteronomy 13:1-3.) Without getting into all of the different anointings found in Scripture, God doesn't anoint or cover (smear Himself on) those that are not in covenant with Him. Just as Lucifer was anointed by God in good faith to serve God's purpose in worship, the Man of Sin will probably have a similar call on his life.

Presently, there are not many people involved in other religions that fit this description. So we as the Church should look first within. (See Matthew 7:3-5.) **1 John 2:18-19** *"Little children, it is the last time: and as ye have heard that antichrist shall come, **even now are there many antichrists**; whereby we know that it is the last time.* [19] ***They went out from us,** but they were not of us; for if they had been of us, they would no doubt have continued with us: but they went out, that they might be made manifest that they were not all of us."* I would dare say the spirits of antichrist that went out from the Church in John the Apostle's day have returned to find it empty, swept, and decorated, just as Jesus warned in Matthew chapter 12. The Apostle Paul warned of the last days in which perilous times would come, saying of the Church in **2 Timothy 3:5**: *"Having a form of godliness, but denying the power thereof: from such turn away."* Oh, they look like God...but so does Satan.

It's a sad concept, but for truth-lovers that find themselves looking for a Church to attend today the question quickly becomes which Church has the least compromise. There was a time not so long ago when the debate within Churches was how to censure willful disobedience by Christians. Today, with the Church asking questions like "Can the Pastor be gay?" it's no wonder the Church, the Word of God, and Christ Himself are ridiculed by the lost. In modern times, blasphemy of God by the world is usually predicated upon the misrepresentation of God by the Church. The apostasy within the modern Church will usher in the Man of Sin; it's a shared or common nature.

The Prototype Relevance

A prototype in the Word of God is a form of prophecy where God uses real life events to represent real life events yet to come. We have already discussed some of these events earlier in this book where the Apostle Paul refers to them as "allegory." Sometimes these events are commonly referred to as "fore-shadowing." The terms are interchangeable and are often called "types and shadows."

The greatest and perhaps easiest to relate prototype or prophetic event pertaining to the Church would be that of National Israel herself. Beginning with Abraham and moving all the way down his lineage to the twelve tribes of Israel, we can see reference after reference to the God/Church relationship. Because faith begins with the Heavenly Father and then proceeds out from

Him, we first look at Abraham, the Father of Faith, as a representation of God the Father.

John chapter 1 tells us that without Jesus, God the Father didn't make anything. All that God the Father desired, in all of His creation, would come through Jesus Christ. Likewise, Abraham asked God, "What will you give me seeing I go childless?" In other words, all that Abraham desired would have to come through his offspring as well.

Then we see Abraham leading Isaac, this same offspring, up the mountain to be offered as a burnt offering. And we know without reservation, this act by Abraham represents God the Father leading His only begotten Son up Calvary's hill to be offered as a sacrifice. Who could deny that this earthly father/son relationship between Abraham and Isaac represents God the Father and God the Son?

From Abraham and Isaac, we then move to Jacob. Abraham begat Isaac, Isaac begat Jacob. Jacob, through the covenant, became heir to the promise. It was he that received the seed and the birthright, because his desire was toward God and not himself. Jacob represents the Church! (I will assert here that if anyone wants to argue over replacement theology, let him argue with the Spirit of Adoption! There is one seed, one faith, one body, and one legitimate heir. As gentiles, we have simply been grafted in! See Romans 11:17-24.) Then as Jacob had twelve sons, the Church also has branched into denominations.

Having this basic understanding of representations, let's look at prototypes and prophecies of the Man of Sin.

Revelation 12:1-6 *"And there appeared a great wonder in heaven; a woman clothed with the sun, and the moon under her feet, and upon her head a crown of twelve stars: ^{2} And she being with child cried, travailing in birth, and pained to be delivered. ^{3} And there appeared another wonder in heaven; and behold a great red dragon, having seven heads and ten horns, and seven crowns upon his heads. ^{4} And his tail drew the third part of the stars of heaven, and did cast them to the earth: and the dragon stood before the woman which was ready to be delivered, for to devour her child as soon as it was born. ^{5} And she brought forth a man child, who was to rule all nations with a rod of iron: and her child was caught up unto God, and to his throne. ^{6} And the woman fled into the wilderness, where she hath a place prepared of God, that they should feed her there a thousand two hundred and threescore days."*

Rev 12:13-17 *"And when the dragon saw that he was cast unto the earth, he persecuted the woman which brought forth the man child. ^{14} And to the woman were given two wings of a great eagle, that she might fly into the* *wilderness, into her place, where she is nourished for a time, and times, and half a time, from the face of the serpent. ¹⁵ And the serpent cast out of his mouth water as a flood after the woman, that he might cause her to be carried away of the flood. ¹⁶ And the earth helped the woman, and the earth opened her mouth, and swallowed up the flood which the dragon cast out of his mouth. ¹⁷ And the dragon was wroth with the woman, and went to make war with the remnant of her seed, which keep the commandments of God, and have the testimony of Jesus Christ."*

It is generally accepted that the Scriptures here are given in prophecy, and that they foretell of the events to come when, at that time, the Man of Sin will be given power to persecute. These Scriptures in Revelation 12 are a prophetic vision, as God gave it to the Apostle John. But, we have seen this story already in the Scriptures. John's vision corresponds to the events recorded in Matthew chapter 2. The events in Matthew 2 had taken place well before the time of John's vision.

Matthew chapter 2 pertains to the birth of Jesus, the attempt by Herod to kill the baby Jesus, the flight of Mary, Joseph, and Jesus into Egypt, and finally the slaughter of the children in Bethlehem by Herod. (Egypt is represented by an eagle in Ezekiel 17.) Hold your thoughts on Matthew 2, as an explanation is in order on God's method of communicating.

Especially on important issues, God repeats Himself. Humans also have picked up on this model of teaching, as our brains are like our stomachs: we do best when we take in small bits or bites at a time, and then allow them to be absorbed as needed. The Apostle Paul said as much to the Corinthian Church in **1 Corinthians 3:1-3**: *"And I, brethren, could not speak unto you as unto spiritual, but as unto carnal, even as unto babes in Christ. ² I have fed you with milk, and not with meat: for hitherto ye were not able to bear it, neither yet now are ye able. ³ For ye are yet carnal: for whereas there is among you envying, and strife, and divisions, are ye not carnal, and walk as men?"* (Carnal is not a type of Christian; it is a stage of Christians.) But God also changes our diet as we grow, while still providing much the same nutrients, just in different ratios and in a different form.

In example, I would refer to the Prophet Daniel's prophecy of the "abomination of desolation." **Daniel 12:11** *"And from the time that the daily sacrifice shall be taken away, and the abomination that maketh desolate set up, there shall be a thousand two hundred and ninety days."* (See also Daniel 9:27, 11:31.) Daniel writes this prophecy somewhere about the time of the sixth century BC.

About 165BC, a man named Antiochus Epiphanes, from the Greek Seleucid Dynasty, came to rule over Israel a while after the death of Alexander the Great, and subsequently offered a sow pig to Zeus on God's brazen altar in the Temple at Jerusalem. (Have you ever wondered why, in the Gospels, they were herding swine in the region of Gadara?) If you can imagine the shock and the emotional fervor that wholly consumed the people of Israel as they learned of the "abomination" in God's Temple, then you can also see why it was considered by the people of that day, and many years after, to be the fulfilling of Daniel's prophecy.

But, Jesus said in **Matthew 24:15-16**: *"When ye therefore shall see the abomination of desolation, spoken of by Daniel the prophet, stand in the holy place, (whoso readeth, let him understand:) [16] Then let them which be in Judaea flee into the mountains:"* Jesus indicates the event known as the "abomination of desolation" is an event yet to come. At this point in history, we have three recorded previews of this same event; two are found in Scripture and one from historical records.

But there is more. The Apostle Paul also writes of the event in **2 Thessalonians 2:3-12**: *"Let no man deceive you by any means: for that day shall not come, except there come a falling away first, and that man of sin be revealed, the son of perdition; [4] Who opposeth and exalteth himself above all that is called God, or that is worshipped; so that he as God sitteth in the temple of God, shewing himself that he is God. [5] Remember ye not, that, when I was yet with you, I told you these things? [6] And now ye know what withholdeth that he might be revealed in his time. [7] For the mystery of iniquity doth already work: only he who now letteth will let, until he be taken out of the way. [8] And then shall that Wicked be revealed, whom the Lord shall consume with the spirit of his mouth, and shall destroy with the brightness of his coming: [9] Even him, whose coming is after the working of Satan with all power and signs and lying wonders, [10] And with all deceivableness of unrighteousness in them that perish; because they received not the love of the truth, that they might be saved. [11] And for this cause God shall send them strong delusion, that they should believe a lie: [12] That they all might be damned who believed not the truth, but had pleasure in unrighteousness."*

Now, there are four records of the future event known as "the Abomination of Desolation." But wait; there's more. In the book that you are holding, we have already paralleled the event in 2 Thessalonians 2:3-12 with the Fall of Lucifer in Ezekiel 28, when he imitated God in the Heavenly Temple. The fall of Lucifer in the heavenly realm is the same event as the abomination of desolation in the earthly realm, which is still yet to come. Now we have three direct mentions of the event from Scripture, we have one account deduced/inferred from the Scripture, and we have one account from history; and each mention or account provides its insights from a slightly different perspective.

I am using Daniel's prophecy to show how God often uses more than one approach to bear witness to an upcoming event. This is why we are able to link the Apostle John's prophetic vision of Revelation 12, which is the woman with child, with the now historical events surrounding the birth of Jesus Christ, as recorded in Matthew 2. From here, we will complete our look at Revelation 12 and 13, and then come back to Matthew chapter 2. Revelation 12 and 13, along with Matthew 2, provide two more references to the Man of Sin and his ministry of death, bringing the total to seven references. They are as follows:

1. Ezekiel 28:11-19 / Isaiah 14:12-14 >< The initial act of rebellion in Heaven. The act will also be fulfilled in the earth, in the macro, at the end of this age. Through pride it is often fulfilled individually, in the micro, daily.

2. Daniel 9:27, 11:31, 12:11 >< From prophetic dreams/visions. Daniel chapters 7-12 details various aspects of the event/person. Daniel is given angelic interpretation of his visions. (See Daniel 8:16, 9:21, 10:14, and 12:7.)

3. The appearance of Antiochus Epiphanes, as recorded in the historical text of 1st Maccabees chapter 1 (from the name Maccabaeus). Antiochus Epiphanes did not just appear out of nowhere and desecrate the temple, but through gifts and other flatteries he ingratiated himself with the people of Israel, as he attempted to Hellenize the region.

4. Matthew chapter 2 details the events of the birth of Jesus as an allegory of the event to come at the end of this age. We know it is used as allegory because the same events are spoken as prophecy in Revelation 12 and 13.

5. **Matthew 24:15-16** *"When ye therefore shall see the abomination of desolation, spoken of by Daniel the prophet, stand in the holy place, (whoso readeth, let him understand:)* [16] *Then let them which be in Judaea flee into the mountains:"*

6. **2 Thessalonians 2:3-12** *"Let no man deceive you by any means: for that day shall not come, except there come a falling away first, and that man of sin be revealed, the son of perdition;* [4] *Who opposeth*

and exalteth himself above all that is called God, or that is worshipped; so that he as God sitteth in the temple of God, shewing himself that he is God."

7. Revelation chapters 12 and 13 From the prophetic visions of the end of this age, by the Apostle John.

The Unholy Trinity

Revelation 12:3 describes the devil as a dragon with seven heads, ten horns, and seven crowns upon his heads. I will refer to him as **7-10-7** (aka "The Dragon").

Revelation 13:1 describes a beast that John saw rising up out of the sea. This beast had seven heads, ten horns, and upon his horns ten crowns. I will refer to this beast as **7-10-10** (aka "The Beast from the Sea").

Revelation 13:11 describes another beast. This beast came up out of the earth and had two horns like a lamb (aka "The Beast from the Earth"). This is the "Antichrist."

Together, these three make the unholy trinity! It is made up of Satan, the beast from the sea, and the beast from the earth. These three are mentioned also in **Revelation 16:13**: *"And I saw three unclean spirits like frogs come out of the mouth of the dragon, and out of the mouth of the beast, and out of the mouth of the false prophet."* In the use of different names for the Man of Sin (beast from the earth, false prophet, etc.) God is revealing to us the different aspects of his person and/or administration. This is true anywhere in Scripture where multiple names are given for an individual person, thing, or event. Remember also Pharaoh's two dreams, one of cows and one of corn, and how they represented the same event. (See Genesis 41.)

Now we have two more names for the Man of Sin: the Beast from the Earth from Revelation 13:11 and the False Prophet from Revelation 16:13. While we have various names for the Man of Sin, there is only one evil trinity. Two parts of this trinity are somewhat obvious but the third part lurks obscurely in plain sight.

The two obvious parts of the evil trinity are easy to identify. Revelation 12:9 says that the dragon (7-10-7) is the devil. That's straightforward and couldn't be any easier.

The Beast from the Earth is given the number of a man in Revelation 13:18, and that number is 666. The significance of this number is that God originally created man on the sixth day. He also created man as the **second trinity**: Spirit, soul, and body. You have but to do the math to see where this is going. As I have previously mentioned, when God brought the Hebrews out of Egyptian bondage and while they were still wandering in the wilderness, God fed them with manna from Heaven. He commanded them to gather enough of the bread for each day, but on the sixth day He told them to gather twice as much. God's intent was for the people to rest on the seventh day. And again, when God brought the Hebrews into the Promised Land, He instructed the Children of Israel to let the land rest the seventh year. To enable a year of rest, God's promise was to provide twice as much in the harvest from the sixth year. The original meaning or significance of the number six was a double portion or double blessing.

But I don't find much, if any, evidence in the Scriptures where the Children of Israel actually observed the command to let the land rest on the seventh year. Thus, the Prophet Jeremiah concluded that Israel would go into Babylonian captivity for seventy years; one year for each of the yearly Sabbaths that Israel had neglected to keep from the time they entered into the Promised Land. As part of this (neglected) Yearly Sabbath observation, the Hebrews were required by God to release their brethren from their debts. (See Deuteronomy 15.) Deuteronomy 15 links the essence of Sabbath (peace) with mercy, compassion, and forgiveness. Ultimately, these qualities within us are dependent on God's mercy, compassion, and forgiveness toward us. Our ability to forgive is contingent on God's forgiveness working in our own lives, but it is still our choice. (See Matthew 18:33; 1 Corinthians 15:3.) No doubt Jesus referred to this in His response, when Peter asked Jesus how often he had to forgive his brother of his trespasses. **Matthew 18:22** *"Jesus saith unto him, I say not unto thee, Until seven times: but, Until seventy times seven."*

The common belief that the 490 times Jesus referred to represents an unlimited number of forgiveness is not supported by the Scriptures; actually, it is the opposite that is observed in Scripture. The transgression 490 times is the invoking of judgment. When the Hebrews failed the Sabbath requirement to release their brethren over a period of 490 years, or seventy seven-year weeks, they set in motion a succession of seventies that would ultimately culminate in the Antichrist himself. (See Daniel 9:24-27.) (See also Daniel 9:2; 2 Chronicles 36:20-21; Ezra 1:1-2; Jeremiah 25:11-12, 29:10.)

I would add Leviticus 26 to this list, also, as the nature of idolatry is covetousness. (See Colossians 3:5; Ephesians 5:5.) It is the love of money that causes us to bring our brethren into bondage. In this greed, man has turned what was the double blessing of the number six into a curse; hence, we have the ministry of the Antichrist from **Revelation 13:16-17**: *"And he causeth all, both small and great, rich and poor, free and bond, to receive a mark in their right hand, or in their foreheads: [17] And that no man might buy or sell, save he* *that had the mark, or the name of the beast, or the number of his name."* If this sounds even a bit familiar, you would be right in assigning this event to that of an evil consequence. But, don't think that the cause and effect are Hebrew oriented. **Romans 3:19** *"Now we know that what things soever the law saith, it saith to them who are under the law: that every mouth may be stopped, and all the world may become guilty before God."*

Just a thought: for those that have not been saved, not taking the mark of the beast, but choosing to die instead, will not merit eternal life. A person that is killed by the Antichrist is no different than any other person that dies. If we die in Christ, that is, with the Blood of Jesus applied to our heart, then we live forever with God in Heaven. If we stand before God without the Blood of Jesus, we will be rejected by God and spend eternity in Hell! (See John 14:6.)

Revelation 13:13-15 tells us of the power of the Antichrist to work miracles. The first miracle mentioned in Revelation 13:13 is the calling down of fire. The Prophet Elijah called fire from Heaven to kill a hundred of King Ahaziah's troops in 2 King 1:10-12. This is the "miracle" that drew the rebuke of Jesus when He told the disciples in **Luke 9:55-56**: *"Ye know not what manner of spirit ye are of. For the Son of man is not come to destroy men's lives, but to save them."* The disciples emulation of Elijah was a portrayal of the legalistic nature which they were operating under, and suggests the same for the Antichrist.

Further miracles of the Antichrist correspond to 2 Thessalonians 2:9 and Deuteronomy 13:1. This is the second obvious part of the evil trinity. The Antichrist is the beast from the earth. So far, we have the Devil and the Antichrist; this begs the question, who or what is 7-10-10? What is the beast from the sea?

Revelation 13:2 *"And the beast which I saw was like unto a leopard, and his feet were as the feet of a bear, and his mouth as the mouth of a lion: and the dragon gave him his power, and his seat, and great authority."*

The three animals that characterize the beast from the sea (7-10-10) from Revelation 13:2 are the same three animals the Prophet Daniel saw as individual beasts in Daniel chapter 7. While there are references in various Bible Scriptures to specific kingdoms, the four beasts in Daniel 7 represent four forms of government.

The lion represents true kingdoms. The bear represents a pseudo-kingdom known as an oligarchy. In a true kingdom, the king is <u>descended</u> from the king. In an oligarchy, the king is <u>ascended</u> from the nobility. The leopard represents democracy. In democracy the king is, or can be, ascended from and by the common people. Daniel's fourth beast was diverse from the other three beasts of his vision, but had the power to subdue the whole earth. The fourth beast of

Daniel 7 has ten horns, just as John's 7-10-10 beast from the sea does. As John saw 7-10-10 rise from the sea, there are also worldwide implications for this beast, as well. In general, the sea represents humanity. **Revelation 17:1** *"And there came one of the seven angels which had the seven vials, and talked with me, saying unto me, Come hither; I will shew unto thee the judgment of the great whore **that sitteth upon many waters**:"* **Revelation 17:15** *"And he saith unto me, **The waters which thou sawest, where the whore sitteth, are peoples, and multitudes, and nations, and tongues.**"* (See also Revelation 4:6; Isaiah 5:26-30; Isaiah 57:20.) But the Apostle John's vision is of a single combined beast. In real practice, the representative republic form of government combines the elements of the three forms of government prior into a singular composite government.

It is commonly taught within circles of evangelical Christianity that the Revised Roman Empire will soon usher in the One-World Leader. This leader will seem to be the only one that can bring peace and financial stability to a world wrought with confusion. Please note the difference between "revived" and "revised." The Roman form of government or representative republic, though morphed, is the predominant form of government worldwide today.

The spirit and ideals of independence (democracy) can and have always moved very swiftly through nations and regions once they have been introduced; hence, it is represented as a leopard with four wings. Just as the dominion of Greece was swift, it quickly ran its course and gave way to Rome. Likewise, in every instance where the spirit of independence (democracy) has taken root, a representative republic has been established.

John's vision is of a beast that embodies characteristics of kingdoms, oligarchies, and democracies. That beast from the sea is the representative republic. The parallels between Scripture and the actual unfolding of events stand in agreement to this concept. Therefore, the unholy or evil trinity is comprised of Satan, the Antichrist, and a Worldwide Ruling Authority. The Worldwide Ruling Authority (Caesar) is the beast from the sea or 7-10-10. This does not mean that every earthly government, at that future time, will be a representative republic. It does imply that the representative republic will be the predominant form of government authorizing the Man of Sin to complete his task. (See Revelation 13:12, 14.)

We have already shown the imitation of God by Satan. The Antichrist will mimic or imitate the ministry of Jesus Christ. And the Worldwide Ruling Authority (Caesar) will attempt to replace or usurp the authority and counsel of the Holy Spirit. For anyone holding to the Scriptures as sacred counsel, this last statement bears great significance for the hour that we live in today. I, too, am sensitive to this struggle.

At this point, it would probably benefit the reader (you) to digest these concepts by prayerfully re-reading Revelation 12 and 13/Matthew 2 and Daniel 7 from your Bible, and see if this chapter of this book provides an accurate conceptualization of the Spiritual visions of the Prophets mentioned.

Back to Matthew Chapter 2

Now that we have looked at the prophecy of the unholy trinity and the inter-relationship of the three from the Apostle John's vision, we can add a layer by looking at the unholy trinity from the perspective of a prophetic event. Matthew chapter 2 pertains to the birth of Jesus, the attempt by Herod to kill the baby Jesus, the flight of Mary, Joseph, and Jesus into Egypt, and finally the slaughter of the children in Bethlehem by Herod. (Egypt is represented by an eagle in Ezekiel 17.) When we combine the prophetic visions of last day events in Revelation 12 and 13 with the prophetic events portrayed in Matthew chapter 2, we find that God has used Satan, Herod, and Caesar to represent this evil trinity!

Herod was appointed king in Israel by Caesar. **Revelation 13:12** *"And he* (the beast from the earth) *exerciseth all the power of the first beast before him, and causeth the earth and them which dwell therein to worship the first beast, whose deadly wound was healed."* **Revelation 13:14** *"And deceiveth them that dwell on the earth by the means of those miracles which he* (the beast from the earth) **had power to do in the sight of the beast** (from the sea)*; saying to them that dwell on the earth, that they should make an image to the beast,* (from the sea)...*"* (All comments in parentheses are mine. DP)

The delegation of authority by Caesar to Herod in the time of Jesus' birth is the same delegation of authority the Worldwide Ruling Authority will convey to the Man of Sin at the end of this age. This act is in imitation of the anointing of Jesus at His baptism by the presence of the Holy Spirit descending and resting upon Him from above. We commonly associate the term "antichrist" with the man that opposes Jesus. But the Greek word "Christ" or "Christos" actually refers to the anointing, as in "Jesus, the Anointed One". In this capacity, antichrist opposes both God the Son and God the Holy Ghost equally. In the physical example of the evil trinity, Caesar represents the Worldwide Ruling Authority (beast from the sea), and Herod represents the Man of Sin, aka the Antichrist (beast from the earth). Remember Saul and Jonathan? In humanity's fallen condition the soul serves the flesh. In the prototype, Herod serves Caesar. In the event to come, the Man of Sin will serve the Worldwide Ruling Authority.

What is the Man of Sin's responsibility? Well, Jesus is the mediator of the New Covenant. **Hebrews 8:6** *"But now hath he obtained a more excellent ministry, by how much also he is the mediator of a better covenant, which was established upon better promises."* (See also Hebrews 9:15, 12:24.) Likewise, the Man of Sin will be the mediator of the covenant between Adam and Satan, on behalf of all whose names are not written in the Lamb's Book of Life. (See Revelation 17:8, 21:27.) The covenant between Adam and Satan has the unfulfilled/soon to be fulfilled aspects of a mark in the flesh (666), and very much bloodshed.

Revelation 12:17 *"And the dragon was wroth with the woman, and went to make war with the remnant of her seed, which keep the commandments of God, and have the testimony of Jesus Christ."*

Matthew 2:16 *"Then Herod, when he saw that he was mocked of the wise men, was exceeding wroth, and sent forth, and slew all the children that were in Bethlehem,..."*

Revelation 12:14 *"And to the woman were given two wings of a great eagle, that she might fly into the wilderness,..."*

Matthew 2:13 *"And when they were departed, behold, the angel of the Lord appeareth to Joseph in a dream, saying, Arise, and take the young child and his mother, and flee into Egypt, and be thou there until I bring thee word: for Herod will seek the young child to destroy him".*

Herod sits as the most prolific of all prototypes of the Antichrist; and yet, we hear so little of him. This we do know of Herod: Herod was an Edomite! History tells us the Herods were the seed of Esau. Remember Esau? **Hebrews 12:16-17** *"Lest there be any fornicator, or profane person, as Esau, who for one morsel of meat sold his birthright. [17] For ye know how that afterward, when he would have inherited the blessing, he was rejected: for he found no place of repentance, though he sought it carefully with tears."* Remember how Esau and Jacob traded places?

Esau wasn't just the brother of Jacob; he was a twin. Even though they were not identical twins, it is likely they would have had a strong resemblance to each other. Further, it is likely the Herods observed circumcision as an outward show of the covenant; Esau was grandson to Abraham. I know that some people believe the Herods were compelled to observe circumcision, but even today, AD 2000, there are many people that trace their ancestry back to Ishmael that still circumcise their male children.

The mimicry continues. In the trinity of man, or rather the current trichotomy, God joined His Holy Spirit to our soul and we live in a body. Caesar is a representative of the flesh. Herod is a representative of the soul. Both of these men govern a realm respective of their nature. In the union of Satan, Caesar, and Herod, the operating system of works is codified into a legal system based on the union of Church and State; that is, a fallen Church and a secular state which are governed by the Dragon. (Many modern legal/political precedents already confirm this idea as valid.) In Herod, the descendant of Esau, we go back to the prototypes of the God/Church relationship. We go back to Abraham, Isaac, and Jacob, and now Esau. Abraham begat Isaac. Isaac begat Esau. We go back to Genesis 25, where we read of Isaac entreating the Lord for Rebekah because she was barren.

Soon after she conceived, "the children struggled together within her," and Rebekah enquired of the Lord. **Gen 25:23-25** *"And the LORD said unto her, Two nations are in thy womb, and two manner of people shall be separated from thy bowels; and the one people shall be stronger than the other people; and the elder shall serve the younger. ²⁴ And when her days to be delivered were fulfilled, behold, there were twins in her womb. ²⁵ **And the first came out red, all over like an hairy garment; and they called his name Esau.**"*

If these prototypes of Abraham, Isaac, and Jacob representing God the Father, God the Son, and the Church hold true, then Esau would represent the "elder" Church. He represents the twin Church, the Church to come after Isaac/Jesus, the Church with its own covering! *"**And the first came out red, all over like an hairy garment; and they called his name Esau.**"* Esau represents the beautiful Church, the fallen Church! (See Revelation 17.) **1 Corinthians 11:15** *"But if a woman have long hair, it is a glory to her: for her hair is given her for a covering."*

I am glad for everyone's sake that there is no nation today called by the name "Esau" or "Edom." Surely, if there was such a nation, some would point the finger, forgetting that such things are an allegory, which is first to teach us about ourselves. Even within present day Churches, many people have been led by pride back into the bondage of religion. We can't go by the sign in the parking lot or by the sign over the door; but is the message from the pulpit liberty in Jesus Christ? Or is it other? And even if the message is spoken in truth, will it be received in truth? Or will it be received in pride?

And even still, where life and truth are proclaimed, the enemy of our soul will surely send his "false apostles, deceitful workers, false prophets, false teachers, false brethren and false christs" to lead astray. (See 2 Cor 11:13; Gal 2:4; 2 Pet 2:1; 1 John 4:1; Acts 20:29-31; Jude 4; Matt 24:11; Mark 13:22.) **Matthew 7:15** *"Beware of false prophets, which come to you in sheep's clothing, but inwardly they are ravening wolves."* We must follow after peace and holiness. God alone, who sees all things in truth, will separate the sheep from the goats and the wheat from the tares when the day comes.

Concerning the Antichrist, Jeremiah 30:7 refers to the coming persecution as "Jacob's trouble." This is a reference to the time when Esau desired to kill Jacob. I would point out here that "Jacob" was a pre-covenant name for Israel.

In Summary

2 Thessalonians 2:9-12 *"Even him, whose coming is after the working of Satan with all power and signs and lying wonders, [10] And with all deceivableness of unrighteousness in them that perish; because they received not the love of the truth, that they might be saved. [11] And for this cause God shall send them strong delusion, that they should believe a lie: [12] That they all might be damned who believed not the truth, but had pleasure in unrighteousness."*

The Man of Sin will come as an angel of light. His light will be the Word of God: in particular, the Law of Moses. The Law in Scripture is represented by the moon. The Law named or set the new moons as signs to govern the timing of all the feasts, fasts, rituals, and ceremonies required by the Law of Moses for the nation of Israel. The woman clothed with the sun and the moon under her feet from Revelation 12:1 is a picture of Redeemed Israel into which the Church has been grafted. She now wears the garment of the bridegroom from Psalms 19:4-5. The relationship between the sun and moon mirrored the relationship between God and Lucifer before Lucifer became Satan. The implication from Revelation 12:1 is that national Israel is now operating by a new system, aka New Covenant.

Through the Word of God, the Man of Sin will lead man to mingle his seed, or mix his covenants. His message will be, "Jesus died for you, but..." And in so doing, he will lead many people that know that Jesus is the Son of God to trust in their own good deeds. Remember how Satan used the Word of God to tempt Jesus? (See Matthew 4:6.) Satan can speak the truth; he cannot speak the truth in truth!

The Man of Sin will facilitate the covenant of Adam and Satan on behalf of all people whose names are not written in the Lamb's Book of Life. He will unite the flesh and soul within the framework of an unholy trinity, resulting in an adulterous bonding of Church and state.

The Man of Sin will walk in the fullness of Satan, and not only in the spirit of antichrist. He is referred to as the Man of Sin, the Son of Perdition, the Lawless One, the Antichrist, the Beast from the Earth, the False Prophet, and the Little Horn of Daniel 7:8. He has been represented in Scripture by Esau, Nimrod, Pharaoh, Nebuchadnezzar, Haman, Antiochus Epiphanes, and Judas Iscariot. The Antichrist is most notably represented in Scripture by the Herods collectively. He will repeat the hateful imitation of God by Lucifer in Heaven, here on the Earth.

The Man of Sin will appear meek and humble, as in "sheep's clothing." He will ingratiate himself to the people through gifts and flatteries. He will use good manners and good works to disarm the simple and the unaware.

Pertaining to his doctrine, he will be a near kinsman to the Jews, but not a Jew. The Edomites were the closest relatives to the Children of Israel. Likewise, Church doctrine aligns closer to Judaism than any other religion. **Mark 8:15** *"And he charged them, saying, Take heed, beware of the **leaven of the Pharisees**, and of the **leaven of Herod**."* **By default, if you share a doctrine, you share a nature. Acts 4:27** *"For of a truth against thy holy child Jesus, whom thou hast anointed, both Herod, and Pontius Pilate, with the Gentiles, and the people of Israel, were gathered together,"* (See also Mark 3:6; Matthew 22:15-21.)

Just as Caesar is a representative of the flesh and uses carnal law to govern from the flesh, the Man of Sin is a representative of the soul and will use religion to govern man from within. Caesar is purely political. Antichrist is religious and will marry the fleshly (political) and the soulish (religious) realms.

Conversely, God promises to change our vile bodies into one fashioned after the likeness of His Glorious Body, as we are joined to Him.

The Beast From the Sea

Daniel 7:7 *"After this I saw in the night visions, and behold a fourth beast, dreadful and terrible, and strong exceedingly; and it had great iron teeth: it devoured and brake in pieces, and stamped the residue with the feet of it: and it was diverse from all the beasts that were before it; and it had ten horns."*

As we have already stated, God Himself has ordained carnal government for carnal people. Not everybody is going to respond to God's goodness in a way that conveys God's presence. Inasmuch as I still have a carnal nature to contend with, the Lord Jesus commands: **1 Peter 2:13** *"Submit yourselves to every ordinance of man for the Lord's sake: whether it be to the king, as supreme;* [14] *Or unto governors, as unto them that are sent by him for the punishment of evildoers, and for the praise of them that do well."* When we looked at the trichotomy of man and the war within, we discovered that the war within is between the Spirit and the flesh. Here and now, I would add that sometimes carnal or offending Christians are routinely delivered by God into the hands of the carnal government for the destruction of the fleshly nature. **Romans 13:1** *"Let every soul be subject unto the higher powers. For there is no power but of God: the powers that be are ordained of God."*

One of the conveniences of democracy, or rather, the representative republic, is that the leadership and the common people usually have shared values. The leadership is not always an exact picture of the populace, but usually it's close enough to be a good representation. In Revelation 13:1-2, the Apostle John saw the beast rise up out of the sea, and the Dragon gave him his power, seat, and authority. At some point in the near future, this carnal government that governs the fleshly realm will be handed over by God to the Dragon. I say "the near future" because every day the fleshly government, man's government, Caesar, etc., becomes more and more corrupt. Today, the moral decay that infects society is prevalent in societies' government as well.

If I could just speak about the American government for a moment pertaining to "the near future," I would point out that we have already past the benchmark of **Isaiah 5:20**: *"Woe unto them that call evil good, and good evil; that put darkness for light, and light for darkness; that put bitter for sweet, and sweet for bitter!"* When an American president praises a young man for coming out of the closet as a sodomite, and the media that serves the public swoons over the example because the general public has an appetite for debauchery, we have missed it. When the same president causes foreign nations to promote homosexuality as a qualifier to receive U.S. monetary aide, we have missed it. When our nation practices infanticide to the tune of **sixty million dead babies**, (these are just babies killed in the U.S. and does not include abortions the American taxpayer has funded outside of our borders), we have missed it. We have now moved into the age of partial birth abortion, which I don't care to describe, but we are missing: actually rejecting the very Grace of God that dignifies all human life! The number one cause of death in the U.S., in recent time, is abortion! Abortion surpasses the next two leading causes of death combined, but it never even makes the list because "they" don't consider the baby to have ever been alive. Sin degrades humanity.

When the U.S. President bathes the White House in the lighted symbol of homosexuality, is he not tempting God? When the U.S. Supreme Court redefined marriage by applying it to same-sex unions, did God consent? Will the blood of sixty million aborted babies not cry louder than "God Bless the

USA?" As America willfully sins and then flaunts it in God's face, do we think we will not reap what we have sown?

Psalms 9:17 *"The wicked shall be turned into hell, and all the nations that forget God."*

How is it, we think we are exempt as Christians, when the New Testament writers warn us of the consequences of apostasy by citing Old Testament examples of judgment? **Hebrews 10:26-29** *"For if we sin wilfully **after that we have received the knowledge of the truth**, there remaineth no more sacrifice for sins, ²⁷ But a certain fearful looking for of judgment and fiery indignation, which shall devour the adversaries. ²⁸ He that despised Moses' law died without mercy under two or three witnesses: ²⁹ Of how much sorer punishment, suppose ye, shall he be thought worthy, who hath trodden under foot the Son of God, and hath counted the blood of the covenant, wherewith he was sanctified, an unholy thing, and hath done despite unto the Spirit of grace?"*

For the Christian that willfully sins, the phrase in Hebrews 10:26, "there remaineth no more sacrifice for sins," demands that we go back to the Cross of Christ. And if we choose not to, then we apply Hebrews 10:27-29 with the same veracity that we originally applied John 3:16 to our lives. Americans can say we are a Christian nation all they want to, but what do our actions say? Yes, we were established on Christian principals. But, where are we today? As a nation, where will we be tomorrow? **Psalm 138:2** *"...**for thou hast magnified thy word above all thy name.**"* The devil can call himself God all he wants to, but that does not make it so. Christians can call themselves Christ-like all they want to, but what do their actions say? God is not into lip service! **Matthew 15:7-8** *"Ye hypocrites, well did Esaias prophesy of you, saying, ⁸ This people draweth nigh unto me with their mouth, and honoureth me with their lips; but their heart is far from me."*

Here is the point. As a nation we are rapidly turning ourselves into reprobates. As a nation, we are crying out for the fulfillment of our own lusts. This longing for sin hastens the coming of the Man of Sin. If the word reprobates offends you, you just made my point! If anyone thinks that sodomy and infanticide and greed and lying and drunkenness and fornication and adultery and so on are OK by God's standards, I would say, "Show me in the Bible!" I didn't say, "Go write your own bible." Love does not rejoice in iniquity! Take heed: nobody stands before the President on Judgment Day!

1 Peter 4:17-18 *"For the time is come that judgment must begin at the house of God: and if it first begin at us, what shall the end be of them that obey* *not the gospel of God?* [18] *And if the righteous scarcely be saved, where shall the ungodly and the sinner appear?"* (See also 2 Kings 24:10-13; Jeremiah 52:13)

A King in Israel

Please allow me to show how the Hebrews would reject the Messiah and cause their own destruction from the Old Testament book of Numbers. This is a prototype from the Old Testament of the events that would take place at the rejection of Jesus Christ, and also of events at the end of this age.

Numbers 11:4-6 *"And the mixt multitude that was among them fell a lusting: and the children of Israel also wept again, and said, Who shall give us flesh to eat?* [5] *We remember the fish, which we did eat in Egypt freely; the cucumbers, and the melons, and the leeks, and the onions, and the garlick:* [6] *But now our soul is dried away: there is nothing at all, beside this manna, before our eyes."*

Numbers 11:18-20 *"And say thou unto the people, Sanctify yourselves against to morrow, and ye shall eat flesh: for ye have wept in the ears of the LORD, saying, Who shall give us flesh to eat? for it was well with us in Egypt: therefore the LORD will give you flesh, and ye shall eat.* [19] *Ye shall not eat one day, nor two days, nor five days, neither ten days, nor twenty days;* [20] *But even a whole month, until it come out at your nostrils, and it be loathsome unto you: because that ye have despised the LORD which is among you, and have wept before him, saying, Why came we forth out of Egypt?"*

Numbers 11:31-34 *"And there went forth a wind from the LORD, and brought quails from the sea, and let them fall by the camp, as it were a day's journey on this side, and as it were a day's journey on the other side, round about the camp, and as it were two cubits high upon the face of the earth.* [32] *And the people stood up all that day, and all that night, and all the next day, and they gathered the quails: he that gathered least gathered ten homers: and they spread them all abroad for themselves round about the camp.* [33] ***And while the flesh was yet between their teeth, ere it was chewed, the wrath of the LORD was kindled against the people, and the LORD smote the people with a very great plague.*** [34] ***And he called the name of that place Kibroth-hattaavah: because there they buried the people that lusted."***

There are several ways that these verses relate to a king in Israel. The event in Numbers 11 happened as God was delivering the Hebrews from the bondage of Egypt, but before they came into the Promised Land. They "fell a lusting" while God was feeding the people manna or "bread" from Heaven.

"Manna" means "to question" or "what is it?" The ministry of Jesus, His crucifixion, and the destruction of Jerusalem parallel this event, as Jesus was determined to bring us into a new relationship with the Father. This new relationship was not based on the servitude of works, but rather as sons desiring to please our Father.

In both settings, God fed the people with a heavenly meal. **Exodus 16:15** *"And when the children of Israel saw it, they said one to another, It is manna: for they wist not what it was. And Moses said unto them, This is the bread which the LORD hath given you to eat."* **John 6:48-51** *"I am that bread of life. [49] Your fathers did eat manna in the wilderness, and are dead. [50] This is the bread which cometh down from heaven, that a man may eat thereof, and not die. [51] I am the living bread which came down from heaven: if any man eat of this bread, he shall live for ever: and the bread that I will give is my flesh, which I will give for the life of the world."*

In both settings the people weren't satisfied. In both settings the people cried out for their own desires. And in both settings destruction would follow.

John 18:39 *"But ye have a custom, that I should release unto you one at the passover: will ye therefore that I release unto you the King of the Jews?"*

John 18:40 <u>*Then cried they all again, saying, Not this man, but Barabbas.*</u> *Now Barabbas was a robber.* (The name Barabbas means "son of the father.")

John 19:14-15 *"And it was the preparation of the passover, and about the sixth hour: and he saith unto the Jews, Behold your King! [15] But they cried out, Away with him, away with him, crucify him.* **Pilate saith unto them, Shall I crucify your King? The chief priests answered, <u>We have no king but Caesar.</u>"**

This prototype is completed in AD 70, as the hand of Caesar laid siege to the city of Jerusalem. God only knows the strife and oppression and brutality that took place inside those walls as thousands died daily. Even though this is the pivotal point in history, it is still a prototype for the much larger event to come at the end of this age. Not that Jesus will be sacrificed again; He will not! But the powers - the beast from the sea and the beast from the earth - the choice, and the destruction will follow this same pattern as we have read from the book of Revelation. **Revelation 16:1** *"And I heard a great voice out of the temple saying to the seven angels, Go your ways, and pour out the vials of the wrath of God upon the earth."* **Proverbs 6:34** *"For jealousy is the rage of a man: therefore he will not spare in the day of vengeance."* The Scriptures testify of Him.

Again, for those that believe you can't fall away, Numbers 11 declares this was a mixed multitude. The same event is recorded also in the Psalms. **Psalm**

78:21-22 *"Therefore the LORD heard this, and was wroth: so a fire was kindled against Jacob, and anger also came up against Israel; ²² Because they believed not in God, and trusted not in his salvation:"* The mixed multitude was made up of Jacob (pre-covenant) and Israel (post-covenant).

Today, Caesar is alive and well, as we all know. Herod's ministry is about to begin. God has made His offer and Jesus shed His Blood for the sins of the world. Satan has made his offer and desires to shed the blood of the world.

John 1:17 *"For the law was given by Moses, but grace and truth came by Jesus Christ."*

Matthew 11:28-30 *"Come unto me, all ye that labour and are heavy laden, and I will give you rest. ²⁹ Take my yoke upon you, and learn of me; for I am meek and lowly in heart: and ye shall find rest unto your souls. ³⁰ For my yoke is easy, and my burden is light."*

We are hearing terms such as "globalization" and "world economy" used more frequently today than ever before. With these concepts, there comes an inseparable dependence on common or international law and currency. Today, sovereign nations are finding more frequent application of international law to their own domestic court proceedings. For many people, global calamities such as war, political unrest, pandemics, global warming, etc. provide the impetus for more authoritative international law. And today, individual rights are being compromised - that is, incrementally surrendered - in lieu of collective necessity.

Couple this with the apostasy of the Church and the moral corruption of society in general, and it becomes clear: the world is ripe for the Man of Sin to facilitate the consummation of the union of Church and State. Already as masses of people look to the State to establish new rules of righteous conduct, they disregard the counsel of the Scriptures and of God's Holy Spirit. Although it will look like God, it will be an unholy union. As far as timing is concerned, I fully expect Jesus to consummate the marriage with His Bride at the same time Satan is consummating the marriage with his bride.

But this is not the end. God has promised a Kingdom to His Son! For human beings, all transitions carry the potential for stress and uncertainty. I doubt this one will be any different!

7

Return of the Melek Tsedek

Assassins, thieves, men-stealers, and the like,
lie in wait, their hope to strike,
in ambush,
their strength and force,
imposed upon the unaware,
of course,
it is not so with Kings!

And with their gain for prize in hand, they scurry from the eyes of man.
In vain they kneel before their lust, as servants to appeasement thrust... into the never
ending.

But from time of old, six thousand years,
we are foretold, He's drawing near,
His Throne to claim, the Rightful Heir;
His Bride awaits, Her heart's prepared,
with great desire,
she then is carried, unto the consummation.

I am but one, who with commission,
extends to you this invitation:
To know the one that died as you. He took your sins and sickness too.
With guilt and shame and condemnation, upon my cross, He was forsaken.
But as He lives today, His mercy beckons:
The escape from wrath, for soon He reckons.

As scoffers wait... .. ..The trumpet sounds!
It's now too late. We've sealed our fate.
We would not hear, when we were told, the Heralds crying from time of old:
"Prepare your hearts! His Majesty is coming!"

And so it is, Great Kings announce their coming!

Psalms 110:1-7 *"The LORD said unto my Lord, Sit thou at my right hand,
until I make thine enemies thy footstool. ² The LORD shall send the rod of thy*

strength out of Zion: rule thou in the midst of thine enemies. ^{3} *Thy people shall be willing in the day of thy power, in the beauties of holiness from the womb of the morning: thou hast the dew of thy youth.* ^{4} ***The LORD hath sworn, and will not repent, Thou art a priest for ever after the order of Melchizedek.*** ^{5} *The Lord at thy right hand shall strike through kings in the day of his wrath.* ^{6} *He shall judge among the heathen, he shall fill the places with the dead bodies; he shall wound the heads over many countries.* ^{7} *He shall drink of the brook in the way: therefore shall he lift up the head."*

The Book of Jasher

So, who was the Melchisedec in the first place? From here I will refer to a written work twice recommended by the Bible.

Joshua 10:13 *"And the sun stood still, and the moon stayed, until the people had avenged themselves upon their enemies.* ***Is not this written in the book of Jasher?"***

2 Samuel 1:18 *"(Also he bade them teach the children of Judah the use of the bow:* ***behold, it is written in the book of Jasher.)"***

The book of Jasher records the period of time from the creation to about the time of Joshua's death and is contemporary with Moses. The book of Jasher is not included in our Canon, and should not be. But as evidenced by Joshua 10:13 and 2 Samuel 1:18 some of the writings in extra-Biblical works can be inspired. If these verses were not inspired, they wouldn't be in our Bible. But that doesn't mean that everything in the book of Jasher is inspired by God. Likewise, the writing of Jude in the New Testament quotes one verse from the book of Enoch. While that one verse is definitely inspired by God, there is nothing to indicate that God intended for the book of Enoch to be included in our Canon. Even Enoch, in his book, says that God would write books out of which He would judge man, but his book would not be one of them. But, these extra-Biblical books do provide valuable historical and contextual insight into the Holy Scriptures.

Jasher 16:11-12 "And Adonizedek king of Jerusalem, **the same was Shem,** went out with his men to meet Abram and his people, with bread and wine, and they remained together in the valley of Melech. ^{12} And Adonizedek blessed Abram, and Abram gave him a tenth from all that he had brought from the spoil of his enemies, for Adonizedek was a priest before God." * **(Emphasis is mine. DP)**

Shem, the son of Noah, was the Melchisedec who received Abraham's tenth of the spoils. If we apply the same standards to interpret the proper title of "Adonizedek" that we used to interpret the proper title of "Melchisedec," then we rend from "Adonizedek" the interpretation of "Lord of Righteousness". Because he is the King of Jerusalem, he is also "King of Peace." Again, with all reverence, I would translate the name to mean "The Righteous Lord of Peace," knowing that his office represents the ministry of the Lord Jesus Christ.

I really <u>don't think</u> there is any significance to the fact that Shem was the Melchisedec to whom Abraham paid tithes. If there was significance, the Bible would have pronounced it. Besides, since it was a father/son order, it is likely that Noah also would have been a Melchisedec. I am not all that interested in knowing which Patriarchs filled the office, but if you are, then I am sure there are Hebrew extra-Biblical texts that will aid your search. What <u>does interest</u> me **is the name used in Jasher, "<u>Adonizedek king of Jerusalem</u>," because that name does appear in the Bible**, and with it significance.

If I have done my job, you will conclude from the "Transition" section of this book, that God never puts two heads on one body. The examples that I gave were that Moses died before Joshua assumed the leadership of Israel in the wilderness, Elijah was taken up and dropped his mantle before Elisha began his ministry, and John the Baptist was beheaded about the time Jesus began His ministry. **Luke 16:16** *"The law and the prophets were until John:.."* And I also wrote that the same thing happened to the Melchisedec when God established the Law of Moses. Here is the account from the Bible:

Joshua 10:1-8 *"Now it came to pass, when **Adoni-zedek king of Jerusalem** had heard how Joshua had taken Ai, and had utterly destroyed it; as he had done to Jericho and her king, so he had done to Ai and her king; and how the inhabitants of Gibeon had made peace with Israel, and were among them; [2] That they feared greatly, because Gibeon was a great city, as one of the royal cities, and because it was greater than Ai, and all the men thereof were mighty. [3] Wherefore **Adoni-zedek king of Jerusalem** sent unto Hoham king of Hebron, and unto Piram king of Jarmuth, and unto Japhia king of Lachish, and unto Debir king of Eglon, saying, [4] Come up unto me, and help me, that we may smite Gibeon: for it hath made peace with Joshua and with the children of Israel. [5] Therefore the five kings of the Amorites, the king of Jerusalem, the king of Hebron, the king of Jarmuth, the king of Lachish, the king of Eglon, gathered themselves together, and went up, they and all their hosts, and encamped before Gibeon, and made war against it. [6] And the men of Gibeon sent unto Joshua to the camp to Gilgal, saying, Slack not thy hand from thy servants;*

come up to us quickly, and save us, and help us: for all the kings of the Amorites that dwell in the mountains are gathered together against us. [7] *So Joshua ascended from Gilgal, he, and all the people of war with him, and all the mighty men of valour.* [8] **And the LORD said unto Joshua, Fear them not: for I have delivered them into thine hand; there shall not a man of them stand before thee."**

Joshua 10:16-18 *"But these five kings fled, and hid themselves in a cave at Makkedah.* [17] *And it was told Joshua, saying, The five kings are found hid in a cave at Makkedah.* [18] *And Joshua said, Roll great stones upon the mouth of the cave, and set men by it for to keep them:"*

Joshua 10:26 *"And afterward Joshua smote them, and slew them, and hanged them on five trees: and they were hanging upon the trees until the evening."*

Both of the names "Melchisedec" and "Adonizedek" are considered to be Amorite names. But the Septuagint doesn't use the word "Amorite" in Joshua 10. The Septuagint calls these peoples "Jebusites." The Jebusites were the pre-inhabitants of the City of David, which is a suburb or district of Jerusalem. Being the King of Jerusalem indicates that the Adonizedek/Melchisedec held the preeminent place among the five "kings."

Never mind though that all human ministries, except that of Jesus Christ, are subject to corruption (Melchisedec was a man). The bigger picture here is that God was moving a people out of a biune condition and into a dichotomous condition. The combined ministry of a king/priest would not be suitable under the Law of Moses. Because the people were now going to be divided within themselves by the Law of Moses, God separated the Kingdom from the Priesthood in the Law of Moses, thus ending the ministry of Melchisedec at that time. The incident is recorded in the Holy Scriptures.

Again I would state that a priest governs the inner man, and a king governs the outer man. In hindsight, we can appreciate this division of authority, knowing the corruption that would entangle both the Levitical priesthood and the kingdom of Israel during this period of time. God has and does still use one power or authority to hold another in check. We have also seen the atrocities that have occurred when this principal was violated or blurred during the European middle ages. Therefore, God instituted the separation of Church and state, and not man. This is in contrast to the powers that be today, that seek to consolidate or consummate their authority within an unholy union. Consider it this way: If the state ever endorses a religion, will it be your religion? Will the state conform to your views?

The realization is that the return to the Melek Tsedek administration of authority is confirmed in this fact: man will not always be a divided being! God is restoring man to his original state of being, which is a Trinity. When this happens, there will also come a legitimate union between Church and State. It will be called, "His Kingdom." This is the significance of the promise: *"Thou art a priest for ever after the order of Melchisedec."*

1 Corinthians 15:49-52 *"And as we have borne the image of the earthy, we shall also bear the image of the heavenly. [50] Now this I say, brethren, that flesh and blood cannot inherit the kingdom of God; neither doth corruption inherit incorruption. [51] Behold, I shew you a mystery; We shall not all sleep, but* ***we shall all be changed,*** *[52] In a moment, in the twinkling of an eye, at the last trump: for the trumpet shall sound, and the dead shall be raised incorruptible, and* ***we shall be changed.***"

1 John 3:2 *"Beloved, now are we the sons of God, and it doth not yet appear* ***what we shall be***: *but we know that, when he shall appear,* ***we shall be like him***; *for we shall see him as he is."*

Psalms 17:15 *"As for me, I will behold thy face in righteousness: I shall be satisfied,* ***when I awake, with thy likeness."***

Psalms 71:20 *"Thou, which hast shewed me great and sore troubles,* ***shalt quicken me again, and shalt bring me up again from the depths of the earth."***

Job 14:14 *"If a man die, shall he live again? all the days of my appointed time will I wait,* ***till my change come."***

Philippians 3:21 ***"Who shall change our vile body, that it may be fashioned like unto his glorious body,*** *according to the working whereby he is able even to subdue all things unto himself."*

Colossians 3:4 *"When Christ, who is our life, shall appear,* ***then shall ye also appear with him in glory."***

1 Corinthians 15:42-44 *"So also is the resurrection of the dead. It is sown in corruption;* ***it is raised in incorruption***: *[43] It is sown in dishonour;* ***it is raised in glory***: *it is sown in weakness;* ***it is raised in power***: *[44] It is sown a natural body;* ***it is raised a spiritual body***. *There is a natural body, and there is a spiritual body."*

Romans 8:11 *"But if the Spirit of him that raised up Jesus from the dead dwell in you,* ***he that raised up Christ from the dead shall also quicken your mortal bodies by his Spirit that dwelleth in you."***

1 Corinthians 15:52 *In a moment, in the twinkling of an eye, at the last trump: for the trumpet shall sound, and the dead shall be raised incorruptible, and **we shall be changed**."*

We shall be changed into a Trinity! When we get our glorified body and bear His image once more, and when death has no more power over us, then we will be like Him. When there is unity within our being, then no covenant will be required. It is covenant that brings two that oppose each other into harmony with each other. This is why there is no covenant initiating the first and last dispensation. When our bodies are changed like unto His glorious body, we will not be antagonistic or contrary to our Loving Creator any more. The last or seventh dispensation begins when the last trump sounds, and the dead in Christ are raised, and we are changed.

1 Thessalonians 4:16-18 *"For the Lord himself shall descend from heaven with a shout, with the voice of the archangel, and with the trump of God: and the dead in Christ shall rise first: [17] Then we which are alive and remain shall be caught up together with them in the clouds, to meet the Lord in the air: and so shall we ever be with the Lord. [18] Wherefore comfort one another with these words."*

Revelation 19:7-9 *"Let us be glad and rejoice, and give honour to him: for the marriage of the Lamb is come, and his wife hath made herself ready. [8] And to her was granted that she should be arrayed in fine linen, clean and white: for the fine linen is the righteousness of saints. [9] And he saith unto me, Write, Blessed are they which are called unto the marriage supper of the Lamb. And he saith unto me, These are the true sayings of God."*

Soon we will be changed. Soon we will be lifted up. Soon we will be ushered into His presence without the hindrance of sinful flesh. But today the restoration of man to bear the image of God is not yet fully complete. Today we are subject to all human frailty. Today we bear ridicule and contempt and scorn, mockery, rejection, anger, hatred and abuse - even danger to our lives. But God Himself is the proper perspective for this, our current existence.

Rom 8:18-23 *"For I reckon that the sufferings of this present time are not worthy to be compared with the glory which shall be revealed in us. [19] For the earnest expectation of the creature waiteth for the manifestation of the sons of God. [20] For the creature was made subject to vanity, not willingly, but by reason of him who hath subjected the same in hope, [21] Because the creature itself also shall be delivered from the bondage of corruption into the glorious liberty of the children of God. [22] **For we know that the whole creation groaneth and***

travaileth in pain together until now. [23] *And not only they, but ourselves also, which have the firstfruits of the Spirit, even we ourselves groan within ourselves, waiting for the adoption, to wit, the redemption of our body."*

The groaning of the creation is articulated by humanity's false prophets through the knowledge of good and evil into the false expectation and false narrative that the world promotes to its own demise. But, the same groaning of the creation prompts the child of Faith, through the Spirit of Truth, to look up, knowing that our redemption draweth nigh.

The Lord hath sworn and will not repent!

So, we look at that promise of God through the man that represents the Melek Tsedek; King David is that representation.

2 Samuel 7:12-13 *"And when thy days be fulfilled, and thou shalt sleep with thy fathers, I will set up thy seed after thee, which shall proceed out of thy bowels, and I will establish his kingdom.* [13] ***He shall build an house for my name, and I will stablish the throne of his kingdom for ever."***

This is the covenant God made with David. It is mentioned as such in Psalm 89:3-4. The promise of God came to David, as David purposed in his heart to build God a dwelling place or "house." Psalm 132 conveys the gratitude and reverence for God that caused David to purpose himself to build God "an habitation." (Since the New Testament is replete with teaching on the essence of the tabernacle or temple, I will forego the usual myriad of references and focus on a couple of inter-related thoughts: A tabernacle is likened to a garment in 2 Corinthians 5:1-4; and virtue always flows from the greater to the lesser, from Hebrews 7:7 and Hebrews 3:3.)

Maybe I won't forego the references; the more I think about it, the more I laugh. Let me sum it up this way: it's a small god that dwells in a small house. King Solomon said the heaven and heaven of heavens could not contain our God. King Solomon was the one everybody credits with building God's Temple in Jerusalem. But King Solomon said it this way, *"But will God indeed dwell on the earth? behold, the heaven and heaven of heavens cannot contain thee; how much less this house that I have builded?"* (**1 Kings 8:27**). Perhaps Solomon had tapped into that supernatural wisdom that God gave him, perhaps. Or, perhaps Solomon had been reading the covenant that God made with Abraham in **Genesis 15:5**: *"And he brought him forth abroad, and said, Look now toward heaven, and tell the stars, if thou be able to number them: and he said unto him, So shall thy seed be."* **Hebrews 3:6** *"But Christ as a son over his own house; **whose house are we, if we...**"*

Back to David. Heretofore, the House of God was the Tabernacle of Moses. It was characterized as the three-part dwelling place of God. It had an outer court, an inner court (called the Holy Place), and a most holy place (called the Holy of Holies). A veil hung in the inner court to "divide" the Holy Place from the Holy of Holies. The Holy of Holies contained the Ark of the Covenant, which was the Throne of God upon the earth. (See Exodus 26:33-34.) This divided tabernacle was an accurate representation of the then-divided being of man. The outer court corresponds to the flesh, the inner court corresponds to the soul, and the most holy place corresponds to the Spirit. Each of these three places within the tabernacle had rituals and services and ordinances that teach us about the natures of the flesh, soul, and Spirit. The responsibility of all aspects of this temple service was delegated to the Levitical Priesthood.

Prior to the covenant that God made with David, the Ark of the Covenant had been at the house of Obed-edom (servant of Edom). When King David realized that it was time to bring the Ark of the Covenant to the City of David, he did so with much gladness and worship. **2 Samuel 6:14** *"And David danced before the LORD with all his might; and David was girded with a linen ephod."*

The linen ephod was a priestly garment. There are at least two other instances of David asking for an ephod and then enquiring of the Lord. (See 1 Samuel 23:6-10, 30:7-8.) (See "The Instruments of Intercession" in the "Appendices" section of this book.)

2 Samuel 6:17 *"And they brought in the ark of the LORD, and set it in his place, **in the midst of the tabernacle that David had pitched for it: and David offered burnt offerings and peace offerings before the LORD.**"*

As I have previously mentioned, there are several priestly aspects to King David's ministry. Here we plainly see King David, of the Tribe of Judah, operating freely in a capacity that the Law of Moses had designated to the Levitical Priesthood. But God went further to validate King David's priestly ministry in **Amos 9:11**: *"**In that day will I raise up the tabernacle of David** that is fallen, and close up the breaches thereof; and I will raise up his ruins, and I will build it as in the days of old:"* This prophecy was spoken during the time of Solomon's Temple and has the appearance that God is looking backwards, but He is not.

Of all the temples or tabernacles found in Scripture, the Tabernacle of David is significant in two ways:

1. The Tabernacle of David is the only tabernacle that God said He would raise. It represents specifically the temple of the Lord Jesus' Body, which He raised after the crucifixion. Therefore, it also

represents the **"Body of Christ,"** as in the Church. **2 Corinthians 11:2** *"For I am jealous over you with godly jealousy: **for I have espoused you to one husband**, that I may present you as a chaste virgin to Christ."*

2.   The Tabernacle of David is the only tabernacle in Scripture-past constructed without a veil. In David's tabernacle there was no separation between the Holy Place and the Most Holy Place. This signifies there will be a time when there is no separation between God and man. It further signifies a time when there will be no division within man. God is looking forward. **Revelation 21: 1-5** *"And I saw a new heaven and a new earth: for the first heaven and the first earth were passed away; and there was no more sea. ² And I John saw the holy city, new Jerusalem, coming down from God out of heaven, prepared as a bride adorned for her husband. ³ And I heard a great voice out of heaven saying, **Behold, the tabernacle of God is with men, and he will dwell with them, and they shall be his people, and God himself shall be with them, and be their God.** ⁴ And God shall wipe away all tears from their eyes; and there shall be no more death, neither sorrow, nor crying, neither shall there be any more pain: for the former things are passed away. ⁵ And he that sat upon the throne said, Behold, I make all things new. And he said unto me, Write: for these words are true and faithful."*

2 Corinthians 5:1-4 *"For we know that if our earthly house of this tabernacle were dissolved, we have a building of God, an house not made with hands, eternal in the heavens. ² For in this we groan, earnestly desiring to be clothed upon with our house which is from heaven: ³ If so be that being clothed we shall not be found naked. ⁴ For we that are in this tabernacle do groan, being burdened: not for that we would be unclothed, but clothed upon, that mortality might be swallowed up of life."*

One greater than David would have to build God's dwelling place. But in His love for David, God allowed David to build a representation of things that presently are, and things that are soon to come. The representations of the Tabernacle of David are fulfilled in the ministry of Jesus Christ, which allows us free access into the Throne Room of our Heavenly Father. **Hebrews 4:16** *"Let us therefore come **boldly unto the throne of grace**, that we may obtain mercy, and find grace to help in time of need."* We don't bypass the Cross as we enter into the Kingdom of God. But, we don't hang out there either. If you were compelled to visit a friend or relative, would you make the trip, and then expect them to stand in their doorway to fellowship with you?

Hebrews 10:19-24 *"Having therefore, brethren, **boldness to enter into the holiest by the blood of Jesus,** ²⁰ By a new and living way, which he hath consecrated for us, through the veil, that is to say, his flesh; ²¹ And having an high priest over the house of God; ²² **Let us draw near** with a true heart in full assurance of faith, having our hearts sprinkled from an evil conscience, and our bodies washed with pure water. ²³ Let us hold fast the profession of our faith without wavering; (for he is faithful that promised;) ²⁴ And let us consider one another to provoke unto love and to good works:"* The "Holiest" (Holy of Holies/Most Holy Place) is God's Throne Room. As Christians, we alone are privileged to have open access to our Heavenly Father, and when we delight ourselves in Him, He is delighted to answer our prayers. (See Psalms 37:4.)

Witnessed in the Gospels

When I read the four Gospels of Jesus Christ in Scripture, I understand that they are written from three different perspectives. Matthew and John write separately, yet distinctly consistent within Jewish train of thought, reasoning, and expectation. Mark's writing reflects a Roman influence, posture, and idealism. Luke's writing reflects a Greek influence, posture, and idealism.

These three perspectives give us the four aspects of Jesus' ministry at His first coming. Matthew's Gospel shows the <u>**kingly**</u> aspects of Jesus' ministry. Mark's Gospel shows the <u>**servant's**</u> aspects of Jesus' ministry. Luke's Gospel shows Jesus' ministry as the <u>**perfect**</u> man. John's Gospel shows the <u>**priestly**</u> aspects of Jesus' ministry.

Through Matthew and John the Jewish perspective is given a dual and divided agency. This signifies, <u>presently,</u> a divided ministry for a divided people; <u>that is a trichotomy.</u> The idea of Jesus as a combined king/priest is witnessed by the fact that as the Apostle John wrote of the priestly aspects of Jesus at His first coming, he also writes of the kingly aspects of Jesus at His second coming; this is in the book that I call the Fifth Gospel, aka the Book of Revelation. This signifies a <u>future fulfillment</u> of a unified ministry for a unified people; <u>that is a trinity.</u>

This is the ministry of the Melek Tsedek. **Zechariah 6:13** *"Even he shall build the temple of the LORD; and he shall bear the glory, and shall sit and rule upon his throne; and he shall be a priest upon his throne:.."* This will be the legitimate union of Church and State. Only an usurper would attempt to accomplish this in hateful imitation of Jesus Christ!

Summary

David went into the "house of God" and ate the showbread that was only lawful for the priests. (See Matthew 12:3-4.) David wore the garment of a priest and made inquiry to the Lord. David established a tabernacle for the Lord and had communion with the Lord without a veil of separation. David was one of few to write concerning the Melek Tsedek.

One last aspect of David's ministry confirms him as a representation of the Melek Tsedek. King David was a man of war! **Psalms 110:1-7** *"The LORD said unto my Lord, Sit thou at my right hand, until I make thine enemies thy footstool. [2] The LORD shall send the rod of thy strength out of Zion: rule thou in the midst of thine enemies. [3] Thy people shall be willing in the day of thy power, in the beauties of holiness from the womb of the morning: <u>thou hast the dew of thy youth.</u> [4] The LORD hath sworn, and will not repent, Thou art a priest for ever after the order of Melchizedek. [5] **The Lord at thy right hand shall strike through kings in the day of his wrath. [6] He shall judge among the heathen, he shall fill the places with the dead bodies; he shall wound the heads over many countries.** [7] He shall drink of the brook in the way: therefore shall he lift up the head."*

In Matthew 22:43, Jesus confirms David as the author of Psalm 110. David was introduced as a warrior when he slew Goliath in the valley between the army of King Saul and the Philistines. He quickly earned the respect of the people and they sang of him, "Saul hath slain his thousands, and David his ten thousands." <u>The dew is a representation of the "anointing."</u> The "dew of thy youth" is a reference to David the shepherd.

As David Was So Shall Jesus Be

Revelation 6:15-17 *"And the kings of the earth, and the great men, and the rich men, and the chief captains, and the mighty men, and every bondman, and every free man, hid themselves in the dens and in the rocks of the mountains; [16] And said to the mountains and rocks, Fall on us, and hide us from the face of him that sitteth on the throne, and **from the wrath of the Lamb: [17] For the great day of his wrath is come; and who shall be able to stand?"***

Revelation 19:11-21 *"And I saw heaven opened, and behold a white horse; and he that sat upon him was called Faithful and True, and in righteousness he doth judge and make war. [12] His eyes were as a flame of fire, and on his head were many crowns; and he had a name written, that no man knew, but he himself. [13] And he was clothed with a vesture dipped in blood: and his name is called The Word of God. [14] And the armies which were in heaven followed him* *upon white horses, clothed in fine linen, white and clean.* ^{15} *And out of his mouth goeth a sharp sword, that with it he should smite the nations: and he shall rule them with a rod of iron: and he treadeth the winepress of the fierceness and wrath of Almighty God.* ^{16} *And he hath on his vesture and on his thigh a name written, KING OF KINGS, AND LORD OF LORDS.* ^{17} *And I saw an angel standing in the sun; and he cried with a loud voice, saying to all the fowls that fly in the midst of heaven, Come and gather yourselves together unto the supper of the great God;* ^{18} *That ye may eat the flesh of kings, and the flesh of captains, and the flesh of mighty men, and the flesh of horses, and of them that sit on them, and the flesh of all men, both free and bond, both small and great.* ^{19} *And I saw the beast, and the kings of the earth, and their armies, gathered together to make war against him that sat on the horse, and against his army.* ^{20} *And the beast was taken, and with him the false prophet that wrought miracles before him, with which he deceived them that had received the mark of the beast, and them that worshipped his image. These both were cast alive into a lake of fire burning with brimstone.* ^{21} *And the remnant were slain with the sword of him that sat upon the horse, which sword proceeded out of his mouth: and all the fowls were filled with their flesh."*

There are many things in Scripture that I don't know. But these I do know. Jesus is alive. He is the Melek Tsedek. He is coming again to claim His Throne. He came the first time as a lamb prepared for the slaughter. He will come the second time as the Lion of the Tribe of Judah!

Expectation of Growth

The writer of Hebrews says in **Hebrews 5:10-14**: *"Called of God an high priest after the order of Melchisedec.* ^{11} *Of whom we have many things to say, and hard to be uttered, seeing ye are dull of hearing.* ^{12} *For when for the time ye ought to be teachers, ye have need that one teach you again which be the first principles of the oracles of God; and are become such as have need of milk, and not of strong meat.* ^{13} *For every one that useth milk is unskilful in the word of righteousness: for he is a babe.* ^{14} *But strong meat belongeth to them that are of full age, even those who by reason of use have their senses exercised to discern both good and evil."*

The method of God to teach and to grow His children is the same for Christians as it is for the world and for Israel. He gives us what we need when we need it. I think it would be unlikely that an infant who refuses his milk would grow or even live long enough to eat his meat. From the commands to "love the Lord our God" and to "love one another as He has loved us," we learn to put one foot in front of the other, and we build line upon line and precept upon precept. But, there is and should be an expectation of maturity from this process, both in the individual and in the dispensational.

Ephesians 4:14-24 *"That we henceforth be no more children, tossed to and fro, and carried about with every wind of doctrine, by the sleight of men, and cunning craftiness, whereby they lie in wait to deceive; [15] But speaking the truth in love, may grow up into him in all things, which is the head, even Christ: [16] From whom the whole body fitly joined together and compacted by that which every joint supplieth, according to the effectual working in the measure of every part, maketh increase of the body unto the edifying of itself in love. [17] This I say therefore, and testify in the Lord, that ye henceforth walk not as other Gentiles walk, in the vanity of their mind, [18] Having the understanding darkened, being alienated from the life of God through the ignorance that is in them, because of the blindness of their heart: [19] Who being past feeling have given themselves over unto lasciviousness, to work all uncleanness with greediness. [20] But ye have not so learned Christ; [21] If so be that ye have heard him, and have been taught by him, as the truth is in Jesus: [22] That ye put off concerning the former conversation the old man, which is corrupt according to the deceitful lusts; [23] And be renewed in the spirit of your mind; [24]* **And that ye put on the new man, which after God is created in righteousness and true holiness.***"*

In the Apostle Paul's day, I can't imagine that the newly birthed Church would have needed the understanding that they were a trichotomy, or that they would become a trinity. Hence, in relation to the knowledge of Melchisedec, we have **Hebrews 5:12** *"...and are become such as have need of milk, and not of strong meat."* Today, however, the Church stands at the threshold of the Dispensation of the Kingdom; the age of trichotomy is at its end. God wants us to know that we have something better to look forward to than the "wretched men that we are!"

Today, Jesus extends His hands in mercy to offer an escape from the terrible judgment we will surely face without Him. Today is a good day to be saved.

Today, there are many divisions among scholars and students of prophecy concerning "tomorrow." If we knew "tomorrow," we could imitate prophetic events and thereby bring about much confusion. God the Father has reserved the knowledge of tomorrow within His own power. The blessing of prophecy is that it only points to our Loving Creator as the Sovereign God over time, space, matter, life, death, and all things created. (See Acts 1:7; Matthew 24:36; Luke 17:20.)

When I was new to Bible study, it bothered me that I didn't understand prophecy. As I prayed about it, the Lord responded to me that I didn't have to understand prophecy to be saved. I just had to trust in Him. After Jesus saved me from my sins, Jesus saved me from "tomorrow." Today I am at peace knowing that He holds my tomorrow(s). Nevertheless, I am admonished again to say, His coming is soon!

"Tell them I'm coming!" says the Lord.

Bibliography

* The Book of Jasher

The Researchers Library of Ancient Texts, Volume One, The Apocrypha, Includes the Books of Enoch, Jasher and Jubilees

Defender / Crane, Mo 65633 / Copyright 2011 Thomas Horn

Appendices

The Holy Spirit in Scripture

Represented by Wine

Genesis 14:18 *"And Melchizedek king of Salem brought forth bread and wine: and he was the priest of the most high God."* The Melek Tsedek ministering the bread and wine to Abraham is a picture of Jesus Christ ministering the Word and the Spirit to His faithful followers.

Acts 2:1-39 *"And when the day of Pentecost was fully come,..... others mocking said, These men are full of new wine...But Peter, standing up with the eleven, lifted up his voice, and said unto them,..... For these are not drunken as ye suppose, seeing it is but the third hour of the day. But this is that which was spoken by the prophet Joel;..."*

Ephesians 5:18 *"And be not drunk with wine, wherein is excess; but be filled with the Spirit;"*

John 2:7-11 *"Jesus saith unto them, Fill the waterpots with water. And they filled them up to the brim. [8] And he saith unto them, Draw out now, and bear unto the governor of the feast. And they bare it. [9] When the ruler of the feast had tasted the water that was made wine, and knew not whence it was: (but the servants which drew the water knew;) the governor of the feast called the bridegroom, [10] And saith unto him, Every man at the beginning doth set forth good wine; and when men have well drunk, then that which is worse: but thou hast kept the good wine until now. [11] This beginning of miracles did Jesus in Cana of Galilee, and **manifested forth his glory;** and his disciples believed on him."*

The first miracle of Jesus represents the transition of ministry from the Law to Grace; that is from the letter of the Law to the Holy Spirit operating within us. When we read of "His Glory" anywhere in Scripture, we should consider it a reference to God's Holy Ghost. **2 Corinthians 3:6-18** *"Who also hath made us able ministers of the new testament; not of the letter, but of the spirit: for the letter killeth, but the spirit giveth life. [7] But if the ministration of death, written and engraven in stones, was glorious, so that the children of Israel could not stedfastly behold the face of Moses for the glory of his countenance; which* *glory was to be done away: [8] How shall not the ministration of the spirit be rather glorious? [9] For if the ministration of condemnation be glory, much more doth the ministration of righteousness exceed in glory. [10] For even that which was made glorious had no glory in this respect, by reason of the glory that excelleth. [11] For if that which is done away was glorious, much more that which remaineth is glorious. [12] Seeing then that we have such hope, we use great plainness of speech: [13] And not as Moses, which put a vail over his face, that the children of Israel could not stedfastly look to the end of that which is abolished: [14] But their minds were blinded: for until this day remaineth the same vail untaken away in the reading of the old testament; which vail is done away in Christ. [15] But even unto this day, when Moses is read, the vail is upon their heart. [16] Nevertheless when it shall turn to the Lord, the vail shall be taken away. [17] Now the Lord is that Spirit: and where the Spirit of the Lord is, there is liberty. [18]* **But we all, with open face beholding as in a glass the glory of the Lord, are changed into the same image from glory to glory, even as by the Spirit of the Lord."**

Represented In the Tabernacle of Moses

Hebrews 9:1-9 *"Then verily the first covenant had also ordinances of divine service, and a worldly sanctuary. [2] For there was a tabernacle made; the first, wherein was the candlestick, and the table, and the shewbread; which is called the sanctuary. [3] And after the second veil, the tabernacle which is called the Holiest of all; [4] Which had the golden censer, and the ark of the covenant overlaid round about with gold, wherein was the golden pot that had manna, and Aaron's rod that budded, and the tables of the covenant; [5] And over it the cherubims of glory shadowing the mercyseat; of which we cannot now speak particularly. [6] Now when these things were thus ordained, the priests went always into the first tabernacle, accomplishing the service of God. [7] But into the second went the high priest alone once every year, not without blood, which he offered for himself, and for the errors of the people: [8]* **The Holy Ghost this signifying, that the way into the holiest of all was not yet made manifest, while as the first tabernacle was yet standing:** *[9] Which was a figure for the time then present,.."* The tabernacle's outer court represents the <u>body</u>, the inner court represents the <u>soul</u>, and the Holy of Holies represents the <u>Holy Spirit</u>. Thus, man could not enter the Spirit while operating under the Old Covenant.

Represented by Lazarus and Eliezer

The name "Lazarus" is the Greek rendering of the Hebrew name "Eliezer," and it means "the helper of God." Both Eliezer in the Old Testament and Lazarus in the New Testament portray a role in Scripture of the Holy Ghost. From the Old Testament, He is the servant of "Father" Abraham which was entrusted with securing a bride for The Son. In the New Testament, He is brother to Mary and Martha. The name "Mary" means "rebellion" and the name "Martha" means "death." The story of Mary and Martha living with their brother, Lazarus, represents the Holy Spirit's presence in the earth with man. But, He was found to have been dead four days at Christ's coming. The resurrection of Lazarus on the fourth day represents the restoration of the Holy Spirit at the end of the fourth millennium; specifically, on the Day of Pentecost. The Holy Ghost had been dead to the world since the fall of Adam. The statement by Martha, *"Lord, by this time he stinketh: for he hath been dead four days."* accurately portrays how the world feels about God's Holy Ghost. Looking at the event through the lens of allegory, it must be the epitome of inversion for "death" to say that "life" stinks. When my son was about four years old, he told me once that I needed to answer him by saying, "Yes sir!" I laughed and hugged him when I responded to him by saying, "No son. It doesn't work that way." **John 11:40** *"Jesus saith unto her, Said I not unto thee, that, if thou wouldest believe, thou shouldest see the **glory of God**?"* **John 11:43** *"...Lazarus, come forth."*

Represented by Nehemiah

The name "Nehemiah" means "the consolation of Yah." As the counselor/consoler/comforter, Nehemiah shouldered the responsibility for the rebuilding of the wall of Jerusalem, as well as re-establishing the proper conduct and way of life for the people of God returning from Babylonian captivity. Nehemiah's credits are too numerous and merits too great to do justice to in an introductory study on the Holy Spirit in Scripture. However, one thought arises to summarize his role as a picture of the Holy Spirit. **Psalm 127:1-2** *"Except the LORD build the house, they labour in vain that build it: except the LORD keep the city, the watchman waketh but in vain. ² It is vain for you to rise up early, to sit up late, to eat the bread of sorrows: for so he giveth his beloved sleep."* Trusting in God's Holy Spirit to accomplish the plans of the Father will keep your obedience-oriented relationship with God from falling into a results-oriented relationship. God is not impressed with what we can do for Him; but rather is glorified in what He does through us. (See Galatians 2:20.)

Represented by the Dove

Matthew 3:16-17 *"And Jesus, when he was baptized, went up straightway out of the water: and, lo, the heavens were opened unto him, and he saw the Spirit of God descending like a dove, and lighting upon him:* [17] *And lo a voice from heaven, saying, This is my beloved Son, in whom I am well pleased."* In this picture of the Trinity of God, the Holy Spirit is represented by the dove. Doves are clean animals by the Law of Moses. Doves are gentile and committed to their mate for life. Birds of the Bible typically represent spirits. (See Revelation 18:2.)

Represented by the Dew

Psalm 133:1-3 *"Behold, how good and how pleasant it is for brethren to dwell together in unity!* [2] *It is like the precious ointment upon the head, that ran down upon the beard, even Aaron's beard: that went down to the skirts of his garments;* [3] *As the dew of Hermon, and as the dew that descended upon the mountains of Zion: for there the LORD commanded the blessing, even life for evermore."* In Psalms 133 the anointing oil is likened to the "dew." As a fleeting image of the Holy Spirit, the dew is not mentioned in the New Testament....unless, it is what Jesus was referring to when He said in **Matthew 6:28-30**: *"And why take ye thought for raiment? Consider the lilies of the field, how they grow; they toil not, neither do they spin:* [29] *And yet I say unto you, That even Solomon in all his glory was not arrayed like one of these.* [30] *Wherefore, if God so clothe the grass of the field, which to day is, and to morrow is cast into the oven, shall he not much more clothe you, O ye of little faith?"*

Represented by the Rainbow

Genesis 9:12-17 *"And God said, This is the **token of the covenant** which I make between me and you and every living creature that is with you, for perpetual generations:* [13] *I do set my bow in the cloud, and it shall be for a **token of a covenant** between me and the earth.* [14] *And it shall come to pass, when I bring a cloud over the earth, that the bow shall be seen in the cloud:* [15] *And I will **remember my covenant**, which is between me and you and every living creature of all flesh; and the waters shall no more become a flood to destroy all flesh.* [16] *And the bow shall be in the cloud; and I will look upon it, that I may **remember** the everlasting **covenant** between God and every living creature of all flesh that is upon the earth.* [17] *And God said unto Noah, This is the **token of the covenant**, which I have established between me and all flesh that is upon the earth."*

The witness or memorial that God established as the token of the covenant with "all flesh" in Genesis 9 also bears witness to the "witness" of the Holy Ghost. **Hebrews 10:15** *"Whereof the Holy Ghost also is a **witness** to us: for after that he had said before,"* The Holy Ghost bears witness to the covenant that God made with "whosoever will" through Jesus Christ.

The physical characteristics of the rainbow reflect the seven-fold ministry of the Holy Spirit. The typical pattern or diagram for showing the colors of solar light involves three overlapping circles arranged in a design similar to a clover. Where any two colors meet or overlap, a new color is formed. Where the three colors meet in the center, the seventh color is formed. This is white or visible light. Only as solar light passes through water do we have the necessary means of seeing the colors of light separately. Thus, in the natural, or as babes, we are only able to know the Holy Spirit, but through the water of the Word (Ephesians 5:26) we are able to see the Seven Spirits of God. (See Revelation 3:1.) From the three that are one comes seven.

The Seven Spirits of God / The Seven Administrations of the Holy Spirit

1.	Spirit of Liberty	Ps 51:12; 2 Cor 3:17
2.	Spirit of Judgment and Burning	Isa 4:4
3.	Spirit of Wisdom	Isa 11:2
4.	Spirit of Grace and Supplications	Zec 12:10
5.	Spirit of Truth	John 14:17
6.	Spirit of Adoption	Rom 8:15
7.	Spirit of Prophecy	Rev 19:10

Sometimes the colors of the rainbow are hard to discern. The conventional model of the Seven Spirits of God being delineated in Isaiah 11:2 is incorrect. What Isaiah 11:2-3 gives us is the seven pillars of Wisdom from Proverbs 9:1. (See Ephesians 1:17-19; Colossians 1:9-11.) The "quick understanding" of Isaiah 11:3 is the Spirit of Revelation in Ephesians 1:17. Perhaps the text in Isaiah could have been translated as, "quickened understanding." While there are other uses of the word "spirit" (spirit of meekness, spirit of faith, etc.) in the Bible, this list reflects my best understanding of the seven-fold ministry of the Holy Spirit at this writing.

Represented by Wind, Air, and Breath

John 3:5-8 *"Jesus answered, Verily, verily, I say unto thee, Except a man be born of water and of the Spirit, he cannot enter into the kingdom of God. ⁶ That which is born of the flesh is flesh; and that which is born of the Spirit is spirit. ⁷ **Marvel not that I said unto thee, Ye must be born again. ⁸ The wind bloweth where it listeth, and thou hearest the sound thereof, but canst not tell whence it cometh, and whither it goeth: so is every one that is born of the Spirit.**"*

Acts 2:1-4 *"And when the day of Pentecost was fully come, they were all with one accord in one place. ² And suddenly there came a sound from heaven as of a **rushing mighty wind,** and it filled all the house where they were sitting. ³ And there appeared unto them cloven tongues like as of fire, and it sat upon each of them. ⁴ And they were all filled with the Holy Ghost, and began to speak with other tongues, as the Spirit gave them utterance."* The event in Acts 2 is the same event in **Genesis 2:7**: *"And the LORD God formed man of the dust of the ground, and breathed into his nostrils the breath of life; and man became a living soul."* In Genesis 2 God breathed life into the body of the first man Adam and in Acts 2 God breathed life into the body of the second man Adam. Jesus is the second man Adam; His body is the Church.

Represented by Fire

Isaiah 4:4 *"When the Lord shall have washed away the filth of the daughters of Zion, and shall have purged the blood of Jerusalem from the midst thereof by the **spirit of judgment, and by the spirit of burning.**"*

Acts 2:3-4 *"And there appeared unto them cloven tongues **like as of fire,** and it sat upon each of them. ⁴ And they were all filled with the Holy Ghost, and began to speak with other tongues, as the Spirit gave them utterance."*

Represented by Oil

Psalm 133:1-2 *"Behold, how good and how pleasant it is for brethren to dwell together in unity! ² It is like the precious ointment upon the head, that ran down upon the beard, even Aaron's beard: that went down to the skirts of his garments;"* (See Leviticus 21:10-12.)

Exodus 25:31,37 *"And thou shalt make a candlestick of pure gold: of beaten work shall the candlestick be made: his shaft, and his branches, his bowls, his knops, and his flowers, shall be of the same.37 And thou shalt make the seven lamps thereof: and they shall light the lamps thereof, that they may give light* *over against it."* Gold in Scripture represents Deity. The oil in the Seven-Branched Lamp represents the presence of the Holy Spirit. Gold, the number seven, oil, fire, and light all represent the presence of God in the Scriptures and are clustered within this seven-branched Menorah.

Many of the examples of the Holy Spirit found in the Scriptures come in clusters. For example, Acts 2 references wind and fire and Psalm 133 references both the dew and the oil. Both Acts 2 and Psalm 133 emphasize unity in the Body of Christ, which is also the theme of 1 Corinthians 12. This chapter outlines the proper context for the operation of the gifts of the Spirit. For example, the word "one" appears more times in 1 Corinthians 12 than in any other single chapter in the New Testament - fifteen in total.

Once God uses something to represent something else in Scripture - once the parallel has been drawn by God - then with diligence we search the Scriptures to see if God reveals more of the parallel in other Scriptures. We don't automatically assume that every mention of one will always equate to the other, but this type of search often reveals the essence of the thing or topic we are studying. As a challenge, grab your concordance, preferably "Strong's", look up the word "maid" or "maiden", then read each verse or verses listed from your Bible, and decide how many times God uses a maid to represent His "still, small voice."

The Instruments of Intercession

Some of the richest symbolism found anywhere in the Scriptures is found in the priestly service of the Tabernacle of Moses. And why not, for the service within the tabernacle represents the interaction between God and man, within man's being. Just as love was to govern everything within the Church beginning the New Testament period, the temple service was the governing consideration of the Levitical Priesthood during the Law of Moses. On this thought, it was necessary for man that God would be very detailed in His instructions for the Tabernacle of Moses and all of its service.

Exodus 28:15-30 *"And thou shalt make the breastplate of judgment with cunning work; after the work of the ephod thou shalt make it; of gold, of blue, and of purple, and of scarlet, and of fine twined linen, shalt thou make it. [16] Foursquare it shall be being doubled; a span shall be the length thereof, and a span shall be the breadth thereof. [17] And thou shalt set in it settings of stones, even four rows of stones: the first row shall be a sardius, a topaz, and a carbuncle: this shall be the first row. [18] And the second row shall be an emerald, a sapphire, and a diamond. [19] And the third row a ligure, an agate, and an* *amethyst. ²⁰ And the fourth row a beryl, and an onyx, and a jasper: they shall be set in gold in their inclosings. ²¹* **And the stones shall be with the names of the children of Israel, twelve, according to their names, like the engravings of a signet; every one with his name shall they be according to the twelve tribes.** *²² And thou shalt make upon the breastplate chains at the ends of wreathen work of pure gold. ²³ And thou shalt make upon the breastplate two rings of gold, and shalt put the two rings on the two ends of the breastplate. ²⁴ And thou shalt put the two wreathen chains of gold in the two rings which are on the ends of the breastplate. ²⁵ And the other two ends of the two wreathen chains thou shalt fasten in the two ouches, and put them on the shoulderpieces of the ephod before it. ²⁶ And thou shalt make two rings of gold, and thou shalt put them upon the two ends of the breastplate in the border thereof, which is in the side of the ephod inward. ²⁷ And two other rings of gold thou shalt make, and shalt put them on the two sides of the ephod underneath, toward the forepart thereof, over against the other coupling thereof, above the curious girdle of the ephod. ²⁸ And they shall bind the breastplate by the rings thereof unto the rings of the ephod with a lace of blue, that it may be above the curious girdle of the ephod, and that the breastplate be not loosed from the ephod. ²⁹ And Aaron shall bear the names of the children of Israel in the breastplate of judgment upon his heart, when he goeth in unto the holy place, for a memorial before the LORD continually. ³⁰* **And thou shalt put in the breastplate of judgment the Urim and the Thummim; and they shall be upon Aaron's heart,** *when he goeth in before the LORD: and Aaron shall bear the judgment of the children of Israel upon his heart before the LORD continually."*

This is the ephod that King David asked for and with which made inquiry. Within the Inner Court, or Holy Place, this ephod was an integral component in the priests' ability to communicate with God; there were four main components.

The seven-branched candlestick is itself a cluster of representations of the Holy Spirit. The candlestick was made of pure gold, which represents deity. The seven branches represent the Seven Spirits of God. It contained oil. The oil kept the fire burning in the lamps, which was the fire that came *"...out from before the LORD, and consumed upon the altar the burnt offering and the fat: which when all the people saw, they shouted, and fell on their faces."* (**Leviticus 9:24**). This is the first component.

The ephod bearing the breastplate of judgment which contained the Urim and Thummim (Lights and Perfections) together was the second component. As the priest, which was the third component, stood praying in the Inner Court, the light from the candlestick would be reflected by the jewels-set-in-gold back on to the candlestick and the Hebrew Aleph-Beth would literally spell out God's response to the priest's inquiries. The letters of the Hebrew Aleph-Beth were engraved, both, into the jewels worn over the priest's heart and upon the "mitre" which was worn on the forehead of the priest. The Urim and Thummim were the jewels-set-in-gold which had the names of the twelve tribes of Israel engraved into them. But there is a caveat; there is a missing letter.

The fourth component of the ensemble, although not named, is easily recognized by anyone who has ever prayed earnestly for someone they love, as "love." The placement of the names of the tribes of Israel upon the heart of the priest is almost a no-brainer. It's almost like fasting. Some people who think a lot (too much) like to classify the different fasts found in Scripture. They name this one and group these ones and compare those ones, assigning each a different significance. But what about the times when we were lost, before we knew God, when adversity came upon us or a loved one, when life and death hung in the balance, and we just didn't think about eating? What about some of those same circumstances that came upon us after we were saved, and somebody suggested we needed to eat, and it made us angry? (Consider King David, Hannah, and King Darius and their motives for fasting.)

Some of the things we read about in Scripture don't need symbolism or classification; they just are. They come from our being; they are recognized as innate to humanity. Jesus said *"for sinners also love..."* (**Luke 6:32-34**).

The picture of the priest in the Holy Place is a picture of a man operating in his soul as he interacts with the Holy Spirit and the Word of God. It shows us God's desire to fellowship with fallen/redeemed humanity. It shows us that God desires to answer our prayers in a way that we can understand. Consider **1 Corinthians 14:15**: *"What is it then? I will pray with the spirit, and I will pray with the understanding also:.."* When the Apostle Paul says, "I will pray with the spirit" he is inferring prayer in the **Most** Holy Place. When he says, "I will pray with the understanding also" he is inferring prayer in the Holy Place. The difference is our understanding. Our mind, will, and emotions constitute our soul; we understand with our mind.

While we have access today, into the Most Holy Place, or the Throne Room of God, we can't understand the things of the Spirit without revelation. To remedy this, the Apostle Paul says, "I will pray with the understanding *also*:". Today, as a "Royal Priesthood," we fulfill this ministry anytime we prayerfully seek God in His written Word as led by the Spirit. Reading our Bible is still the listening part of our prayers.

But, intercessory prayer allows us to approach the Throne of God on behalf of other people. When I pray for or about things in my own life, I have to contend with my own doubts, fears, misguided desires, confusions, regrets, erroneous beliefs, etc. But, when I pray for someone else, these competing voices lack standing; they just begin to fade into the distance. It allows me to hear God's still, small voice with a greater clarity as I bear the burdens of God's people in His presence. **Galatians 6:2** *"Bear ye one another's burdens, and so fulfil the law of Christ."*

Within my own circle of support, I regularly request, "I want some of you to pray with me, but I want most of you to pray for me." The preeminent role that Urim and Thummim played in the temple ministry suggests that God delights to see us bring the needs of others to His capability. The preeminent role that Urim and Thummim played in the temple ministry suggests that God delights to see His Bride set Her realm in order by seeking His specific intentions and instructions. We, the Church, you as an individual, have an open invitation to hear from God by applying ourselves to prayer and study of His Word. No great thing done in the flesh will ever garner merit in any eternal evaluation when compared to the simplest act of obedience accomplished by God's Holy Spirit through us.

The Missing Letters

The Hebrew alphabet is comprised of twenty-two letters. In many of the older alphabets the letters were often pictorial representations before they came to represent sounds and syllables. In the Hebrew Aleph-Beit many of those pictures represent a virtue or quality that the pictured object would posses. For example, the Hebrew word for "father" is "Ab." The Hebrew letter for the "A" was a picture of an ox, which conveyed the essence of "strength." The Hebrew letter "B" was a picture of a house. When combined the "Ab" is recognized as "the strength of the house" or the "father." Further combinations of letters would produce similar variations in the meaning of words. In Genesis 17:5, God changed Abram's name to Abraham by adding the "h" and the "a." With the "h" representing the "breath of God" and the "a" representing "strength" we would see that by virtue of the "strength of God's Breath" (Spirit) Abram went from being "father of a multitude" to Abraham and "father of a multitude of nations."

Certainly this brief explanation is an over-simplification of a method of communicating, or teaching of precepts, that God embedded within His Word. It is this author's assertion that Man did not achieve or accomplish, either written or spoken, language outside of God's Providence. But rather, language was imparted to man as part of the package of "God's Image." In Genesis 2:18-23, God interacts with Adam verbally as Adam exercised authority to assign designations to "every living creature" before Eve was formed from Adam. But, language also would not escape the corruption that befell humanity, and it was only a matter of time before God had to deal with that corruption. Genesis 11 implicates Adam's Divine gift of language as the enabling force behind the city and tower with the heavenly in its top, aka Babel.

The narrative within Genesis 11 indicates the people were working toward a means to interact with the evil spirits that God had recently disembodied at the Great Flood. The tower of Babel was to be a "high place" of idol worship. As for the language, when you read Genesis 11 from your Bible, compare verse 4 with verses 8-9. The themes within Genesis 11:1-9 are common language, unity of purpose, and a common name, to which, God "scattered." Beginning in Genesis 11:10 thru Genesis 12:2, the culmination of God's response to man's wayward attempt at producing an enlightened nation is to introduce the "generations" that would produce Abram and God's Promise to him. **Genesis 12:2** *"And I will **make of thee a great nation**, and I will bless thee, and **make thy name great**; and thou shalt be a blessing:"*

This is the nation of people that the Apostle Paul says in **Romans 3:2**: *"...**because that unto them were committed the oracles of God**."*. (See also Hebrews 5:11-14 and Acts 7:37-38.) **2 Timothy 3:15** *"And that from a child thou hast known the holy scriptures, which are able to make thee wise unto salvation through faith which is in Christ Jesus. [16] **All scripture is given by inspiration of God**, and is profitable for doctrine, for reproof, for correction, for instruction in righteousness: [17] That the man of God may be perfect, throughly furnished unto all good works."*

The Hebrew language of the Old Testament is either the original Divine Adamic language that was retained by Shem or it is a language that was imparted to Shem at the tower of Babel incident. In either case, the Hebrew language and its alphabet are Divinely Inspired. Over many centuries, critical analysis of the Hebrew language and alphabet used in the Torah and used by the Prophets has shown a consistency of application that exceeds human ingenuity and capabilities. The accuracy to which the essence of letters and their corresponding numbers is applied through words to events that would not occur for hundreds or thousands of years is mind boggling and can only be ascribed to an all-knowing, all-powerful, wonderful, and loving Creator who has put His signature on every building block of His creation.

Rather than trying to list numerous examples of God's unique signature found in Scripture, I will list several written works on the subject by various authors at the end of this appendix; and I am afraid that these together will not be able to "scratch the surface" on the subject.

Ultimately, it is the Word of God that defines itself. It is how God uses words and letters that assigns their virtue to them. (See 1 Corinthians 2:13.) For simplicity we will use Psalm 119 to determine the virtue of the letters in question. Psalm 119 is considered an "alphabetic" psalm. The twenty-two subheadings of the psalm are the twenty-two letters of the Hebrew alphabet. In many of the sub-divisions the text following the subheadings declares the virtue of the subheading. For ease of reference, I will use the spelling of the letters as found in the subheadings of Psalm 119.

The jewels that the priest wore on his heart as he ministered in the Holy Place were engraved with eighteen of the twenty-two letters of the Hebrew alphabet. The plate of pure gold that was worn on the front of the mitre (worn on the forehead) was engraved with eleven letters, but only added two more letters to the total. The missing letters from the priest's repertoire were the "Teth" and the "Tzaddi". The Teth was the ninth letter of the Hebrew alphabet and had a numeric value of nine. The Tzaddi was the eighteenth letter and had a numeric value of ninety. Already the correlation of the two letters is evident.

Psalm 119 verses 65-72 ascribe to the letter "Teth" the virtue of "objective good." Objective good is not the "good" that leads "every man to do what is right in his own eyes." (See Judges 21:25.) It is the "good" that God says is good. It is the "good" that He desires to impart to us through His Word, but will impart to us through His correction, if necessary. **Psalms 119:71** *"It is good for me that I have been afflicted; that I might learn thy statutes."*

Psalm 119 verses 137-144 ascribe to the letter "Tzaddi" the virtue of "righteousness." The word "right," in various forms, appears six times in the eight verses of this subdivision of the alphabetic psalm. **Psalms 119:137-138** *"Righteous art thou, O LORD, and upright are thy judgments. [138] Thy testimonies that thou hast commanded are righteous and very faithful."* **Psalms 119:144** *"The righteousness of thy testimonies is everlasting: give me understanding, and I shall live."*

On the surface, this aspect of the temple service implies that the Sons of Jacob were insufficient or incomplete in the virtues of God, hence, objective good and righteousness were not innate to them. This is an idea the Writer of Hebrews agrees with. **Hebrews 7:19** *"For the law made nothing perfect, but the bringing in of a better hope did; by the which we draw nigh unto God."* If we look beyond the surface, we find the hand of God producing, in the nation of Israel, the same virtues that they lacked on their own. For example, the solid gold plate that was worn on the front of the mitre of the Priest was called, in

Hebrew, the "**tzitz**." In Hebrew the spelling is, "tzaddi, jod, tzaddi." The Hebrew letter "jod" (yad, yod, or iota in the Greek) is represented by the "hand" in the early pictures of the letters. (See Psalm 119:73 under the subheading "Jod".) **The complete picture of the mitre on the forehead of the priest is that "righteousness, the hand of God, righteousness" produces or is the foundation of "HOLINESS TO THE LORD".** (See Exodus 28:36-38.) **Isaiah 41:10** *"Fear thou not; for I am with thee: be not dismayed; for I am thy God: I will strengthen thee; yea, I will help thee; yea, I will uphold thee with the **right hand of my righteousness.**"* It is no coincidence that Jesus sits at the right hand of the Father!

Studies into the deeper elements of God's Word are fascinating, at the least. They can be rewarding and full of revelation and insight. However, these studies should always point us to "the simplicity that is in Christ." When the Apostle John was sent to the Isle of Patmos, he encountered the Lord Jesus after the manner of the High Priest in the temple. John says, *"I was in the Spirit on the Lord's day, and heard behind me a great voice, as of a trumpet," "And I turned to see the voice that spake with me. And being turned, I saw seven golden candlesticks;* [13] *And in the midst of the seven candlesticks one like unto the Son of man, clothed with a garment down to the foot, and girt about the paps with a golden girdle." "Saying, I am Alpha and Omega, the first and the last:"* (**Revelation 1:10,12,11**). No doubt Jesus spoke to John in John's "mother tongue" of Hebrew, and not the Koine Greek of the day. (John writes from the priestly perspective.) The Aleph and Tav are the first and last letters of the Hebrew alphabet. Being super-imposed upon the seven-branched candlestick, after the manner of the Priest, Jesus (The Word of God) indicated there are no missing letters in Him. **We have the fullness of God's Person and revelation in Jesus Christ. He is the Right Hand of God's Righteousness.**

Recommended for Reading and Reference

Your Holy Bible / Nothing will ever benefit your person more than the intimate, prayerful reading of God's Word. As you apply the Scriptures personally, you will develop discernment of the voice of the Holy Ghost. For topical studies within God's Word, word for word translations are best. DP

The Temple: Its Ministry and Services, Updated Edition / By Alfred Edersheim / Copyright 1994 by Hendrickson Publishers, Inc. / PO Box 3473 Peabody, Massachusetts 01961-3473 / ISBN 978-1-56563-826-6

The Tabernacle of Moses / By Kevin J. Conner / Copyright 1976 by Kevin J. Conner / Published by City Bible Publishing, 9200 NE Fremont Portland, Oregon 97220 / ISBN 0-914936-93-X

The Mystery of the Menorah...and the Hebrew Alphabet / By J.R. Church and Gary Stearman / First Edition, 1993 / Copyright 1993 by Prophecy in the News, Inc. / Published by Prophecy Publications, PO Box 7000, Oklahoma City, OK. 73153 / ISBN 0-941241-13-0

Number in Scripture: Its Supernatural Design and Spiritual Significance / By E.W. Bullinger / Published in 1967 by Kregel Publications, a division of Kregel, Inc., 2450 Oak Industrial Dr. NE, Grand Rapids, Mi. 49505 / ISBN 978-0-8254-2047-4

Biblical Mathematics Keys to Scripture Numerics / By Dr. Ed F. Vallowe / Copyright 1998 by Dr. Ed F. Vallowe / Published by The Olive Press, PO Box 280008, Columbia, SC. 29228 / ISBN 0-937422-38-X

Cosmic Codes Hidden Messages From The Edge Of Eternity / By Dr. Chuck Missler / Copyright 1999 by Koinonia House Revised 2004 / Published by Koinonia House PO Box D, Coeur d' Alene, Id. 83816-0347 / ISBN 978-1-57821-255-2

The Companion Bible / The Authorized Version of 1611 (KJV) with the Structures and Critical, Explanatory, and Suggestive Notes and with 198 Appendixes / Originally Published in 1922 / Notes and appendixes by E.W. Bullinger / Published by Kregel Publications Grand Rapids, Mi. 49501

Wycliffe Bible Dictionary / Copyright 1975 by Moody Bible Institute of Chicago / Published by Hendrickson Publishers, Inc. PO Box 3473 Peabody, Massachusetts 01961-3473 / ISBN 1-56563-362-8

Smith's Bible Dictionary / Crusade Bible Publishers, Inc. / Mt. Juliet (Nashville), Tn. 37122 (No copyright is given in this edition. This is an older edition; which is preferred, as many of the entries have been altered in the newer editions. There are no SBN or ISBN numbers offered.)

Strong's Exhaustive Concordance of the Bible / By James Strong, S.T.D., LL.D / Hendrickson Publishers PO Box 3473 Peabody, MA 01961-3473 / ISBN 0-917006-01-1 / Or the Updated and Expanded Edition 978-1-59856-378-8

* Note: Any revelation or understanding or deeper meaning or deeper insight or doctrine or even a passing thought that contradicts the **plain text**

reading of the Holy Scriptures should be rejected. Even in good faith, and with the best intentions, men make mistakes.

The Problem With Some Existing Models of the Antichrist

Deuteronomy 19:15 *"One witness shall not rise up against a man for any iniquity, or for any sin, in any sin that he sinneth: at the mouth of two witnesses, or at the mouth of three witnesses, shall the matter be established."*

The principle of God that men use to make good faith determinations or to verify a matter is the "two or three witnesses" principle. In a world where deceit and treachery and confusion and all manner of maliciousness are so prevalent, it is a good principal to use to bear witness of the truth. It is a principle that God Himself has used in writing His Book. In my twenty short years of Bible study, I can't find a single idea, concept, doctrine, or legitimate theory that is found in only a single place in the Scripture. Legitimate doctrines will always be supported from more than one place in the Scriptures. The Scriptures bear witness of the Scriptures. In this manner, the Scriptures also define themselves. A single example of this, among many, is when we used Genesis 1:28, James 3:7, and Revelation 12:3,9 to show that Leviathan from Job 41 is not an earthly animal. **2 Peter 1:20** *"Knowing this first, that no prophecy of the scripture is of any private interpretation.* [21] *For the prophecy came not in old time by the will of man: but holy men of God spake as they were moved by the Holy Ghost."*

In the New Testament, Jesus reiterated and applied the two or three witnesses concept to inter-personal relationships. (See Matthew 18:16.) And, in Revelation 11:3-13 there is a ministry given to "two witnesses" to prophesy for one thousand, two hundred, and sixty days. The idea is that the testimony of the two witnesses will agree.

When an expositor focuses solely on an example of the Antichrist from a single Scriptural reference, often the prototype is carried too far. For example: King David is a prototype of Jesus Christ. But, we don't assume that just because King David sinned that Jesus also would commit sin. At some point, the representation by the prototype comes to an end and the prototype reverts to simply being itself. This concept applies to any representation in Scripture and not just representations of Jesus Christ or the Antichrist. Knowing where to draw the line in a representation is a matter of finding witness of the individual elements within other representations or within that which is represented.

If an expositor builds a model of the Antichrist from a single Scriptural reference, it doesn't necessarily mean that his/her ideas are wrong. But until every element within the model is supported or validated by a corroborating witness from the Scriptures, the model should be considered incomplete.

Thoughts on Divorce

Isn't it curious that two people, either madly in love or madly in heat, will run to the nearest **preacher** to "tie the knot" or "seal the deal". (There is an unseen force that creates in us a longing for legitimacy.) But those same two people, when it goes awry, will run headlong to the nearest **judge**. Isn't it telling that what began in love and good faith would end in legalistic fervor and tragedy. It doesn't have to be said that one or both participants in the covenant of marriage has moved into the realm of carnality. Sadly, it doesn't always take two to tango when we consider the nature of conflict within marriage. A person can be doing everything within them to be right, and to do right, and to get it right, and happily do it all in a right way and someone else, through vice or folly or some breach in character can come by, out of the blue, and mess it up. It takes two in agreement to be married. It only takes one to bring division.

As a child, I suffered through two very painful divorces. My father had been the beneficiary of two women, in succession, that loved him and would have followed him in his integrity, had he chosen to live that life. I will always remember, as a child, how my step-mother would eat food from my plate that I could not tolerate so my father would not whip me. His new family was my family and we loved each other as a family. But, ultimately it was my father's lust and depravity that would bring tumult and destruction to our house. In this I offer my condolences to any and all that have or will experience divorce.

Underlying the debates on divorce, i.e. are they allowed by God, are they forgivable, what are the effects on re-marriage, etc., is the question..."are covenants forever?" If you have read this book through, you understand that the covenant God cut at Mt. Sinai was temporary in nature, and that it had to relinquish authority over us when we came to Christ. Furthermore, each successive dispensation, from the Fall of Adam, was governed by a covenant that replaced the one prior to it. It is only in a perfect world we could say that covenants last forever...but then, in a perfect world we wouldn't need covenants in the first place. By virtue of creation, Eve was Adam's wife and not by covenant. Covenants are here **because we are fallen.**

The Difference in Divorce and Putting Away

In western simplicity, we are often taught these two terms, from the Scriptures, have the same meaning. In reality, the two can have the same essence, but putting away retains the authority of covenant and divorce dissolves the authority of the covenant. Consider **Matthew 19:7**: *"They say unto him, Why did Moses then command to give a writing of divorcement, **and to put her away?**"* The "and" is insignificant until we pair it with **Isaiah 50:1**: *"Thus saith the LORD, **Where is the bill of your mother's divorcement,** whom I **have** put away? or which of my creditors is it to whom I have sold you? Behold, for your iniquities have ye sold yourselves, and <u>for your transgressions is your mother put away."</u>* It is the Lord that draws the distinction between divorce and putting away. In addition to Isaiah 50:1, an example of putting away without divorce is **2 Samuel 20:3**: *"And David came to his house at Jerusalem; and the king took the ten women his concubines, whom he had left to keep the house, and put them in ward, and fed them, but went not in unto them. So they were shut up unto the day of their death, living in widowhood."*

Since it is Moses that set the standard, let's look at what he said. **Deuteronomy 24:1** *"When a man hath taken a wife, and married her, and it come to pass that she find no favour in his eyes, because he hath found some uncleanness in her: then let him write her a bill of divorcement, and give it in her hand, and send her out of his house. [2] **And when she is departed out of his house, she may go and be another man's wife.** [3] And if the latter husband hate her, and write her a bill of divorcement, and giveth it in her hand, and sendeth her out of his house; or if the latter husband die, which took her to be his wife; [4] Her former husband, which sent her away, **may not take her again to be his wife,** after that she is defiled; <u>for that is abomination before the LORD</u>: and thou shalt not cause the land to sin, which the LORD thy God giveth thee for an inheritance."*

1. In the first emphasized verse, **God through Moses established divorce for the point of re-marriage.** It's like God is saying if Moses finds too much fault in you, then you can marry My Son.

2. In the second emphasized verse, **once you have left Moses you cannot go back.** It is adultery without fornication to try and turn from Christ back to Moses. For people who try, the law they turn to will ultimately reject them.

The essence of divorce and putting away is established in the Law of Moses. Since the Covenant of Christ is independent of Moses, we may return to Christ and be renewed from our transgressions. This is the application, in the macro, of **1 Corinthians 7:10-11**: *"And unto the married I command, yet not I, but the Lord, Let not the wife depart from her husband: [11] But and if she depart, let her remain unmarried, or be reconciled to her husband: and let not* *the husband put away his wife."* Since there are no contradictions in Scripture, and seeing that Jesus allowed for "putting away" in Matthew 19:9 in cases of sex outside of marriage, and the Apostle Paul allowed for re-marriage in cases of abandonment in 1 Corinthians 7:15 and 1 Corinthians 7:39, it would appear that 1 Corinthians 7:10-11 applies to the Christ/Church relationship.

While it is good for Christians to apply every principal in Scripture to and through their lives, regrettably there are an innumerable amount of unfaithful offences that are inflicted by spouses upon their spouse. Without getting into all the "what ifs" of marriage, I would ask, "Does a piece of paper make two people married if they are divorced in their heart?" "Is God OK when an infidel uses covenant to gain the advantage over a believer?" "If one person is content in the marriage, and the other is abusive because they want something else outside the marriage, are they both at fault?" There is no agreement without agreement. It takes two to agree.

If the Church attempts to answer the problem of divorce in legalistic terms, is that not a divorce itself? Should the Church rather approach the dilemma, in the individual, from the operating principles of faith, love, and grace? If we are going to abandon the principles of grace, to which we are espoused, and return to legalism, is that not a rejection of the essence of Jesus Christ? Divorce in this life is never a convenience. **And rest assured, God still hates divorce.** (See Malachi 2:11-16.) But sometimes, it is necessary. That's why God made it.

God is the Judge. He will defend, apply, or strike down our relationships as He sees fit. (See Isaiah 28:14-19.) As the Church, our job is to love and pray for those in adversity, while every man is persuaded in his own heart of his own standing in Jesus Christ. Maybe you were in the right, maybe you got it wrong, but God wants all the victims of divorce to know, *"...Yea, I have loved thee with an everlasting love: therefore with lovingkindness have I drawn thee."* **(Jeremiah 31:3).**

Romans 5:1 *"Therefore being justified by faith, we have peace with God through our Lord Jesus Christ:"*

Closing Thoughts

Jeremiah 3:14 *"Turn, O backsliding children, saith the LORD; for I am married unto you: and I will take you one of a city, and two of a family, and I will bring you to Zion:"*

Jeremiah 18:7-8 *"At what instant I shall speak concerning a nation, and concerning a kingdom, to pluck up, and to pull down, and to destroy it;* [8] *If that* *nation, against whom I have pronounced, turn from their evil, I will repent of the evil that I thought to do unto them."*

Revelation 2:1*"Unto the angel of the **church** of Ephesus write;..."* **Revelation 2:5** *"Remember therefore from whence thou art fallen, and **repent**, and do the first works; or else I will come unto thee quickly, and will remove thy candlestick out of his place, **except thou repent.**"*

Revelation 2:12 *"And to the angel of the **church** in Pergamos write;..."* **Revelation 2:16** *"**Repent**; or else I will come unto thee quickly, and will fight against them with the sword of my mouth."*

Revelation 2:18 *"And unto the angel of the **church** in Thyatira write;..."* **Revelation 2:21-23** *"And I gave her space to **repent** of her fornication; and she repented not. ²² Behold, I will cast her into a bed, and them that commit adultery with her into great tribulation, except they repent of their deeds. ²³ And I will kill her children with death; and all the churches shall know that I am he which searcheth the reins and hearts: and I will give unto every one of you according to your works."*

Revelation 3:1*"And unto the angel of the **church** in Sardis write;..."* **Revelation 3:2-3** *"Be watchful, and strengthen the things which remain, that are ready to die: for I have not found thy works perfect before God. ³ Remember therefore how thou hast received and heard, and hold fast, and **repent.** If therefore thou shalt not watch, I will come on thee as a thief, and thou shalt not know what hour I will come upon thee."*

Revelation 3:14 *"And unto the angel of the **church** of the Laodiceans write;..."* **Revelation 3:19** *"**As many as I love, I rebuke and chasten**: be zealous therefore, and **repent.**"*

The message to the Church and to America and to the World is the same today as it was to Israel before She was destroyed by the Babylonians. I hear a lot of preaching these days about God's mercy upon Israel during the Babylonian captivity. But, before they got there, the death and carnage that was unleashed upon them was terrible.

The Prophet Elisha wept when he considered the consequences of Israel's unfaithfulness at the hands of Hazael. (See 2 Kings 8:12.) Hazael, the Syrian, had been anointed by the Prophet Elijah to be king in Syria for the purpose of destroying the unfaithful of Israel. (See 1 Kings 19:15-17.) In the destruction of Israel, we are not talking about military conflict between competing armies on a battlefield; we are talking about a blood-crazed army unleashed upon a helpless civilian population with the intent of satisfying their every demonic lust upon them. And of the Hebrews that survived the Babylonian carnage, only the youngest adults would live long enough to ever come home again. To this, God said "Why will ye die?" God was faithful to warn Israel of her impending judgment and to offer an escape, but she would not.

Mercy rejoices against judgment. But, we have to invoke mercy by our repentance. By definition that means "putting on God's Righteousness," which He offers freely to all that call upon the name of the Lord Jesus Christ as personal Savior. Everything else is insufficient.

Today there are some wonderful ministries and ministers and congregations and individual servants of Jesus Christ. I hold, with great admiration and thanksgiving, those Christians that stand without compromise in the highest esteem. To many of you, I am indebted to your faithfulness. Thank you!

The message is, "There is a reckoning coming." Two thousand years as a trichotomy is long enough. To the Christians that live in compromise, I would ask: "Where will you stand when judgment begins at the 'House of God?'" Today, the Door of Salvation is open.

Revelation 22:17 *"And the Spirit and the Bride say, Come..."*

Dewayne A. Pattie is available for interviews or personal appearances. For more information send questions to: info@advbooks.com

To purchase additional copies of this book, or to see a list of all current titles visit our bookstore website at www.advbookstore.com

Advantage
BOOKS

Longwood, Florida, USA
"we bring dreams to life"™
www.advbookstore.com